Learning from
the Learners

Learning from the Learners

Successful College Students Share Their Effective Learning Habits

Edited by Elizabeth Berry, Bettina J. Huber, and Cynthia Z. Rawitch

ROWMAN & LITTLEFIELD
Lanham • Boulder • New York • London

Published by Rowman & Littlefield
A wholly owned subsidiary of The Rowman & Littlefield Publishing Group, Inc.
4501 Forbes Boulevard, Suite 200, Lanham, Maryland 20706
www.rowman.com

Unit A, Whitacre Mews, 26-34 Stannary Street, London SE11 4AB

British Library Cataloguing in Publication Information Available

Library of Congress Cataloging-in-Publication Data

Names: Berry, Elizabeth, editor. | Huber, Bettina J., editor. | Rawitch, Cynthia Z., 1946–, editor.
Title: Learning from the learners : successful college students share their effective learning habits / edited by Elizabeth Berry, Bettina J. Huber, and Cynthia Z. Rawitch.
Description: Lanham : Rowman & Littlefield Publishing Group, Inc., [2018] | Includes bibliographical references and index.
Identifiers: LCCN 2017025215 (print) | LCCN 2017044288 (ebook) | ISBN 9781442278622 (electronic) | ISBN 9781442278608 (hardcover : alk. paper) | ISBN 9781442278615 (pbk. : alk. paper)
Subjects: LCSH: Study skills—Evaluation. | Learning, Psychology of. | College students.
Classification: LCC LB2395 (ebook) | LCC LB2395 .L385 2018 (print) | DDC 378.1/98—dc23
LC record available at https://lccn.loc.gov/2017025215

∞™ The paper used in this publication meets the minimum requirements of American National Standard for Information Sciences—Permanence of Paper for Printed Library Materials, ANSI/NISO Z39.48-1992.

Printed in the United States of America

Contents

Illustrations

FIGURES

TABLES

Foreword

In 2007/2008, as provost, I visited several times with a team of current and retired faculty and staff at California State University, Northridge (CSUN), led by the then director of institutional research. They were interested in learning about the learning habits of successful students and intended to interview hundreds of students, following them for several years; they wanted to know what strategies, according to the students, helped them to learn. This approach struck me as remarkable, worthy of central support for a number of reasons.

First, the humility of the project impressed me. Imagine: we—professors, administrators, and staff members—can learn from students. Sure, this view is scripture in the progressivist canon. But for members of the university to act on this belief, my, what got into the water? Second, like most public comprehensive universities, we were fixated institutionally on the learning impediments of "remedial students." These students populated a liminal category that the university constructed, I believe, to signify the slow sinking of the whole enterprise into the marsh of poor preparation. How refreshing it was to focus on signs of success, especially in a comprehensive public university. Usually, such institutions "don't get no respect." A study such as this one made sense at Harvard. But Northridge? Like Edgar Allan Poe's purloined letter, the rationale for such a project was so obvious, and therefore easily overlooked. Third, like a little Napoleon halted on the wintry plains of Russia, I was stymied in my campaign to instill the wisdom of Ernest Boyer's *Scholarship Reconsidered* (1990) in campus culture. Surely, a public comprehensive university, as tied to its community as is CSUN, should respect the scholarships of application, integration, and teaching and learning as complements to discovery.

The Learning Habits Project showcased the value of group research and exemplified the social value and academic professionalism of the scholarships of application, integration, and teaching and learning. It helped to break the ice that encased scholarship. At the same time, we organized another team of faculty and staff to mine the big data that tie the academic paths and performance of thousands of graduates and nongraduates to careers and earnings later in life. And we were working with the Carnegie Corporation of New York on studying the effect of teacher-preparation programs on K–12 pupil learning. By 2010, CSUN had several hundred faculty members, staff members, and students involved in scholarly work that would have been previously dismissed as service.

The project on learning habits also enabled us to make better sense out of the results that we got from participating in the Collegiate Learning Assessment (CLA) and the NSSE (National Survey of Student Engagement). The learning habits team recorded many poignant stories that these surveys never could capture. Fortunately, aging narrows one's memories, so I could not be expansive on this topic of students' stories, even if I tried. But what struck me reading and hearing about the interviews with students was the role of "thoughtfulness."

Thoughtfulness consisted of students' academic behavior "recollected in tranquility" during the interviews. In these conversations, students reviewed their experiences and distilled the actions that led to success. Such disclosure came to light during face-to-face dialogue with another person. Empathy in the listener and self-confidence in the teller commingled. The teller confided the "secret sauce" to the listener. The teller consciously understood the ingredients, perhaps for the first time; it was a moment of self-discovery. The student, the teller, became the authority. The empathy of the listener drew out thoughtfulness so it could be shared with others. The teller took pride in knowing that her or his knowledge would help others to learn. The community of scholars/learners expanded.

I am confident that the many passages in this book about such thoughtfulness will help you in your quest. I have seen the practice work at Northridge. The next question is, how can an institution institutionalize such thoughtfulness over the long haul? The CSUN team that researched, wrote, and edited this book will have to answer this question in a volume 2! Inquiring minds want to know.

Harold Hellenbrand
provost emeritus, California State University, Northridge

Preface

Recent studies of learning at the college level focus on what students need to do to succeed from the point of view of education professionals—higher education experts who often provide valuable advice and support to struggling students. This edited collection, however, is based on what the student learners—experts of another type—tell us about what they *do* to succeed. In effect, these chapters stand the traditional approach on its head by examining the learning habits of successful students based on what they tell us about their learning strategies, on what they do to succeed in college, and on the teaching approaches they think best foster their learning.

This unique 10-year study, known as the Learning Habits Project (LHP), rests on a rich qualitative data set that includes both open-ended survey responses and in-depth interviews with more than 700 students at California State University, Northridge (CSUN), a large metropolitan university in Southern California. With one or two exceptions, no other volume on the widely discussed hot topic of student success relies on such a wealth of data about what works from the point of view of students. The study is unique in another respect: those who conducted it and report on findings in these chapters constitute a cross-section of university personnel—the faculty, the staff, and administrators—across multiple academic and administrative divisions that are too often perceived as silos. Throughout the life of the project, participants met in monthly seminars that provided both training in good interview practices and a forum for discussing, from a variety of perspectives, the new issues and insights emerging from the ongoing face-to-face interviews. As you will see later, these meetings not only informed and improved the interaction with students participating in the project, but also changed the way faculty members and administrators approached their own teaching and work, proving to be a rich and powerful agent of change.

CALIFORNIA STATE UNIVERSITY, NORTHRIDGE (CSUN)

Cal State Northridge, the university hosting the Learning Habits Project, is one of the largest institutions in the 23-campus California State University (CSU) system. Founded in 1958, CSUN is located at the northern edge of Los Angeles County in the San Fernando Valley. During the past decade, CSUN has become one of the largest comprehensive universities in the country, drawing most of its students from a highly diverse urban environment and offering degrees in well over 100 academic programs. Enrollment has hovered around 40,000 undergraduate and graduate students since fall 2014, making CSUN first or second largest in the CSU system, depending on the year. Since the mid-2000s, the majority of incoming freshmen have stemmed from backgrounds traditionally underserved by higher education, accounting for two-thirds of all entering freshmen in the fall of 2016; students from Latina/o backgrounds account for the vast majority. Many of these new students are first-generation college-goers from immigrant backgrounds. Many also enter with deficiencies in their preparation for college, with 33–37 percent of the fall 2016 entrants not fully prepared for college-level work in mathematics or English/language arts. Given these characteristics, the university typifies the new urban reality for higher education.

THE PROJECT

The initial impetus for the Learning Habits Project emerged from the tonal dichotomy that permeates comprehensive institutions such as ours every spring: the usual preoccupation with the reasons so many students are struggling to persist is augmented by a stream of anecdotes about the remarkable achievements of the nearly 10,000 students who are about to graduate. After pondering this annual shift in focus for several years, the then director of institutional research concluded that a project such as this might "teach us something that my studies of failing students weren't." She approached several faculty members, some retired, and administrators about the idea of questioning those students who were clearly persisting to graduation on how they managed it, sometimes against considerable odds. The results, she said, might yield insights that could be profitably shared with the many students who struggle. And, thus, the Learning Habits Project was born.

While inspired by Richard Light's book about Harvard University students and how they experience college,[1] the Learning Habits Project involved students who are not usually the subjects of long-range studies, that is, highly diverse students at a large, comprehensive university. It focuses on student strengths, not their struggles, although you will see they were also asked how they met any challenges they faced. And since the learning habits (LH) students share many of the characteristics of their peers at comparable state universities, here and elsewhere in the United States, the findings discussed will be of particular interest to educators everywhere who are trying to help the growing number of similar students to succeed.

In its final form, the overarching aim of the project was to track, over four to six years, several groups of newly enrolled freshmen who were most likely to succeed at the university. The hope was to gain insight into their characteristics and academic approaches. We sought to find out about their *learning habits* and, most especially, how and why they work. As such, the project has been an integral part of CSUN's ongoing efforts to assess the success of its varied academic and cocurricular programs in fostering student learning. Through the years, the university has devoted substantial resources to helping at-risk students. However, until the establishment of the Learning Habits Project, it had not conducted any systematic study of students who score well on placement exams and are not considered "at risk." This is not to suggest that the performance of these "good" students is not tracked and routinely assessed within the context of both their majors and general education.

Since the project was formally launched in late fall 2007, more than 700 incoming freshmen have signed onto it. All participants joined in one of four fall terms: 2007, 2008, 2010, and 2011. Collectively, these students participated in more than 600 face-to-face interviews early in the spring semester of their freshman year and close to 525 similar interviews at the beginning of their third year, when most were juniors. By the end of the 2015/2016 academic year, 280 face-to-face interviews had been conducted with LH graduating seniors for a total of 1,433 personal and individual interviews.

In addition to participating in these periodic interviews, LH students responded to open-ended questions about their learning at the end of each fall and spring term during their first six years, as long as they remained at CSUN. Some questions were repeated from term to term (e.g., whether and why specific courses completed during the preceding term provided unusually good learning experiences), while others were asked only once. The latter included questions about changes in students' approaches to different types of assignments (e.g., writing and critical thinking), all of which were posed at the end of students' third or fourth semester at the university.

A note about the nonstudent participants: many of the faculty members, staff members, and administrators who began with the first set of students stayed with the project to the end, while others left after several years for a variety of reasons, usually competing demands. All seemed to benefit. Faculty members who participated in the study reported that they came to appreciate the need for clarity and organization; they learned the importance of designing clear assignments. One history professor commented, "My experience with the Learning Habits Project has taught me to be less concerned about covering every little piece of content. Rather, I like my students to learn strategies of how to learn. If they miss a bit of Russian history because of shifting focus, so be it."

And what did the participating students gain from the experience? Apart from the "early registration" that ongoing participation guaranteed (serious coin of the realm at CSUN), one of the most interesting reactions emerging from the graduating senior interviews was the students' conviction that their participation made them more thoughtful about their learning, an emphasis that may help account for their unusual success, as discussion elsewhere in this book will show.

OVERVIEW OF THE BOOK

Given the scope of the data that the Learning Habits Project generated during the 10 years of its existence, summarizing all of them in the chapters that follow would be impossible. Building on the collaboration that informed the data-collection phase of the Learning Habits Project, participants were invited to prepare chapters focusing on a theme or topic that was of particular interest to them. The resulting chapters in *Learning from the Learners* reflect the authors' distinct perspective and disciplinary approach to selected themes evident in the rich and varied data sets.

Part 1 of the book is designed to provide context for the chapters that follow. Thus, its first chapter describes the procedures we used to organize and summarize the extensive qualitative data that we assembled. Although we relied on content analysis procedures throughout, we approached the interview data differently than the more focused responses generated by the open-ended questions included in the end-of-term surveys. Each set of procedures, along with other procedural issues, is described in some detail.

Chapter 2 describes key elements of the LH students' background and academic success, comparing them to those evident within the larger group of incoming freshmen invited to participate in the project but, for various reasons, not doing so. The data indicate that the LH students outperformed these comparable students on several of the persistence indicators considered. Equally important, further analysis reveals that, despite clear variation in background and preparation, differences in achievement between LH students from traditionally underserved and better-served backgrounds are remarkably small. These findings give rise to a question considered in the last section of the chapter: can some of the unusually high levels of achievement evident among the LH students be ascribed to their participation in the project? Or is their greater success simply a function of their better entry-level preparation for college work? The answer: it's a little of both. The question of how participation in the project may have benefited students is taken up again in chapter 12.

The second section of the book focuses on similarities and differences among key student subgroups, with the introduction indicating why racial and ethnic background is not a focus of discussion. Part of the reason is that first-generation status, the topic examined in chapter 3, is so closely intertwined with racial and ethnic background in the CSUN context. Interesting insight into factors contributing to the accomplishments of the first-generation LH students emerges from the student responses summarized in chapter 3. After addressing the ambiguities of defining first-generation status, the chapter moves on to a consideration of how family matters, not only for first-generation students, but also for others. A key finding revolves around how the level of parental educational achievement affects students' ability to navigate college, although not in ways we commonly assume, nor in what previous research has indicated. Although the parents of first-generation students may lack the knowledge to advise their children about the challenges of college, they can and do encourage and support their determination to succeed.

Chapter 4 focuses on differences by gender, with the initial section of the chapter documenting the usual differences in college persistence. Although women outpace men in the larger cohorts from which the LH students are drawn, the differences in performance are diminished among the LH students. Thanks to the availability of data from the CIRP freshman survey, it is possible to identify typical gender differences among CSUN's entering freshmen, with men more self-confident than women but less academically engaged. Again, these differences are attenuated among the LH students. The remainder of the chapter uses LH data to show how students build on their differing strengths at entry to navigate their college experiences.

The final chapter of this second section focuses on a specific end-of-term question: how did campus diversity affect your learning? The discussion in this fifth chapter reveals that most students value campus diversity, although the degree to which they do so varies strongly by major among the men, largely because STEM (science, technology, engineering, and mathematics) majors are of the opinion that campus diversity has no bearing on their learning.

The introduction to part 3, which focuses on broad themes emerging from the face-to-face interviews, provides context for the following discussion by outlining students' comments about the teaching practices they consider most helpful.

Reading at the college level—the focus of chapter 6—especially complex academic texts, presents even the good LH students with challenges that negatively affect learning. Here the challenges are twofold: students struggle with both comprehension and volume. The data suggest that students are unprepared for the second because so little reading is required of them in high school. And this limited experience, in turn, undercuts their ability to fully comprehend the more complex texts that they encounter in college. Out of necessity, therefore, many look to instructors for guidance about how to proceed and for clear expectations. Although faculty members are not generally "reading experts," it is important that more of them recognize the challenges students face and take steps to promote comprehension of the difficult academic texts that they assign.

By and large, students come to CSUN better prepared to deal with college-level writing than to deal with college-level reading. Chapter 7 focuses on their progress in the former by systematically examining the differences between essays prepared in first-year composition courses and those prepared for the more advanced courses attempted during the junior year. The greatest gains appear to be in improved use of sources and evidence. The issue of "transfer" from one writing context to another is a focus of discussion, as is the importance of creating better writing prompts to help students successfully meet their instructors' expectations.

Technology has been a mixed blessing in the college classroom, where it took firm root during the years in which the Learning Habits Project was underway. It should not come as a surprise, therefore, that students voiced a range of responses to its use during their interviews. Chapters 8 and 9 review them, noting that students had a great deal to say, especially about the use of PowerPoint. The first part of chapter 8 takes a historical view, tracing the recent evolution of academic technology with the aid of selected student comments. Thereafter, attention turns to students' views of electronic tools, the pros and cons of partially or fully online classes, and coping with the distractions and challenges of today's readily available online tools. Discussion in chapter 9 also outlines a valuable technique that helps to ensure the more effective use of technology.

In part 4, attention turns to student learning outside the classroom, with a brief introduction providing an overview of the types of cocurricular activities found valuable by the LH students. The chapters themselves focus on student practices that influence their persistence and success.

Why students do or do not seek help outside the classroom when they struggle academically is the subject of chapter 10. As students persist, the data suggest, they overcome their initial reluctance to look to others for advice. Persistence to graduation, it appears, is related, at least in part, to students' positive support, whether it is from the faculty, peers, the counseling center, or other services.

Chapter 11 reveals that, although the LH students may not be aware of it, they engage in metacognitive behaviors as they come to terms with the various academic challenges they encounter. The authors suggest that in so doing the LH students develop self-regulation strategies, internal motivation, and responsibility. It is clear that as they reflect on their own learning, something that participation in the project fostered according to discussion in the next chapter, they devise successful strategies for achieving their academic goals.

One of the most interesting results of the Learning Habits Project emerged from a question posed to graduating seniors about possible benefits of project participation. Chapter 12 summarizes responses to this question, the most frequent of which was that participation in the project made students more thoughtful about their learning. This in turn enabled them to choose their courses more successfully, thereby ensuring their timely graduation. Discussion in this chapter locates students' reflections in the context of recent neuroscientific findings about brain function.

In the final chapter of the book, we reflect on what we learned and suggest how these insights could be, or are being, applied to changes in policy and faculty practice.

NOTE

1. Richard Light, *Making the Most of College: Students Speak Their Minds* (Cambridge, MA: Harvard University Press, 2001).

Acknowledgments

Learning from the Learners is the result of collaboration, cooperation, and dedication by a cross-section of university personnel to whom we offer our deepest appreciation and gratitude.

First, our former provost, Harold Hellenbrand, enthusiastically embraced the idea for this study and supported it throughout with funds, encouragement, and valuable suggestions. His active promotion of the project's research value lent credibility and inspiration. We deeply thank him for his continuing support and validation.

Throughout the 10 years of this project, CSUN's top leadership sustained us, beginning with retired president Jolene Koester and continuing under current president Dianne F. Harrison and provost Yi Li.

We extend heartfelt thanks to Ana Quiran and Sabrina Rife, two exceptional young women with whom we had the pleasure of working. As staff to the Learning Habits Project and the Office of Institutional Research, they were often asked to take on tasks not in their "job descriptions" and did so with remarkable competence and grace. This project could not have been completed without them.

At the beginning of this study, we recruited some of the finest members of the CSUN community to participate. We knew we wanted colleagues who were passionate about teaching and learning, and who would commit their time to interviews and dialogue, whether faculty members, professional staff members, or administrators. These "seminarians" met regularly and demonstrated extraordinary skills, insights, and humor. We are extremely grateful for all their contributions, many of which you will read about in this volume.

Of course, "the learners"—the subjects of the research—were key to its success. We thank them for their willingness to share their stories. Their candor revealed amazing fortitude and persistence. They were truly delightful collaborators and took pride in their participation.

The extensive data generated by the Learning Habits Project provided opportunities for further research, and we thank Janet Oh, director of Institutional Research, for initiating and managing the Learning Habits Fellows Program. And we also thank those faculty members who were awarded fellowships and conducted research in their own disciplines or specialties.

The graduate student transcript coders were critical in analyzing the data that informs this book. Particular appreciation goes to Vana Khachatourian, Andrew Takimoto, Patricia Lara, and José Perez.

And, finally, we extend a special thank-you to Charles Harmon at Rowman & Littlefield, who recognized the value of this research, kept us on track, and was flexible when we occasionally "fell off."

Part One

PROJECT PARAMETERS

1

The Evolution of the Learning Habits Project

Methods and Procedures

Bettina J. Huber

Launched in the fall of 2007, the Learning Habits Project was designed to track, over a four-to-six-year period, several groups of newly enrolled students likely to succeed at California State University, Northridge (CSUN). As noted in the preface, its purpose was to gain insight into the characteristics and practices of these promising students—that is, we sought to find out about their learning habits. The project became an integral part of the university's ongoing efforts to assess the success of its academic programs and related activities in fostering student learning. Thus, it served as a complement to the many campus initiatives for at-risk students.

GENESIS OF THE PROJECT

As plans for what became the Learning Habits Project (LHP) evolved during mid-2007, we drew on both the insights and procedures of two earlier projects undertaken at major research universities: one at Harvard from the mid-1980s to the early 1990s and the other at the University of Washington during the early 2000s. The more important study for our face-to-face student interviews and seminar discussions was the Harvard project, initiated in 1986 by then president Derek Bok and spearheaded by Richard Light (2001). This project extended over 10 years, during which 1,600 students participated in in-depth interviews focusing on their study habits and reflections on their learning and coursework. Our study adopted two key practices from the Harvard project: (1) regular seminar discussions for the participating researchers/interviewers, during which we initially focused on exchanging interview insights; and (2) the creation of common, required questions for each student interview, coupled with the freedom to explore aspects of particular interest to individual interviewers.

The second project to provide useful background for ours was the UW SOUL project (Study of Undergraduate Learning) at the University of Washington (Beyer, Gillmore, and Fisher 2007), begun in 1999. This project tracked more than 300 entering freshmen for four years in order to collect detailed information about their undergraduate learning. Half of the students participated in annual individual or group interviews and assembled portfolios of their coursework, along with reflective essays on the portfolios' contents. Multiple modes of data collection provided a rich array of material that informed a wide range of curricular discussions at the University of Washington. The UW SOUL project provided source material for a number of our end-of-term survey questions. And, like it, we adopted a mixed-methods approach to data collection.

However, what makes CSUN's Learning Habits Project unique is not the combination of elements drawn from its predecessors. Rather, it is the setting in which the project took place: students in comprehensive, state-supported institutions rarely receive attention from researchers. A study combining elements of those undertaken by our two predecessors at a university such as ours, with its unusually diverse and often underprepared student population, seemed timely and valuable.

The nature of our student body also gave rise to the project's focus on successful students, well prepared for college-level work. In a setting in which many freshmen do not make it past the first year, it was crucial for us to focus on those entrants most likely to last until graduation in order to gather responses from the same students throughout their college careers. It was the project's dependence on long-term student persistence for its viability that gave rise to the requirement that freshman participants meet one of two entry criteria: a high school GPA of at least 3.5 *or* full readiness at entry for college-level work in English and mathematics.[1] (One-third of all learning habits [LH] students met both criteria.)

Before discussing the procedures used to select project participants, we need to mention two other recent studies of student learning, underway contemporaneously with ours. Although they concern themselves with different student populations and rely on more quantitative methodological strategies than the LHP, the topics they explore are similar in character. One, the Wabash National Study of Liberal Arts Education, focuses on selective liberal arts colleges, while the other is student driven, aiming to provide advice to faculty about becoming more effective teachers. This second study, discussed in a recently published book titled *To My Professor* (Michigan State School of Journalism 2016), synthesizes a mountain of suggestions generated through social media and face-to-face student-led conversations at Michigan State University, a selective state-supported institution. All data summarized in the study were generated by seeking student responses to the prompt "To my professor . . ." The resulting advice, offered to faculty and based on actual college experiences, is summarized in a series of chapters focusing on the major recurrent themes identified by the undergraduate authors. These range from a discussion of course structure and good syllabi to students' financial challenges and the health and wellness issues many face. Another key theme, running through several chapters, is the importance of making all types of students feel welcome in their new college surroundings. The book also contains advice from assorted experts about handling tricky situations (e.g., in-class confrontations about race and class).

The Wabash Study was carried out between 2006 and 2012 and led by the Center of Inquiry at Wabash College. As the name implies, this large-scale, longitudinal research project was designed to investigate the collegiate experiences that are integral to a liberal arts education, with a focus on assessing student learning in particular areas (e.g., critical thinking and leadership). Students from a fair number of institutions participated in this highly quantitative study, with the majority enrolled at small liberal arts colleges (18 of 26 institutions in 2008).

A book based on the study, and focusing on student affairs issues, appeared several years ago (Martin and Hevel 2014), while a set of initial findings were summarized in *Change* (Pascarella and Blaich 2013).[2] Of these, two are particularly relevant to discussion in this book. First, the quality of classroom instruction matters, with clear and organized instruction fostering cognitive growth and persistence. And second, the characteristics that selected subgroups of students bring with them to college often mitigate or enhance the benefits of the college experiences to which they are exposed.

SELECTION OF THE LH STUDENTS

Initial student participants were recruited into the Learning Habits Project early in the spring 2008 semester from freshmen who entered CSUN the preceding fall. Potential participants were recruited from entrants meeting one of the criteria outlined above and intending to specialize in majors with the highest one-year continuation rates at the time: those in the colleges of humanities and science and mathematics, along with undeclared majors. In subsequent years, this restriction by major was dropped, with additional participants drawn from all majors.

Once the initial 526 eligible freshmen had been identified (out of a freshmen class of 4,119), each received a letter from the university's provost inviting participation. Students accepting the invitation agreed to three requirements.[3] They had to

- complete a brief set of open-ended survey questions at the end of each term;
- participate in two to three face-to-face interviews during their years at CSUN; and
- submit selected class assignments with the aid of electronic portfolio software.

In addition to the above, we extracted a range of information on participating students from CSUN's student data files (e.g., background characteristics, courses attempted, and grades received). In return for completing the above tasks, project participants received free access to an e-portfolio (for which CSUN students normally paid $90) and early class registration, beginning in the fall of 2008. Eighty-two freshmen accepted this very first invitation to participate, with most persisting to the end of their college careers. (Throughout the years, early registration proved to be the biggest lure for all new and continuing LH students.)

Using the same criteria, we enrolled an additional 165 entering freshmen in fall 2008. And then, after a one-year hiatus, another 223 entering freshmen accepted the invitation to join the project in fall 2010, as did close to 300 of those entering in fall 2011. All signed release forms and gave permission to have their interviews recorded. In sum, 721 entering freshmen have been systematically tracked and interviewed during the decade-long life of the Learning Habits Project.[4]

SELECTION AND TRAINING OF FACULTY AND STAFF PARTICIPANTS

Once preliminary parameters were defined and initial funding secured from the Office of the Provost, the leadership of four of the campus's eight academic colleges (Mike Curb College of Arts, Media, and Communication; Humanities; Science and Mathematics; and Social and Behavioral Sciences) was asked to nominate one or more faculty members likely to be particularly well suited for and interested in the project. From those nominated and other suggestions, 12 faculty members were invited to participate. An additional 10 participants were recruited from among the university staff and faculty with "reassigned time" administrative positions (e.g., the director of the Office of Faculty Development).

From the beginning, participation was conditioned on a commitment to take part in monthly seminars and to conduct a minimum number of individual student interviews during a semester, usually five to ten. Faculty members received stipends for their participation, with the good lunches provided at all seminar meetings an unusual bonus for all. There has been some variation in seminar membership from year to year; however, almost half of the initial faculty and staff participants (nine out of 20) remained involved to the end.[5] A complete list of LHP participants appears in appendix 1.

In preparation for the inaugural round of face-to-face interviews, the first spring 2008 meeting of the Learning Habits Seminar was devoted to discussing and demonstrating effective interviewing techniques. This session included a mock interview, followed by debriefing facilitated by two seminar members experienced in qualitative research. The mock interview was conducted by the director of the university's counseling center, himself a seminar participant, with a student employee from the Office of Undergraduate Studies playing the role of interviewee. This exercise proved extremely helpful for onlookers, demonstrating the importance of listening and responding appropriately. During the debriefing period, guidelines for conducting interviews were presented and discussed, and the agreed-upon list of interview questions was distributed. The mock interview was recorded and available to assist in the training of new LHP members through the years.

During the remainder of the spring 2008 semester, 70 freshmen were interviewed by the project's faculty and staff, all of whom gained considerable confidence and expertise in the process. Through time, the faculty and staff interviewers found that most freshmen were hesitant and tended to give brief responses. Getting more than one-word responses from some was a bit like pulling teeth, with the result that freshman interviews typically lasted only 20–30 minutes. Juniors and seniors, in contrast, talked easily and reflectively about their experience at CSUN. As a result, most of their interviews went on for an hour or more. Throughout the project, interviews were recorded, transformed into written transcripts, and uploaded into a software program designed to handle qualitative data.[6]

The full set of interview questions that eventually evolved appears in appendix 2. Some of the questions elicited simple demographic information, but most delved into students' study habits and views of faculty teaching practices. Key questions in the freshman interviews focused on how students' high school study habits changed in college, while some of the questions posed to juniors asked if and how their learning habits had changed since college entry. One of these questions, to which the upper division students responded with interest and insight, was, If you ran into your freshman self at the [coffee shop] here on campus, what advice would you give that younger self about improving your academic performance?

SUMMARIZING THE DATA

Traditional content analysis procedures guided identification of the major themes emerging from both face-to-face interviews and responses to the open-ended, end-of-term survey questions (Weber 1990). The software used to store the interview transcripts and survey responses also provided functionality that facilitated organization of the two data sets. Since coding procedures differed, in keeping with differences in response format, they are discussed separately below.

End-of-Term Responses

The end-of-term questions that students answered online were of two types: questions that were repeated from term to term and questions that were asked only once. Questions posed every term included the following:

- Thinking back on the courses you took this past term, was there one in which you learned a great deal more than in the other courses you took? If yes, what was it about this course that made it such a good learning experience for you?
- In the courses you attempted this past term (other than the one mentioned above), were there techniques, exercises, or approaches that your instructors used in one or more that made a significant contribution to your learning? If yes, please describe the techniques or exercises that were so helpful.
- Were there other aspects of your college experience this term (e.g., cocurricular activities and paid employment) that made a significant contribution to your learning? If yes, please describe the most important such experience.

Questions that were asked only once included those addressing the following topics:

- The student's approaches to certain skill sets, including writing, reading, critical thinking, quantitative reasoning, information literacy, and civic responsibility

- Aspects of the student's experience during the first college year that contributed to the decision to return the following fall
- Changes in approaches to studying during the transition from a focus on general education courses to a focus on courses in the student's chosen major
- Changes in the student's notions of what college success means
- Effects/impact of campus diversity on the student's learning
- Topics or areas of study that graduating seniors wished they had learned more about and the reasons they singled these out

The full set of end-of-term questions appears in appendix 3. Given the richness of the resulting data set and this book's emphasis on the interview data, not all of the above topics are discussed in the following pages.

Since the end-of-term responses were relatively short and confined to a limited number of topics, initial data analysis involved developing a set of categories and subcategories that encompassed relevant responses to particular questions. Although several people participated in the development and application of the coding schemes used, only one person handled each phase, in an effort to maximize reliability. Such an approach proved feasible because the staff members who handled most of the coding remained in place throughout the life of the project.

Initially, one person used a random sample of responses to identify a preliminary set of coding categories. In most cases, a second person then used and, where appropriate, expanded the initial set, while coding all responses to a given question or subquestion. In a few instances, having a single person code all responses to the questions posed repeatedly from term to term did not prove feasible. In those cases, separate people coded all responses for individual cohorts, collaborating closely during the process. Finally, once the initial coding was complete, still another person often reviewed all coded excerpts for accuracy and consistency.

The final set of categories and subcategories provided the basis for a quantitative summary of the responses to any given question. Individual responses dealing with more than one of the identified categories or subcategories were counted as many times as appropriate; all percentages, however, are based on the total number of respondents answering a given question.

Interview Themes

In contrast to the specificity of the end-of-term questions, those posed in the face-to-face interviews were quite broad and designed to elicit a wide range of responses. A number of these questions included topical prompts, both to facilitate student responses and to ensure that key concerns were consistently covered. Questions posed in student interviews included the following:

- Describe your study habits in high school. How have they changed since you became a college student? (freshman)
- Describe approaches or techniques used by some of your instructors that were particularly helpful in enhancing your learning. (freshman)
- Are there things you routinely do in your classes that help you learn? (freshman)
- Describe strategies you used inside and outside of the classroom to complete assignments and prepare for tests. (junior)
- How do you balance the academic demands of college with your other responsibilities? (junior)
- As you think back over your time at college, what learning strategies have served you best during your college years? (senior)
- If you were starting college over, what, if anything, would you do differently? (senior)

As noted above, the full set of interview questions appears in appendix 2.

Given the range of responses to any given question, compiling an overall summary for each one made little sense. Instead, seminar participants developed a set of themes that addressed topics of particular interest to them. The major topics eventually considered were:

- Changes in approaches to reading and writing assignments
- Effective learning strategies
- Help-seeking behaviors and strategies
- Self-directed learning strategies
- Experiences of first-generation college students
- Teaching practices that benefit student learning
- Using technology to foster student learning
- Campus activities that contributed to learning

As you will see, many of these major topics are the focus of individual chapters in this book.

Each of the broad themes outlined above included a set of subthemes to guide coding. For example, the teaching practices theme included four subthemes dealing with the benefits of (1) how instructors approach their courses; (2) how the course structure impacted the student; (3) the value of instructor attention to means of successfully completing course requirements; and (4) other teaching practices that facilitated student learning. More specific emphases within various subthemes were often defined as coding progressed.

Once all elements of the themes were in place, several student assistants read through each interview transcript in its entirety, highlighting all interview excerpts relating to particular themes and subthemes. Throughout the multiterm coding process, student assistants met with two of the project leaders to review questions/issues around the meaning of specific subthemes.

This process also served to ensure coding consistency, despite the changes in personnel that are to be expected over the life of a 10-year-long project. Initial training for new staff members also helped ensure coding consistency. Whenever new student employees came on board, they received a small set of already-coded interviews to examine and code on their own. Every effort was made to ensure that this initial task focused on a specific interview type or a small set of themes. Once it was completed, the new person met with one of the project managers to discuss and resolve inconsistencies that were evident before he or she began coding new interviews. Insofar as feasible, we also tried to vary the work of the student coders, so they did not spend more than a few hours at a time reviewing interview transcripts.

Once the coding was complete, numerical summaries were again compiled for all themes and subthemes. Although these summaries, along with those for the end-of-term responses, were made available to all chapter authors, not all relied on them. Some, especially those engaging with the data while coding was still underway, preferred to rely on more traditional means of dealing directly with qualitative data. Nonetheless, many of the themes outlined above are dealt with in the following pages. Within the context of these discussions, a range of specific student comments enriches the text.

NOTES

1. Freshmen admitted to the university system of which our campus is a part are required to complete two ETS tests prior to registration if their SAT or ACT scores are not sufficiently high: the Entry-Level Mathematics test (ELM) and the English Proficiency Test (EPT). Scores on both determine whether incoming students are fully prepared for college work. Those who aren't must complete a certain amount of remedial/developmental work during their first college year.

2. In addition, the Wabash Study has given rise to a large number of articles and conference presentations, references to which can be found at the following website: "Research and Publications," Center of Inquiry at Wabash College, 2016, http://www.liberalarts.wabash.edu/research-and-publications.

3. Midway through the project, the university introduced a universally available and cost-free learning management system (LMS). Thus, we switched from the electronic portfolio system to the LMS, since students rely on it for other purposes.

4. In all four cohorts, a number of students failed to complete any of the tasks they had committed to during their first year at CSUN (n = 41). With one exception, they

were dropped from inclusion in the final LH sample as a result. The exception was the initial comparisons of students' background and entry characteristics, along with their persistence rates, for which the full initial sample was retained.

5. A number of the membership changes are the result of the inevitable turnover in administrative positions occupied by faculty members.

6. We are using Dedoose, a relatively new product developed by scholars at UCLA and SocioCultural Research Consultants, LLC. (An early version of the software was known as EthnoNotes; the current version is available at http://www.dedoose.com/.)

REFERENCES

Beyer, Catharine H., Gerald M. Gillmore, and Andrew Fisher. 2007. *Inside the Undergraduate Experience: The University of Washington's Study of Undergraduate Learning*. Bolton, MA: Anker Press.

Light, Richard J. 2001. *Making the Most of College: Students Speak Their Minds*. Cambridge, MA: Harvard University Press.

Martin, G. I., and M. S. Hevel, eds. 2014. *Research-Driven Practice in Student Affairs: Implications from the Wabash National Study of Liberal Arts Education*. San Francisco: Jossey-Bass.

Michigan State School of Journalism (Joe Grimm, ed.). 2016. *To My Professor: Student Voices for Great College Teaching*. Canton, MI: Read the Spirit Books.

Pascarella, Ernest T., and Charles Blaich. 2013. "Lessons from the Wabash National Study of Liberal Arts Education." *Change: The Magazine of Higher Learning* 45 (March–April): 6–15.

Weber, Robert Philip. 1990. *Basic Content Analysis*. 2nd ed. Newbury Park, CA: Sage.

2

Who Are the Learning Habits Students, and Why Do They Persist?

Bettina J. Huber

How do the key characteristics of the learning habits (LH) students' backgrounds and academic success differ from the larger group of incoming freshmen invited to participate in the project but who did not do so?[1] What are the key differences by racial and ethnic background within the LH group? Both of these questions are addressed in this chapter. Thereafter, in light of the reported findings, we also examine if and to what degree the outstanding academic success of LH students can be ascribed to their project experience, their unusually good preparation for college work, or something else.

LH students were recruited over multiple years and in different ways, as we saw in chapter 1. Initial data analysis addressed the question of whether participants recruited in different entry terms significantly differed from one another. However, no such differences were evident for the key characteristics considered (i.e., proficiency at entry and high school GPA). Some differences by cohort were evident for students' scores on the mandated California State University system-wide placement exams, one focusing on mathematics and one on English/language arts. Participants drawn from the fall 2011 freshman class were less likely than those recruited earlier to be required to take either test because their SAT performance exempted them.

Two more modest differences by background were also evident for the two most recent entry cohorts, fall 2010 and fall 2011. Participants drawn from those years were somewhat more likely than those drawn from the two earlier cohorts to be Pell Grant recipients (38 vs. 24–32 percent) and to come from "traditionally underserved" racial and ethnic groups (39–42 percent vs. 29–34 percent).[2] These shifts in student background are parallel to shifts in the composition of freshmen entering the university during the 2007–2011 period. During those five years, the overall composition of the incoming freshman

class shifted from 53 percent traditionally underserved to 62 percent. Therefore, the modest differences by cohort year do not appear to have a distorting
effect on the data and receive no further attention.

KEY CHARACTERISTICS OF LEARNING HABITS STUDENTS

Entry Characteristics and Background

Project participants were among the most highly qualified incoming students
at California State University, Northridge (CSUN): at entry, all have high
school GPAs of at least 3.50 and/or fully prepared for college-level work in
mathematics and English. Table 2.1 compares these students with two other
groups of incoming freshmen: those who were invited to participate in LH
but did not and those who were not invited to participate because they did
not meet the entry criteria. Since the last group clearly differs from the other
two, discussion focuses only on students eligible to participate in the project.

As the first two sections of table 2.1 indicate, a clear majority of LH participants (55 percent) had high school GPAs of 3.50 or higher, and 79 percent
were fully proficient in mathematics and English at entry. The majority of LH
students attained this status because of their SAT scores, as is evident from
the next three sections of table 2.1. Among the few participants needing remediation at entry, the majority needed work in one subject only. In terms of
planned majors, one in five LH students entered without declaring a specific
major. Of those who did specify a major, most planned to specialize in fields
housed in three disciplinary clusters: arts, media, and communication; science
and mathematics; and business and economics.

Comparing students who did and did not participate in the project shows
only modest differences in entry characteristics. Statistically significant differences are evident for the characteristics shown in table 2.1, but all are modest in character. LH students are somewhat more likely than nonparticipants
to have high school GPAs of 3.50 or higher (55 vs. 49 percent), to be fully
proficient at entry (79 vs. 70 percent), and to be exempt from the two CSU
placement exams (55–61 vs. 47–48 percent), thanks to their strong performance on the SAT. In addition, LH students are somewhat more likely than
nonparticipants to plan majors housed in science and mathematics (15 vs. 11
percent) but somewhat less likely to plan majors housed in engineering and
computer science (7 vs. 11 percent).

As can be seen in the first two sections of table 2.2, 64 percent of LH
freshmen are women, and 37 percent stem from backgrounds traditionally
underserved by higher education, with just over 30 percent from Latina/o
background. Only one-third are Pell Grant recipients, and as is evident in

Table 2.1. Entry characteristics of new first-time freshmen by LH participation status

Entry Characteristic	Actual Participants	Invited to Participate	Not Invited
High School GPA			
F = 40.81 (.001); df = 1; Eta = .075			
2.74 or less	5.0	9.5	23.1
2.75–2.99	7.6	10.8	25.2
3.00–3.24	16.7	17.0	32.6
3.25–3.49	15.7	14.1	19.1
3.50–3.74	27.4	30.5	0.0
3.75 or higher	27.5	18.2	0.0
Total	100.0	100.0	100.0
(No. of participants)	(759)	(6,532)	(11,896)
Mean	3.47	3.36	2.95
Median	3.52	3.45	3.00
Interquartile range	3.2–3.8	3.1–3.7	2.8–3.2
Proficiency at Entry			
Chi square = 24.75 (.001); df = 1; Cramer's V = .058			
Fully Proficient	79.1	70.4	0.0
Needs remediation in:	21.0	29.6	100.0
English only	7.3	9.9	22.2
Mathematics only	7.1	4.9	15.7
Both subjects	6.6	14.8	62.2
Total	100.0	100.0	100.0
(No. of participants)	(759)	(6,532)	(11,896)
SAT Composite Scores			
F = 47.88 (.001); df = 1; Eta = .081			
Below 700	7.9	15.7	22.4
700–799	1.7	3.7	17.4
800–899	6.7	8.5	25.8
900–999	13.6	16.2	23.1
1000–1099	27.9	23.9	9.5
1100–1199	25.3	20.1	1.7
1200 or higher	16.9	11.9	0.1
Total	100.0	100.0	100.0
(No. of participants)	(759)	(6,532)	(11,896)
Mean	996.9	896.0	742.8
Median	1070.0	1020.0	840.0
Interquartile range	960–1160	870–1120	720–930
Scores on English Proficiency Test (EPT)			
F = 33.63 (.001); df = 1; Eta = .095			
Below 141	5.0	12.8	45.6
141–150	12.1	18.4	40.4
151 or higher (GE eligible)	21.7	21.3	6.5
Exempt from EPT (due to SAT score)	61.1	47.5	7.5
Total	100.0	100.0	100.0
(No. of participants)	(759)	(6,532)	(11,896)

(continued)

Table 2.1. *Continued*

Entry Characteristic	Actual Participants	Invited to Participate	Not Invited
Mean	149.2	146.3	140.2
Median	151.0	148.0	141.0
Interquartile range	146–154	141–153	135–146

Scores on Entry-Level Mathematics Examination (ELM)
F = 11.62 (.001); df = 1; Eta = .055

	Actual Participants	Invited to Participate	Not Invited
Below 34 (two remed courses)	2.8	7.4	35.2
34–49 (one remed course)	13.2	14.6	43.2
50 or higher (GE Math)	29.5	31.1	12.4
Exempt from ELM (due to SAT score)	54.6	46.9	9.2
Total	100.0	100.0	100.0
(No. of participants)	(759)	(6,532)	(11,896)
Mean	51.6	49.1	36.9
Median	52.0	52.0	36.0
Interquartile range	42–60	40–58	28–44

College Housing Planned Major
Chi square = 24.21 (.002); df = 8; Cramer's V = .058

	Actual Participants	Invited to Participate	Not Invited
Arts, Media, and Communication	16.5	16.9	12.5
Business and Economics	13.4	15.1	14.9
Education	1.6	0.9	0.7
Engineering and Computer Science	7.0	10.7	7.0
Health and Human Development	11.2	10.2	11.4
Humanities	5.3	5.2	4.2
Science and Mathematics	14.9	11.0	7.8
Social and Behavioral Sciences	11.1	11.6	15.4
Undeclared	19.1	18.4	26.0
Total	100.0	100.0	100.0
(No. of participants)	(759)	(6,532)	(11,896)

Note: The summary statistics shown below each variable listed focus on the differences between the groups of students who did and did not choose to participate in the Learning Habits Project.

the third section of table 2.2, just over half have at least one parent with a four-year college degree. These background characteristics set LH students apart from comparable freshmen who were invited to participate but did not. Although the differences between the two groups are statistically significant, the magnitude of the differences is again modest. LH students are somewhat more likely than nonparticipants to be women (64 vs. 51 percent) or to have at least one parent with a college education (51 vs. 40 percent) but somewhat less likely to stem from traditionally underserved backgrounds (37 vs. 45 percent) or to be Pell Grant recipients (34 vs. 43 percent).

Table 2.2. Background characteristics of new first-time freshmen by LH participation status

Background Characteristic	Actual Participants	Invited to Participate	Not Invited
Gender			
Chi square = 46.62 (.001); df = 1; Cramer's V = .080			
Women	64.2	51.1	57.9
Men	35.8	48.9	42.1
Total	100.0	100.0	100.0
(No. of participants)	(759)	(6,532)	(11,896)
Racial and Ethnic Background			
Chi square = 24.82 (.001); df = 1; Cramer's V = .060			
Traditionally Underserved	37.4	45.3	66.3
American Indian	*0.1*	*0.3*	*0.3*
Pacific Islander	*0.0*	*0.3*	*0.3*
African American	*4.6*	*6.1*	*15.2*
Latina/o	*30.8*	*37.3*	*49.3*
Multirace	*1.8*	*1.3*	*1.2*
Better Served	61.8	50.5	29.9
Asian	*13.4*	*14.0*	*10.3*
White	*39.1*	*28.9*	*14.3*
Multirace (i.e., Asian and white)	*1.8*	*1.3*	*0.4*
Decline to state	*7.4*	*6.3*	*5.0*
International	0.8	4.3	3.8
Total	100.0	100.0	100.0
(No. of participants)	(759)	(6,532)	(11,896)
Pell Grant Status (proxy for low income)			
Chi square = 20.28 (.001); df = 1; Cramer's V = .053			
Pell Grant recipient	34.4	42.9	58.6
No grant received	65.6	57.1	41.4
Total	100.0	100.0	100.0
(No. of participants)	(759)	(6,532)	(11,896)
Percent Traditionally Underserved	62.8	66.4	81.5
among Pell Grant recipients	(261)	(2,803)	(6,970)
Parental Education (indicator of first-generation college status)			
Chi square = 34.11 (.001); df = 2; Cramer's V = .071			
Both parents: high school or less	21.5	29.1	43.0
One/both parents: some college	22.1	23.6	23.5
One/both parents: four-year degree	51.0	39.9	25.7
Unknown	5.4	7.4	7.8
Total	100.0	100.0	100.0
(No. of participants)	(759)	(6,532)	(11,896)

(continued)

Table 2.2.   *Continued*

Background Characteristic	Actual Participants	Invited to Participate	Not Invited
Country in Which Parents' Grew Up			
Raised in the United States	40.6	—	—
Raised in another country	59.4	—	—
Total	100.0		
(No. of participants)	(716)		
Learning Habits Students' Native Language			
English	80.1	—	—
Another language	19.9	—	—
Total	100.0		
(No. of participants)	(718)		
Language Spoken in Students' Home while Growing Up			
English	47.9	—	—
Another language	52.1	—	—
Total	100.0		
(No. of participants)	(703)		

Note: The summary statistics shown below each variable listed focus on the differences between the groups of students who did and did not choose to participate in the Learning Habits Project.

Information provided by participants when they formally joined the project indicates that approximately three-fifths have at least one parent who grew up in another country. While English is the native language of 80 percent of project participants, the last sections of table 2.2 indicate that just over half grew up in homes in which a language other than English was spoken. Of those who heard non-English languages at home, a little over three-fifths (62 percent) heard one of two languages: Spanish or Armenian.[3] Given the character of the university's student body, there is no reason to think that LH respondents differ from others in these respects.

Taken together, the data summarized in tables 2.1 and 2.2 suggest that LH students entered college somewhat better prepared than comparable students in their entry cohorts and came from somewhat more privileged socioeconomic backgrounds. Presumably such advantages, although modest, can be expected to affect the LH students' subsequent college performance, and as you will see, this presumption proves to be true in a number of instances.

Academic Achievement

Table 2.3 summarizes various aspects of LH students' academic performance, along with those of the other two groups considered in the preceding section. When compared to nonparticipants, LH students differ significantly on all

Table 2.3. Persistence and academic success by LH participation status

Persistence Measure	Actual Participants	Invited to Participate	Not Invited
One-Year Continuation Rate			
Chi square = 88.91 (.001); df = 1; Cramer's V = .110			
Enrolled at beginning of second year	93.3	78.9	68.5
Not enrolled at beginning of second year	6.7	21.1	31.5
Total	100.0	100.0	100.0
(No. of participants)	(759)	(6,532)	(11,896)
Academic Standing at End of First Year			
Chi square = 108.5 (.001); df = 2; Cramer's V = .122			
In good standing	95.8	80.5	67.0
On probation	2.9	10.5	15.7
Disqualified	1.3	9.0	17.3
Total	100.0	100.0	100.0
(No. of participants)	(759)	(6,489)	(11,848)
CSUN GPA at End of First Year			
F = 266.73 (.001); df = 1; Eta = .188			
1.99 or less	4.1	16.9	29.9
2.00–2.49	5.8	13.0	21.0
2.50–2.99	16.5	22.7	25.5
3.00–3.49	34.4	28.0	18.2
3.50–3.74	19.5	12.1	3.8
3.75 or higher	19.8	7.3	1.6
Total	100.0	100.0	100.0
(No. of participants)	(759)	(6,359)	(11,445)
Mean	3.26	2.77	2.35
Median	3.35	2.94	2.48
Interquartile range	3.0–3.7	2.3–3.4	1.8–3.0
Cumulative CSUN Units Earned at End of First Year			
F = 197.90 (.001); df = 1; Eta = .163			
15 or fewer units	1.8	15.2	20.7
16–24 units	19.2	30.8	37.5
25–30 units	63.5	46.1	35.7
31 or more units	15.4	8.0	6.2
Total	100.0	100.0	100.0
(No. of participants)	(759)	(6,532)	(11,896)
Mean	26.9	23.0	21.3
Median	27.0	25.0	23.0
Interquartile range	25–29	21–28	17–27

(continued)

Table 2.3. *Continued*

Persistence Measure	*Actual Participants*	*Invited to Participate*	*Not Invited*
Degree Status (at end of 2015–16)			
Chi square = 120.35 (.001); df = 1; Cramer's V = .128			
Baccalaureate degree completed	75.9	55.1	42.3
Degree not completed	24.1	44.9	57.7
but still enrolled at CSUN (13th term after entry)	*3.6*	*4.4*	*3.9*
and no longer enrolled at CSUN	*20.6*	*40.5*	*53.8*
Total	100.0	100.0	100.0
(No. of participants)	(759)	(6,531)	(11,896)
Status of Students Who Have Yet to Earn Baccalaureate Degrees*			
Still Enrolled at CSUN			
Chi square = 3.03 (NS); df = 2; Cramer's V = .0985			
In good standing	85.2	88.3	87.2
On probation	14.8	7.2	6.4
Disqualified	0.0	4.5	6.4
Total	100.0	100.0	100.0
(No. of participants)	(27)	(290)	(468)
No Longer Enrolled at CSUN			
Chi square = 36.88 (.001); df = 2; Cramer's V = .115			
In good standing	79.5	54.8	38.5
On probation	7.7	20.2	24.6
Disqualified	12.8	25.0	36.9
Total	100.0	100.0	100.0
(No. of participants)	(156)	(2,644)	(6,400)
Four-Year Graduation Rate			
Chi square = 167.88 (.001); df = 1; Cramer's V = .152			
Graduated in Four Years or Less	37.6	17.8	6.9
Did Not Graduate within Four Years	62.5	82.3	93.1
Total	100.0	100.0	100.0
(No. of participants)	(759)	(6,531)	(11,896)
Five-Year Graduation Rate			
Chi square = 143.32 (.001); df = 1 Cramer's V = .140			
Graduated in Five Years or Less	67.7	44.8	28.9
Did Not Graduate within Five Years	32.3	55.2	71.1
Total	100.0	100.0	100.0
(No. of participants)	(759)	(6,531)	(11,896)
Likely Graduation Rate			
Chi square = 109.96 (.001); df = 1; Cramer's V = .122			
Graduated or Enrolled in 13th term after entry	77.5	57.8	45.7

Persistence Measure	Actual Participants	Invited to Participate	Not Invited
No longer enrolled at CSUN	22.5	42.2	54.3
Total	100.0	100.0	100.0
(No. of participants)	(759)	(6,531)	(11,896)

Baccalaureate Degree Recipients*

CSUN GPA at Graduation
$F = 85.14 \ (.001); \ df = 1; \ Eta = .141$

1.99 or less	0.2	0.2	0.2
2.00–2.49	4.0	7.3	17.4
2.50–2.99	16.2	27.5	42.8
3.00–3.49	38.5	39.7	31.8
3.50–3.74	22.1	17.1	6.0
3.75 or higher	19.1	8.3	1.8
Total	100.0	100.0	100.0
(No. of participants)	(576)	(3,597)	(5,028)
Mean	3.34	3.16	2.89
Median	3.37	3.18	2.88
Interquartile range	3.1–3.7	2.9–3.5	2.6–3.2

Cumulative CSUN Units Earned**
$F = 0.71 \ (NS); \ df = 1; \ Eta = .013$

110 or fewer units	0.0	0.2	0.1
111–120 units	11.3	10.5	0.6
121–130 units	41.3	41.1	36.2
131 or more units	47.4	48.3	63.2
Total	100.0	100.0	100.0
(No. of participants)	(576)	(3,597)	(5,028)
Mean	133.5	133.0	135.4
Median	129.5	130.0	133.0
Interquartile range	122–141	123–140	128–140

Time to Degree
$F = 52.04 \ (.001); \ df = 1; \ Eta = .139$

Four years or less	49.5	32.2	16.3
Four to six years	48.1	62.8	74.9
More than six years	2.4	5.0	8.8
Total	100.0	100.0	100.0
(No. of participants)	(576)	(3,597)	(5,028)
Mean	4.5	4.8	5.2
Median	4.5	5.0	5.0
Interquartile range	4.0–5.0	4.0–5.0	4.5–5.5

Note: The summary statistics shown below each variable listed focus on the differences between the groups of students who did and did not choose to participate in the Learning Habits Project.

*In evaluating these measures, it is important to bear in mind that only the first three entry cohorts have been enrolled for at least six years. Students from most recent (2011) had been enrolled for five years only at the end of 2015–2016.
**These unit counts include advanced placement and community college units earned by students.

four of the first-year indicators considered. As is evident from the first section, almost all ended their first year in good standing, with close to three-quarters earning GPAs of 3.00 or higher. Nearly four in five earned at least 25 credit units during this initial year, and more than nine in 10 returned for a second year of college. Although LH students performed better on all measurements than comparably qualified students, the differences in one-year continuation rates and academic standing are the more modest. Those for the other two persistence measures examined are clear-cut. Thus, LH students are considerably more likely than nonparticipants to have earned a GPA of 3.00 or higher at the end of their first year (74 vs. 47 percent) and to have earned 25 or more units during that period (79 vs. 54 percent).

Examining persistence measures related to graduation, three-quarters of LH students (76 percent) earned baccalaureate degrees by the end of the 2015/2016 academic year. Of those who had yet to graduate, very few were still enrolled in the thirteenth term after entry; of those who remained enrolled, however, the vast majority were in good standing. Close to two-fifths of LH students (38 percent) graduated within four years, according to table 2.3, while approximately two-thirds graduated within five years and close to four-fifths are likely to graduate.[4] Once again, LH students outperformed nonparticipants, although the degree of difference between the two groups is modest, with one important exception. LH students were twice as likely as nonparticipants to have graduated within four years (38 percent vs. 18 percent).[5]

The last sections of table 2.3 summarize three characteristics of the baccalaureate degree recipients. These indicate that four in five LH graduates ended their undergraduate careers with GPAs of 3.00 or higher, while most accumulated more than the minimum 120 units required for graduation, although the overage was generally within 10 units of the minimum required. Finally, half of the graduates earned their degrees in four years or less. When compared to nonparticipants, LH graduates were considerably more likely to have GPAs of at least 3.00 (80 vs. 65 percent) and somewhat more likely to have earned their degrees within four years (50 vs. 32 percent). The two groups do not differ in terms of the number of units accumulated at graduation.

In short, LH students outperformed comparable students in their entry cohorts on several of the persistence indicators considered in table 2.3. These include GPA and earned units at the end of the first college year, along with graduating within four years and cumulative GPA at graduation. More modest differences, all favoring the LH students, are evident for most of the other persistence indicators considered.

To some degree, these rather striking differences in achievement can be attributed to the fact that LH students tended to arrive better prepared for college than the eligible, but nonparticipating, students. However, since such differences in preparation are relatively modest, the question arises of whether some of the differences in achievement can be ascribed to participation in the project. This issue is addressed in the last section of this chapter.

Before turning to this issue, one more set of key subgroup differences needs to be examined: differences by racial and ethnic background, the focus of the next section.

DIFFERENCES BY RACIAL AND ETHNIC BACKGROUND

Although preceding discussion indicated that students from backgrounds traditionally underserved by higher education are underrepresented among LH participants, their numbers are still sufficient to examine whether and how they differ from students from better-served backgrounds. To keep differences that do emerge in perspective, comparable figures appear in tables 2.4–2.6 for all freshmen entering the university in the four fall terms during which LH students were recruited.

Entry Characteristics and Background

The data summarized in table 2.4 indicate there are clear differences in background between the two groups of LH students being considered.[6] Those from traditionally underserved backgrounds are considerably more likely than their better-served counterparts to be Pell Grant recipients (58 vs. 21 percent) and to have parents with no more than a high school education (45 vs. 8 percent). Similarly, strong differences are evident for the larger freshman group, as the figures on the right side of the table indicate. Differences by gender are less pronounced but still evident. Although women are more numerous than men within both the traditionally underserved and the better-served LH groups, women are somewhat more predominant among the former (70 vs. 61 percent).

There are clear differences in entry-level preparation between the traditionally underserved and better-served students, whether they are LH students or part of the larger freshman group. The one exception, as the second section of table 2.5 indicates, is high school GPA, largely because of its gatekeeper role. Thus, among LH students, the majority of both the traditionally underserved and the better served entered with GPAs of 3.50 or higher (56 and 55 percent, respectively). Among the larger freshman group, in contrast, a modest difference is evident, with better-served students outperforming the traditionally underserved (22 percent vs. 16 percent entering with GPAs of

Table 2.4. Background characteristics of LH participants and all first-time freshmen in their entry cohorts by racial and ethnic background

Background Characteristic	Learning Habits Participants		All Entering Freshmen	
	Traditionally Underserved	Better Served	Traditionally Underserved	Better Served
Racial and Ethnic Background*				
Traditionally Underserved				
American Indian	0.4	0.0	0.5	0.0
Pacific Islander	0.0	0.0	0.6	0.0
African American	12.3	0.0	20.1	0.0
Latina/o	82.4	0.0	76.7	0.0
Multirace	4.9	0.0	2.2	0.0
Better Served				
Asian	0.0	21.8	0.0	30.5
White	0.0	63.3	0.0	53.0
Multirace (i.e., Asian and white)	0.0	3.0	0.0	2.0
Decline to state	0.0	11.9	0.0	14.6
Total	100.0	100.0	100.0	100.0
(No. of participants)	(284)	(469)	(11,128)	(7,326)
Pell Grant Status (proxy for low income)				
Pell Grant recipient	57.8	20.7	69.2	31.6
No grant received	42.3	79.3	30.8	68.4
Total	100.0	100.0	100.0	100.0
(No. of participants)	(284)	(469)	(11,128)	(7,326)
	Chi square = 107.30 (.001); df = 1 Cramer's V = .377		Chi square = 2514.31 (.001); df = 1 Cramer's V = .369	
Parental Education (indicator of First-Generation College Status)				
Both parents: high school or less	44.7	7.5	53.5	14.3
One/both parents: some college	24.3	20.7	24.6	23.1
One/both parents: four-year degree	28.9	64.8	16.5	53.2
Unknown	2.1	7.0	5.3	9.4
Total	100.0	100.0	100.0	100.0
(No. of participants)	(284)	(469)	(11,128)	(7,326)
	Chi square = 157.39 (.001); df = 2 Cramer's V = .470		Chi square = 3741.64 (.001); df = 2 Cramer's V = .467	
Gender				
Women	70.4	60.6	60.0	51.4
Men	29.6	39.5	40.0	48.6
Total	100.0	100.0	100.0	100.0
(No. of participants)	(284)	(469)	(11,128)	(7,326)

Background Characteristic	Learning Habits Participants		All Entering Freshmen	
	Traditionally Underserved	Better Served	Traditionally Underserved	Better Served
Entry Term				
Fall 2007	9.9	11.5	19.1	25.2
Fall 2008	16.9	23.7	23.0	26.2
Fall 2010	31.0	29.0	28.3	25.4
Fall 2011	42.3	35.8	29.6	23.3
Total	100.0	100.0	100.0	100.0
(No. of participants)	(284)	(469)	(11,128)	(7,326)
	Chi square = 6.43 (.093); df = 3 Cramer's V = .092		Chi square = 175.54 (.001); df = 3 Cramer's V = .098	

*International students have been excluded from consideration in these breakdowns by racial and ethnic background.

Table 2.5.   Entry characteristics of LH participants and all first-time freshmen in their entry cohorts by racial and ethnic background

Entry Characteristic	Learning Habits Participants		All Entering Freshmen	
	Traditionally Underserved	Better Served	Traditionally Underserved	Better Served
Participation Criteria				
High School GPA of 3.5 or higher				
and Proficient at entry	24.6	40.1	—	—
but Needed remediation	31.3	14.5	—	—
High School GPA below 3.5 but				
Proficient at entry	44.0	45.4	—	—
Total	100.0	100.0		
(No. of participants)	(284)	(469)		
	Chi square = 36.44 (.001); df = 2 Cramer's V = .220			
High School GPA				
2.74 or less	4.9	4.7	19.1	16.1
2.75–2.99	5.6	8.7	21.0	18.6
3.00–3.24	16.9	16.6	27.1	25.6
3.25–3.49	16.6	15.4	17.2	17.7
3.50–3.74	31.7	25.0	10.1	12.4
3.75 or higher	24.3	29.6	5.5	9.7
Total	100.0	100.0	100.0	100.0
(No. of participants)	(284)	(469)	(11,128)	(7,326)

(continued)

Table 2.5. *Continued*

Entry Characteristic	Learning Habits Participants		All Entering Freshmen	
	Traditionally Underserved	*Better Served*	*Traditionally Underserved*	*Better Served*
Mean	3.46	3.48	3.08	3.16
Median	3.54	3.50	3.05	3.13
Interquartile range	3.2–3.7	3.2–3.8	2.8–3.3	2.9–3.4
	F = 0.51 (NS); df = 1 Eta = .014		F = 167.99 (.001); df = 1 Eta = .095	
Proficiency at Entry				
Fully Proficient	68.3	85.5	18.2	42.1
Needs remediation in:	31.7	14.5	81.8	57.9
English only	*8.8*	*6.4*	*14.8*	*19.9*
Mathematics only	*9.9*	*5.3*	*12.1*	*11.9*
Both subjects	*13.0*	*2.8*	*54.9*	*26.1*
Total	100.0	100.0	100.0	100.0
(No. of participants)	(284)	(469)	(11,128)	(7,326)
	Chi square = 31.53 (.001); df = 1 Cramer's V = .205		Chi square = 1256.41 (.001); df = 1 Cramer's V = .261	
SAT Composite Scores				
Below 700	8.8	7.3	20.9	13.6
700–799	3.9	0.4	16.7	5.8
800–899	12.0	3.6	23.5	13.5
900–999	19.0	10.2	20.5	21.2
1000–1099	26.1	29.2	11.7	21.2
1100–1199	21.8	27.3	5.0	15.1
1200 or higher	8.5	22.0	1.8	9.6
Total	100.0	100.0	100.0	100.0
(No. of participants)	(284)	(469)	(11,128)	(7,326)
Mean	941.9	1031.2	774.9	889.8
Median	1020.0	1090.0	850.0	980.0
Interquartile range	900–1110	1010–1180	730–960	840–1090
	F = 14.62 (.001); df = 1 Eta = .138		F = 534.61 (.001); df = 1 Eta = .168	
College Housing Planned Major				
Arts, Media, and Communication	14.1	17.9	12.0	17.8
Business and Economics	14.4	12.8	12.1	16.9
Education	1.1	1.9	0.5	1.3
Engineering and Computer Science	3.9	8.7	7.3	8.2
Health and Human Development	11.6	11.1	10.7	11.9

Entry Characteristic	Learning Habits Participants		All Entering Freshmen	
	Traditionally Underserved	*Better Served*	*Traditionally Underserved*	*Better Served*
Humanities	5.3	5.3	4.7	4.7
Science and Mathematics	10.6	17.3	8.9	9.8
Social and Behavioral Sciences	16.2	7.9	17.6	9.0
Undeclared	22.9	17.1	26.2	20.3
Total	100.0	100.0	100.0	100.0
(No. of participants)	(284)	(469)	(11,128)	(7,326)
	Chi square = 28.47 (.001); df = 8 Cramer's V = .194		Chi square = 519.01 (.001); df = 8 Cramer's V = .168	

3.50 or higher). For the other two entry characteristics considered, stronger differences are evident. Thus, the better-served LH students are more likely than their traditionally underserved counterparts to be fully proficient at entry (86 vs. 68 percent) and to score 1000 or higher on the SAT (79 vs. 56 percent). These differences in performance, while clear-cut, are weaker among LH students than within the larger freshman group. By way of example, within the larger freshman grouping, 42 percent of the better-served students entered fully proficient compared to only 18 percent of the traditionally underserved.

The differences by major evident among LH students are not typical of those in the larger freshman group. The last section of table 2.5 indicates that LH students from traditionally underserved backgrounds are more likely than those from better-served backgrounds to plan majors housed in the College of Social and Behavioral Sciences (16 vs. 8 percent) and less likely to plan majors in two other colleges: science and mathematics (11 vs. 17 percent) or engineering and computer science (4 vs. 9 percent).[7]

ACADEMIC ACHIEVEMENT

Once attention shifts to academic performance, differences within the larger freshman group are not regularly mirrored among the LH students. This is evident from the persistence measures summarized in table 2.6. Of the four first-year measures shown, only one gives rise to a statistically significant difference among LH students. In this instance, students from better-served backgrounds earned somewhat higher GPAs at the end of their first year than did those from traditionally underserved backgrounds: 76 versus 69 percent had GPAs exceeding 3.00. For the other three indicators, no differences in performance are evident. Both groups of LH students have nearly identical one-year continuation rates (94 vs. 92 percent) and end their first year in good academic standing (94 vs. 97 percent) and with 25 or more earned units in hand (79 percent for both). Within the larger freshman group, in contrast, clear differences in performance persist on all four indicators, with better-served students consistently outperforming those from traditionally under-served backgrounds. The smallest gap in performance is found in one-year continuation rates (a difference of nine percentage points), while the gaps for the other three indicators range from 14 to 16 percentage points.

When it comes to persistence to graduation, similar differences in performance are evident in most cases. According to the middle sections of table 2.6, better-served LH students were somewhat more likely than their traditionally underserved counterparts to have a baccalaureate degree in hand by the end of the 2015/2016 college year (79 vs. 70 percent), to have graduated within four years (41 vs. 32 percent), and to have graduated within five years (63 vs. 53 percent). When it comes to the "likely" graduation rate, which includes students who remained enrolled in their thirteenth term after entry, differences in performance attenuate even further, with 73–80 percent considered likely to graduate. This stands in contrast to the larger freshman group, where a gap of 14 percentage points remains for the "likely" graduation rate. A similar, though less dramatic, contrast is seen for degree status, where the gap between the better served and traditionally underserved in the proportion of students completing the baccalaureate degree is 9 percent for LH students compared to 16 percent for the larger group.

The last three sections of table 2.6 summarize characteristics of degree recipients. Here, differences in performance remain evident for final GPA: 83 percent of LH students from better-served backgrounds graduated with a GPA of at least 3.00 compared to 74 percent of their traditionally underserved counterparts. The gap in performance is smaller, however, than the one seen within the larger freshman grouping (59 vs. 46 percent with a 3.0 GPA). A similar pattern is evident for the time-to-degree measure. The better-served LH students are somewhat more likely than their traditionally underserved counterparts to have graduated within four years (52 vs. 46 percent). This gap, however, is smaller than the size of the one for the larger freshman grouping (29 vs. 20 percent graduating in four years). The third measure—cumulative units earned—shows no real gaps in performance, undoubtedly because the university-imposed ceiling on unit accumulation prevents them from emerging.

In sum, this discussion reveals typical differences in both the background and college preparedness of the LH students stemming from different racial and ethnic backgrounds: students from traditionally underserved backgrounds are more likely than those from better-served backgrounds to be Pell Grant

Table 2.6. Persistence and academic success of LH participants and all first-time freshmen in their entry cohorts by racial and ethnic background

	Learning Habits Participants		All Entering Freshmen	
Persistence Measure	Traditionally Underserved	Better Served	Traditionally Underserved	Better Served
One-Year Continuation Rate				
Enrolled at beginning of second year	92.3	93.8	69.5	78.6
Not enrolled at beginning of second year	7.8	6.2	30.5	21.4
Total	100.0	100.0	100.0	100.0
(No. of participants)	(284)	(469)	(11,128)	(7,326)
	Chi square = 0.68 (NS); df = 1 Cramer's V = .030		Chi square = 187.56 (.001); df = 1 Cramer's V = .101	
Academic Standing at End of First Year				
In good standing	94.4	96.8	67.1	80.8
On probation	3.5	2.4	15.8	9.8
Disqualified	2.1	0.9	17.1	9.4
Total	100.0	100.0	100.0	100.0
(No. of participants)	(284)	(469)	(11,090)	(7,275)
	Chi square = 3.10 (NS); df = 2 Cramer's V = .064		Chi square = 414.29 (.001); df = 2 Cramer's V = .150	
CSUN GPA at End of First Year				
1.99 or less	5.6	3.0	29.6	17.1
2.00–2.49	7.4	4.9	19.6	14.9
2.50–2.99	17.6	15.8	23.8	24.6
3.00–3.49	37.7	32.4	19.5	26.2
3.50–3.74	16.2	21.5	4.9	10.7
3.75 or higher	15.5	22.4	2.6	6.5
Total	100.0	100.0	100.0	100.0
(No. of participants)	(284)	(469)	(10,707)	(7,149)
Mean	3.16	3.32	2.39	2.73
Median	3.23	3.42	2.51	2.87
Interquartile range	2.9–3.6	3.0–3.7	1.8–3.0	2.3–3.3
	$F = 15.56$ (.001); df = 1 Eta = .142		$F = 683.33$ (.001); df = 1 Eta = .189	
Cumulative CSUN Units Earned at End of First Year				
15 or fewer units	2.1	1.7	20.3	14.5
16–24 units	19.0	19.4	37.9	29.5
25–30 units	67.6	61.0	35.9	47.0
31 or more units	11.3	17.9	5.9	8.9
Total	100.0	100.0	100.0	100.0
(No. of participants)	(284)	(469)	(11,128)	(7,326)

(continued)

Table 2.6. *Continued*

Persistence Measure	Learning Habits Participants		All Entering Freshmen	
	Traditionally Underserved	Better Served	Traditionally Underserved	Better Served
Mean	26.4	27.1	21.3	23.3
Median	27.0	27.0	24.0	25.0
Interquartile range	25–29	25–30	18–27	21–28
	F = 4.96 (.03); df = 1 Eta = .081		F = 309.43 (.001); df = 1 Eta = .128	

Degree Status (at end of 2015–2016)

Baccalaureate Degree completed	70.4	79.1	41.6	57.5
Degree not completed	29.6	20.9	58.4	42.5
but still enrolled at CSUN (13th term after entry)	*2.5*	*1.1*	*4.7*	*3.1*
and no longer enrolled at CSUN	*27.1*	*19.8*	*53.7*	*39.4*
Total	100.0	100.0	100.0	100.0
(No. of participants)	(284)	(469)	(11,128)	(7,325)
	Chi square = 7.28 (.008); df = 1 Cramer's V = .098		Chi square = 442.87 (.001); df = 1 Cramer's V = .155	

Four-Year Graduation Rate

Graduated in Four Years or Less	32.4	40.7	8.1	16.9
Did Not Graduate within Four Years	67.6	59.3	91.9	83.1
Total	100.0	100.0	100.0	100.0
(No. of participants)	(284)	(469)	(11,128)	(7,325)
	Chi square = 5.23 (.024); df = 1 Cramer's V = .083		Chi square = 333.31 (.001); df = 1 Cramer's V = .134	

Five-Year Graduation Rate

Graduated in Five Years or Less	52.8	62.5	30.0	44.5
Did Not Graduate within Five Years	47.2	37.5	70.0	55.5
Total	100.0	100.0	100.0	100.0
(No. of participants)	(284)	(469)	(11,128)	(7,325)
	Chi square = 6.81 (.009); df = 1 Cramer's V = .095		Chi square = 403.53 (.001); df = 1 Cramer's V = .148	

Likely Graduation Rate

Graduated or Enrolled in 13th term after entry	72.9	80.2	48.4	62.2
No longer enrolled at CSUN	27.1	19.8	51.7	37.8

Persistence Measure	Learning Habits Participants		All Entering Freshmen	
	Traditionally Underserved	Better Served	Traditionally Underserved	Better Served
Total	100.0	100.0	100.0	100.0
(No. of participants)	(284)	(469)	(11,128)	(7,325)
	Chi square = 5.37 (.024); df = 1 Cramer's V = .031		Chi square = 339.69 (.001); df = 1 Cramer's V = .136	

Baccalaureate Degree Recipients

CSUN GPA at Graduation

Persistence Measure	Traditionally Underserved	Better Served	Traditionally Underserved	Better Served
1.99 or less	0.0	0.3	0.2	0.1
2.00–2.49	5.5	3.2	15.3	9.5
2.50–2.99	20.5	13.8	39.1	31.1
3.00–3.49	40.0	37.7	33.2	37.5
3.50–3.74	20.5	22.9	8.7	14.3
3.75 or higher	13.5	22.1	3.6	7.5
Total	100.0	100.0	100.0	100.0
(No. of participants)	(200)	(371)	(4,634)	(4,209)
Mean	3.26	3.38	2.95	3.1
Median	3.29	3.43	2.94	3.11
Interquartile range	3.0–3.6	3.1–3.7	2.6–3.3	2.8–3.4
	$F = 10.15$ (.002); df = 1 Eta = .132		$F = 246.41$ (.001); df = 1 Eta = .165	

Cumulative CSUN Units Earned

Persistence Measure	Traditionally Underserved	Better Served	Traditionally Underserved	Better Served
110 or fewer units	0.0	0.0	0.0	0.2
111–120 units	9.5	12.1	3.0	7.6
121–130 units	42.5	40.7	36.7	40.7
131 or more units	48.0	47.2	60.2	51.6
Total	100.0	100.0	100.0	100.0
(No. of participants)	(200)	(371)	(4,634)	(4,209)
Mean	133.8	133.3	134.7	133.7
Median	130.0	128.0	132.0	131.0
Interquartile range	123–141	122–142	127–140	125–140
	$F = .220$ (NS); df = 1 Eta = .020		$F = 16.72$ (.001); df = 1 Eta = .043	

Time to Degree

Persistence Measure	Traditionally Underserved	Better Served	Traditionally Underserved	Better Served
Four years or less	46.0	51.5	19.5	29.4
Four to six years	38.5	32.9	72.8	64.6
More than six years	15.5	15.6	7.8	6.0
Total	100.0	100.0	100.0	100.0
(No. of participants)	(200)	(371)	(4,634)	(4,209)
Mean	4.6	4.5	5.1	4.9
Median	4.5	4.0	5.0	5.0
Interquartile range	4.0–5.0	4.0–5.0	4.5–5.5	4.0–5.0
	$F = 6.00$ (.015); df = 1 Eta = .102		$F = 117.64$ (.001); df = 1 Eta = .115	

recipients and to have parents with no more than a high school education. Further, they enter college more likely to need developmental work in at least one subject and to have composite SAT scores below 1000. Despite these clear differences in background and preparation, differences in achievement between LH students from either background are remarkably small, with a number disappearing entirely.

DID PARTICIPATION IN THE LEARNING HABITS PROJECT ENHANCE STUDENTS' PERSISTENCE TO GRADUATION?

The findings discussed in this chapter add import to the question posed here: can some of the unusually high levels of achievement among LH students be ascribed to their participation in the project? Or is their greater success simply a function of their better preparation for college work?

A multivariate regression analysis focusing on all freshmen eligible to participate in the Learning Habits Project provided a preliminary answer to these questions. The analysis focused on two outcome measures: the four-year graduation rate and the "likely" graduation rate, both as of fall 2015. Five antecedent variables were entered into the model in two steps: two background variables (i.e., gender and racial/ethnic background), followed by three measures of preparedness for college work at entry: proficiency in mathematics and English, SAT scores, and high school GPA, with the last being the most influential. Participation in LH was the final factor entered into the model. For both persistence measures, the variance explained was modest: 8 percent for the four-year graduation rate and 5 percent for the "likely" graduation rate. In both instances, however, LH status accounted for one-fifth and one-seventh, respectively, of the variance explained, suggesting that the experience itself contributed to the academic persistence and success of participants. The fact that both models explain relatively little variance overall may well be a sign that the road to college graduation has multiple forks, with a greater range of factors in play at each juncture than the model took into account.

Table 2.5 pinpointed some of the persistence measures on which LH students excelled in comparison to incoming freshmen who were invited to participate but chose not to. Statistically significant differences were evident for most of the indicators considered, with notable differences evident for the following: GPA and earned units at the end of the first year, the four-year graduation rate, and cumulative GPA at graduation. Given the importance of high school GPA in the regression analysis, figures 2.1 and 2.2 trace the two measures of longer-term persistence examined across the full high school

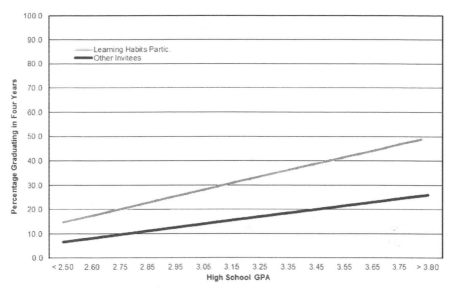

Figure 2.1.   The percent of incoming freshmen graduating within four years by learning habits status of qualified students.

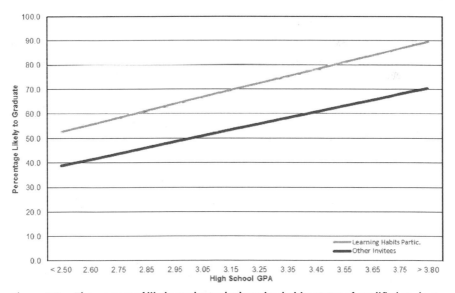

Figure 2.2.   The percent of likely graduates by learning habits status of qualified students.

GPA spectrum. Both figures indicate that LH students, shown in gray, consistently outperform nonparticipants, shown in black. Since variation in preparedness has been controlled for, the space between the two smoothed lines represents the gain attributable to participation in the project. The gradual increase in the gap suggests that better-prepared freshman entrants gained disproportionately from participation in the project.

The summary figures shown in table 2.7 examine the nature of the project's effect from another perspective: the gap in performance between traditionally underserved and better-served students who did and did not participate in the project. Such gaps are currently receiving considerable attention in the scholarly literature and proving hard to attenuate. Thus, it is of particular interest that some gaps shown on the right side of table 2.7 are smaller among LH students than among nonparticipants. Evidence of this comes from two sources. First, among nonparticipants, differences in persistence between traditionally underserved and better-served students are statistically significant at the .001 level for almost all indicators shown. Among the LH students, in contrast, such a significance level is approximated in only two cases: the cumulative GPA figures for the end of the first college year and at graduation.

Comparing the gaps shown on the right side of the table reveals a similar trend: for six of the eight indicators examined, the gap is at least modestly smaller among LH students than it is among nonparticipants, with better-served students outperforming traditionally underserved in all cases. The relatively small gap in one-year continuation rates is reduced by almost half among LH students and eliminated entirely in the case of cumulative units earned at the end of the first year. Similarly, a 7.6 percent gap in the proportion of four-year graduates among the nonparticipating degree recipients is reduced to 5.5 percent among LH students, a reduction of one-quarter.

In sum, the data suggest that much of the reason LH students performed exceptionally well in college, despite some typical gaps in their preparation at entry, stems from the fact that they entered better prepared than students who could have joined the project but did not. And these differences in preparation clearly explain the performance difference between the LH students and those in their entry cohorts who did not meet the project's participation criteria.

However, the data also suggest that aspects of the LH experience facilitated participants' persistence to graduation. Two sources of evidence support this conclusion: participants' unusually high comparative academic success and the reduction in the usual performance gap between traditionally underserved and better-served project participants.

LH features that played a role in fostering student success are the focus of chapter 12, which summarizes students' own reports of how the project facilitated their persistence to graduation. For the moment, it is sufficient

Table 2.7. Persistence and academic success of freshmen eligible to participate in Learning Habits Project by participation status and racial and ethnic background

Persistence Measure	Learning Habits Participants		Invited to Join; Did Not		Performance Gap (Better Served–Tradit. Under)	
	Traditionally Underserved	Better Served	Traditionally Underserved	Better Served	Partic.	Invited
One-Year Continuation Rate						
Enrolled at beginning of second year	92.3	93.8	77.6	80.4	1.6	2.8
Not enrolled at beginning of second year	7.8	6.2	22.4	19.6		
Total	100.0	100.0	100.0	100.0		
(No. of participants)	(284)	(469)	(2,958)	(3,296)		
	Chi square = 0.68 (NS); df = 1 Cramer's V = .030		Chi square = 7.46 (.007); df = 1 Cramer's V = .035			
CSUN GPA at End of First Year						
Mean	3.16	3.32	2.64	2.88		
Median	3.23	3.42	2.81	3.05	0.19	0.24
Interquartile range	2.9–3.6	3.0–3.7	2.1–3.3	2.5–3.5		
(Number of students on which averages based)	(284)	(469)	(2,873)	(3,216)		
	$F = 15.56$ (.001); df = 1 Eta = .142		$F = 108.916$ (.001); df = 1 Eta = .131			
Cumulative CSUN Units Earned at End of First Year						
Mean	26.4	27.1	22.4	23.6		
Median	27.0	27.0	24.0	25.0	0.0	1.0
Interquartile range	25–29	25–30	20–27	22–28		
(Number of students on which averages based)	(284)	(469)	(2,958)	(3,296)		
	$F = 4.96$ (.03); df = 1 Eta = .081		$F = 42.68$ (.001); df = 1 Eta = .082			

(continued)

Table 2.7. *Continued*

Persistence Measure	Learning Habits Participants		Invited to Join; Did Not		Performance Gap (Better Served– Tradit. Under)	
	Traditionally Underserved	Better Served	Traditionally Underserved	Better Served	Partic.	Invited
Degree Status (at end of 2015–2016)						
Baccalaureate Degree completed	70.4	79.1	50.0	60.0	8.7	10.0
Degree not completed	29.6	20.9	50.0	40.0		
but still enrolled at CSUN (13th term after entry)	*2.5*	*1.1*	*5.5*	*3.3*		
and no longer enrolled at CSUN	*27.1*	*19.8*	*44.5*	*36.7*		
Total	100.0	100.0	100.0	100.0		
(No. of participants)	(284)	(469)	(2,958)	(3,295)		
	Chi square = 7.28 (.008); df = 1 Cramer's V = .098		Chi square = 63.47 (.001); df = 1 Cramer's V = .101			
Likely Graduation Rate						
Graduated or Enrolled in 13th term after entry	72.9	80.2	57.2	64.6	7.3	7.3
No longer enrolled at CSUN	27.1	19.8	42.8	35.5		
Total	100.0	100.0	100.0	100.0		
(No. of participants)	(284)	(469)	(2,958)	(3,295)		
	Chi square = 5.37 (.024); df = 1 Cramer's V = .084		Chi square = 35.43 (.001); df = 1 Cramer's V = .075			
Four-Year Graduation Rate						
Graduated in Four Years or Less	32.4	40.7	13.9	21.2	8.3	7.4
Did Not Graduate within Four Years	67.6	59.3	86.1	78.8		
Total	100.0	100.0	100.0	100.0		

Persistence Measure	Learning Habits Participants		Invited to Join; Did Not		Performance Gap (Better Served–Tradit. Under)	
	Traditionally Underserved	Better Served	Traditionally Underserved	Better Served	Partic.	Invited
(No. of participants)	(284)	(469)	(2,958)	(3,295)		
	Chi square = 5.23 (.024); df = 1 Cramer's V = .083		Chi square = 57.63 (.001); df = 1 Cramer's V = .096			
Time to Degree						
Four years or less	46.0	51.5	27.8	35.4	5.5	7.6
Four to six years	38.5	32.9	67.0	59.6		
More than six years	15.5	15.6	5.2	5.0		
Total	100.0	100.0	100.0	100.0		
(No. of participants)	(200)	(371)	(1,478)	(1,977)		
Mean	4.6	4.5	4.9	4.7		
Median	4.5	4.0	5.0	4.5		
Interquartile range	4.0–5.0	4.0–5.0	4.0–5.0	4.0–5.0		
	F = 6.00 (.015); df = 1 Eta = .102		F = 16.82 (.001); df = 1 Eta = .070			
CSUN GPA at Graduation*						
1.99 or less	0.0	0.3	0.2	0.2		
2.00–2.49	5.5	3.2	8.9	6.0		
2.50–2.99	20.5	13.8	31.6	24.6		
3.00–3.49	40.0	37.7	38.7	40.4	8.8	9.9
3.50–3.74	20.5	22.9	14.3	19.3		
3.75 or higher	13.5	22.1	6.4	9.6		
Total	100.0	100.0	100.0	100.0		
(No. of participants)	(200)	(371)	(1,478)	(1,977)		
Mean	3.26	3.38	3.11	3.20		
Median	3.29	3.43	3.11	3.23		
Interquartile range	3.0–3.6	3.1–3.7	2.8–3.4	2.9–3.5		
	F = 10.15 (.002); df = 1 Eta = .132		F = 42.88 (.001); df = 1 Eta = .111			

*The gap for CSUN GPA focused on the percentage of graduates with cumulative GPAs of 3.00 or higher.

to note an important implication of the LH students' college success: their reports of what works for them, both inside and outside the classroom, deserve serious consideration.

NOTES

1. Especially during recruitment of the last two LH cohorts, we closed the enrollment period rather quickly to avoid being overwhelmed by interested freshmen. Thus, although some of the freshmen among the invited nonparticipants chose not to participate, some undoubtedly intended to do so but did not commit as expeditiously as required.

2. Five subgroups make up the larger set of students stemming from traditionally underserved backgrounds: American Indians, Pacific Islanders, African Americans, Latina/o, and multirace. Others are referred to as stemming from "better-served" backgrounds.

3. The prevalence of Armenian is explained by CSUN's proximity to Glendale, a Los Angeles suburb with a high concentration of Armenian immigrants.

4. In this instance, "likely" graduates are those who had graduated by the end of the 2015/2016 academic year or were still enrolled at the university in their 13th term after entry.

5. Although the numbers are not large, it is worth noting that LH students who are no longer enrolled are somewhat more likely than nonparticipants to have been in good academic standing at departure (80 vs. 55 percent).

6. The summary figures appearing at the bottom of table 2.4 are shown to document that the traditionally underserved and better-served LH students are not disproportionately drawn from different entry cohorts. The small differences that appear are not statistically significant.

7. The relative disinterest in STEM disciplines among the traditionally underserved LH students likely derives from their greater need of remediation in mathematics at entry (23 vs. 8 percent for the better served).

Part Two

DIFFERING PATTERNS OF ENGAGEMENT WITHIN MAJOR STUDENT SUBGROUPS

Now that the basic parameters of the Learning Habits Project have been outlined, the three chapters in this section drill down into the data to examine the distinctive patterns among key student subgroups. Chapter 3 examines the views of first-generation students in the project, paying particular attention to the mechanisms they develop in response to the special challenges that many face. It also looks briefly at an unusual "advantage" first-generation students might have. Chapter 4 examines differences by gender, highlighting the distinctive preparation and learning habits that may enable women to persist at higher rates than men, both at California State University, Northridge (CSUN) and elsewhere. Finally, chapter 5 examines variation in responses to a question about the contribution of campus diversity to student learning. Although several sources of variation in these responses are examined, the combined impact of gender and planned major are shown to be the most consequential.

No chapter is devoted to differences by racial and ethnic background, largely because doing so would be duplicative, given the substantial overlap between racial and ethnic background and first-generation status, the importance of which is examined in detail. As is evident from the first section of the following table, close to a fifth of the learning habits (LH) students are first-generation college students, as we define it (i.e., both parents with no more than a high school education). Of these students, close to three in four stem from Latina/o backgrounds, making the two subcategories largely identical. The reverse also holds to a substantial degree: the majority of LH students from Latina/o backgrounds, who constitute four-fifths of participants stemming from traditionally underserved backgrounds, are first generation. This stands in stark contrast to students from other racial and ethnic backgrounds, less than one-tenth of whom are first generation and two-thirds of whom have at least one parent with a four-year degree.

Parental education levels and racial and ethnic background of the LH students*

	Parental Education (proxy for first-generation status)			
	High school or less — both parents	Some college — one or both	Four-year degree — one or both	Total
Racial and Ethnic Background				
Latina/o	51.3	23.5	25.2	100.0
Other	9.1	23.1	67.8	100.0
Total	22.7	23.2	54.1	100.0
(No. of students)				
Traditionally Underserved	78.4	41.6	21.2	38.9
Latina/o	*72.8*	*32.5*	*15.0*	*32.2*
Other	*5.6*	*9.0*	*6.2*	*6.7*
Better Served	21.6	58.4	78.8	61.1
Total	100.0	100.0	100.0	100.0
(No. of students)	(162)	(166)	(386)	(714)

**Note:* Students whose parental educational status is unknown (n = 44) are excluded from this table.

We did, of course, examine the LH data with an eye toward identifying differences in the study habits of students stemming from backgrounds that have been traditionally underserved or better served by higher education.[1] Surprisingly, little meaningful variation is evident within either the interview or the end-of-term data. Moreover, none of the modest differences that could be discerned were sufficiently strong to be considered statistically significant.

Although the lack of variation by racial and ethnic background was initially surprising, there may be a simple explanation for it: by and large, well-prepared college students, which the LH students clearly are, rely on similar techniques to succeed. As a result, the effective learning habits highlighted in the next sections of this volume would likely benefit less well-prepared students from all backgrounds, traditionally underserved or better served.

NOTE

1. Five subgroups make up the larger set of students stemming from backgrounds traditionally underserved by higher education: American Indians, Pacific Islanders, African Americans, Latina/o, and multirace. Others are referred to as stemming from better-served backgrounds.

3

Being the First to Go to College

Steven Graves

"Why are you [even] going to college? Just go work."

"The product of [my parents'] hard work . . . inspires me to keep working hard . . . to get into university. . . . My mom had to sell her wedding bands. So, my parents are willing to give up that much so that I can keep studying. It's heavy motivation."

The demographics of the United States are changing rapidly, and few places have witnessed this transition as dramatically as Los Angeles's San Fernando Valley, once dubbed "America's suburb" because it was the idyllic prototype of the postwar American community. Even a decade after its founding, our rapidly growing institution had startlingly little diversity in 1967. Of the 15,600 students, only 34 were black or Latina/o (*Los Angeles Times* 1998). Today, the valley remains largely prosperous, but it is far more working class, and the percentage of white residents has fallen below 50 percent. What was once ground zero for white, middle-class, nuclear families now foreshadows an America with a kaleidoscope of identities and familial backgrounds.

California State University, Northridge (CSUN), the flagship institution of the San Fernando Valley, presents a compelling case study of demographic changes in a comprehensive four-year, urban university setting. Among the numerous elements of change we are experiencing is a revolution in diversity. CSUN's percentage of white, non-Hispanic students fell below 50 percent in the early 1990s, and now Latino/a, African American, and other traditionally underserved students top 50 percent (CSUN Office of Institutional Research 2017). Classrooms like those at CSUN present a bounty of learning opportunities for everyone, but this diversity presents challenges as well. Many of the assumptions about students that have guided educators for decades may prove poor models for educational policy making and pedagogic strategy in the 21st century. How students adapt to the challenges of college when they come from homes where their parents have had little formal education figures prominently among these issues. The purpose of this chapter is to examine the role of family in the academic pathways taken by students in the Learning Habits Project (LHP), so we may learn how to better serve future students.

Our curiosity was driven by questions about how the educational attainment of family members of learning habits (LH) students affected a host of achievement measures and coping mechanisms, as well as other important pathway decisions, such as choice of major, cocurricular involvement, employment, living arrangements, and study habits. We also sought to better understand how demographic factors such as ethnicity, gender, language, income, and citizenship cross-cut against familial background in conditioning student success and pathways.

To answer our questions, we analyzed a host of data points collected from students in our study, in addition to analyzing hours of interview transcripts. Among the variables considered were the educational attainment of parents and siblings, along with the students' GPA at several points in their academic career, SAT scores, proficiency in math and English at entry, progress toward degree, and choice of major. After analysis of more than 700 students in the project, we found several important trends we believe are worthy of attention because of their implications for both educational policy and pedagogic strategies.

Our core finding is simple: family matters. Parents and siblings exercise considerable influence on the types of tools for success college students bring to campus from home. Our analysis shows that the level of parental educational attainment (PEA) has a number of effects on how students navigate college but that in numerous ways these effects appear to be different than they are commonly assumed to be, and different from what some prior research indicates. While it is clear that many first-generation students have stresses and obstacles differing from those experienced by students from families with a history of attending college, for some there is little advantage to having parents or siblings with college experience. We also found that students who are the first in their family to attend college derive occasional *benefits* from their first-generation status. On the whole, however, we must conclude that college is somewhat easier if the voice of experience is at home, or just a phone call away.

The benefits that accrue to students with a family history of college come in a variety of forms. Well-educated parents are helpful in very obvious ways: filling out applications, proofreading papers, helping with assignments, or even assisting with advanced work where students are following a career path blazed by a parent or older sibling. However, many students at CSUN, including among our LH students, come from families where parents primarily speak a language other than English. In these cases, parents are generally ineffective in helping students overcome *obvious* academic obstacles. These are dynamics we expected to find, and we did so regularly in the course of our interviews. Still, we found a number of other student-family interactions a bit more surprising, which we will elaborate on later. For the moment, we can argue quite forcefully that although student tools for success vary significantly by family background, almost all LH students found creative ways to leverage whatever advantages they had in their quests to succeed. Parents with degrees may pass on critical knowledge sets or academic skills to their children. But other parents, perhaps with modest educational backgrounds, have given their children the gifts of grit, persistence, and determination, which often prove just as critical to succeeding in college. Most LH students used multiple success tool kits, but different strategies for success appeared more regularly in some groups than in others. We discuss these strategies in the pages that follow.

ACCURATELY IDENTIFYING FIRST-GENERATION STUDENTS: LIMITATIONS OF COMMON PRACTICES

During the course of our work, we found that the standard, governmental definition of first-generation student (FGS)—the "child of family in which neither parent holds a 'First Bachelor's Degree'"—is too broad to be truly useful, at least in the California context. In particular, we find that first-generation students defined in the usual manner are not as homogeneous as they are assumed to be by the federal government and by researchers who rely on this standard definition. Looking more closely at *levels* of PEA, we found an unacceptably large within-group variation among students labeled first generation in the traditional sense. We believe that a more nuanced classification system is more informative.

We argue that students from families whose parents have had some exposure to higher education, even if only a few classes at a local community college, should not be considered first generation in the same sense as students whose parents have no more than a high school education. Their numbers are not trivial. Among LH students, they constitute close to one-quarter of the total, equal in number to the students whose parents have no more than a high school education. Further, among the freshman cohorts from which the LH students were drawn, one-quarter of all entrants have one or more parents with some college experience. So, even without degree attainment, students with such parents would appear to accrue significant advantages over those whose parents did not go to college at all.

As you will see in the next sections of this chapter, students whose parents have some college often display characteristics that more closely mimic patterns exhibited by their peers from families where parents have college degrees. This is true of average SAT scores, for example, along with some of the persistence measures considered (see tables 3.2 and 3.3). On the other hand, students from families where parents have had no exposure to college, or even high school, tend to exhibit distinct patterns in terms of GPA, major, and other metrics. As such, they should perhaps be the only ones considered truly first-generation students.

We are not the first to recognize the mismatch between government categories and the lived realities on campuses. Penny McConnell (2000) offers a reasonably comprehensive review of the literature from 1982 to 1999. She found variations in the way "first generation" was defined from "first in *family* to *attend* college" to "neither parent attended college" and "neither parent graduated college," the last of which was used by the U.S. Department of Education (McConnell 2000, 76). A more recent examination of the issue lends support to our findings (Ward, Siegal, and Davenport 2012).

Siblings

Another inadequacy of the federal definition of first-generation students is that it seems to assume there are no older children in these families. This is hardly the case. The LH data provide some insight into the experience of participants' siblings because we asked about them as a prelude to face-to-face interviews. Although there are some discrepancies in the two sets of responses, as the second and third sections of table 3.1 indicate, between 20 and 25 percent have siblings who attended college. Further, if one combines the two sets of responses and eliminates the missing information, the data suggest that two-fifths of the supposedly "true" first-generation students have immediate family members with college experience. Although the qualitative data discussed below document the benefits of being able to watch older siblings make the transition to college, the LH data do not provide evidence that first-generation students with college-attending siblings persist at higher rates than other first-generation students. Such a pattern may well be atypical, however, given the uniformly high college preparedness of the LH students in general.

In addition to the presence of college-attending siblings, first-generation students among LH respondents vary in several aspects of family background. As the fifth section of table 3.1 indicates, four in five have parents who were raised outside the United States. Only three-fifths are native English speakers,

Table 3.1. Characteristics associated with first-generation status by parental education

Characteristic	Both parents: high school or less	One or both parents with: some college	One or both parents with: a four-year college degree (college grad)	All Learning Habits Partic.
1. All Learning Habits Participants				
Percent	22.7	23.4	53.9	100.0
(Number)	(163)	(168)	(387)	(718)
2. First-Generation Status in Eyes of Respondents at Time of Freshman-Year Interviews				
First in family to attend college	35.6	16.1	2.6	13.2
Siblings attending college	21.5	13.7	5.4	11.0
Parents/grandparents attended college	2.5	23.8	38.2	26.7
Parents and siblings attended college	3.1	5.4	10.6	7.7
Family members have attended college (no other details provided)	3.1	4.2	7.2	5.6
No information	34.4	36.9	35.9	35.8
No Freshman interview	*12.3*	*10.1*	*11.9*	*11.6*
No information provided at time of interview	*22.1*	*26.8*	*24.0*	*24.2*
Total	100.0	100.0	100.0	100.0
(No. of participants)	(163)	(168)	(387)	(718)
3. First-Generation Status in Eyes of Respondents at Time of Junior-Year Interviews				
First in family to attend college	33.7	13.7	2.1	12.0
Siblings attending college*	26.4	14.3	5.9	12.5
Parents/grandparents attended college	4.3	23.2	42.9	29.5
Family members have attended college (no other details provided)	3.7	3.6	8.5	6.3
No information	31.9	45.2	40.6	39.7
No Freshman interview	*27.6*	*38.1*	*28.4*	*30.5*
No information provided at time of interview	*4.3*	*7.1*	*12.1*	*9.2*
Total	100.0	100.0	100.0	100.0
(No. of participants)	(163)	(168)	(387)	(718)

(*continued*)

Table 3.1. *Continued*

Characteristic	Both parents: high school or less	One or both parents with:		All
		some college	a four-year college degree (college grad)	Learning Habits Partic.
4. Refinement of First-Generation Designation (i.e., combination of first- and third-year responses)				
True First Generation	57.0	—	—	—
College Experience in Immediate Family	43.0	—	—	—
Total	100.0	—	—	—
(No. of participants)	(135)			
5. Country in Which Parents Grew Up				
Raised in the United States	19.0	44.0	48.3	40.6
Raised in Another Country	81.0	56.0	51.7	59.4
Total	100.0	100.0	100.0	100.0
(No. of participants)	(163)	(166)	(387)	(716)
6. LH Students' Native Language				
English	57.7	81.0	89.2	80.1
Another language	42.3	19.1	10.9	19.9
Total	100.0	100.0	100.0	100.0
(No. of participants)	(163)	(168)	(387)	(718)
7. Language Spoken in Students' Home while Growing Up				
English	21.7	54.7	56.2	47.9
Another language	78.3	45.3	43.8	52.1
Total	100.0	100.0	100.0	100.0
(No. of participants)	(161)	(161)	(381)	(703)
8. Languages Other Than English Spoken in Home				
Spanish	86.3	57.8	19.5	50.4
Armenian	6.5	23.4	11.9	12.1
Tagalog^	0.0	3.1	19.5	9.5
Korean	0.8	3.1	4.4	2.9
Arabic	1.6	3.1	3.1	2.6
Russian	0.0	1.6	5.0	2.6
Farsi^^	0.8	1.6	4.4	2.6
Vietnamese	1.6	1.6	2.5	2.0
Japanese	0.0	0.0	3.1	1.4
Assyrian	0.0	3.1	0.6	0.9
French	0.0	0.0	1.3	0.6
Gujarati	0.0	0.0	1.3	0.6

Characteristic	Both parents: high school or less	One or both parents with:		All Learning Habits Partic.
		some college	a four-year college degree (college grad)	
Italian	0.0	0.0	1.3	0.6
Mandarin	0.0	0.0	1.3	0.6
Thai	0.0	0.0	1.3	0.6
Two or more languages spoken	0.8	6.3	10.7	6.3
Other languages (only mentioned once)	3.2	6.3	12.6	8.1
Total	100.0	100.0	100.0	100.0
(No. of participants)	(124)	(64)	(159)	(347)

*In some of the respondents in this category, parents, as well as siblings, have attended college.
^A few students in the Tagalog grouping specified Filipino as their home language (0.9 percent).
^^A few students in the Farsi grouping specified Persian as their home language (0.6 percent).

First Generation—Freshman Interview: Chi square = 191.50 (.001); df = 8; Cramer's V = .456
First Generation—Junior Interview: Chi square = 181.71 (.001); df = 6; Cramer's V = .466
Country in Which Parents Grew Up: Chi square = 41.820 (.001); df = 2; Cramer's V = .242
Students' Native Language: Chi square = 71.36 (.001); df = 2; Cramer's V = .315
Languages Spoken in Home while Growing Up: Chi square = 57.53 (.001); df = 2; Cramer's V = .286

while close to four-fifths routinely heard a language other than English while growing up (see sections 6 and 7 of table 3.1). Not surprisingly, given the composition of the CSUN student body, the language most frequently heard is Spanish, with Armenian a distant second.[1]

A REVIEW OF THE LITERATURE

Numerous researchers have recognized that current and future generations of college students will look quite different from the largely white, middle-class college kids of the late 20th century. A quick search of Google Scholar suggests there were over 50,000 entries returned between 2000 and 2016 for the search term "first-generation college students." While the length and quality of those pieces vary substantially, a number of these studies informed our research.

The ways in which first-generation students differ from their counterparts is a common fascination among those studying college students. Some findings are well known. Numerous studies have shown that first-generation college students are more likely to be from underrepresented ethnic or racial backgrounds (see, e.g., Horn and Nuñez 2000); others have shown that first-generation students also tend to come from less economically well-off families (Terenzini et al. 1996). These findings concur with a large study done by the National Center for Educational Statistics (NCES; 1998), which found that first-generation students are also more likely to be women and a bit older on average than their counterparts. The same NCES study suggested that first-generation students are more strongly motivated to go to college by specific career aspirations than are their counterparts.

More germane to our research questions are studies that sought to explain *how* family background affects student success. In particular, we were interested in how families help their college students accrue "social capital" or "cultural capital" that allows these students to navigate both campus bureaucracies and collegiate value systems. For example, one study conducted on sophomores enrolled at five California State University campuses found there were significant differences between first-generation students and their counterparts in terms of GPA and perceived rate of persistence to graduation, and that these differences stemmed at least partly from differing degrees of perceived self-efficacy (Vuong, Brown-Welty, and Tracz 2010).

Perceptions of self-efficacy overlap in confusing ways with college preparation. Phillip Pratt and Thomas Skaggs (1989) claimed that little differences were evident in the high school experiences, academic abilities, and intellectual confidence of FGS but that these students tended to have many doubts about their preparation for college. There is some evidence to validate FGS reservations about their high school preparation. Patrick Terenzini and colleagues found that FGS had lower skills in terms of precollege math and reading, had taken fewer preparatory courses in the humanities and fine arts, and spent fewer hours per week studying (1996, 10). Karin Hsiao (1992) also found FGS more frequently lacking in time management skills.

Some studies essentially argue that perhaps the controlling variables for college success are really cultural and are strongly conflated with first-generation status. For example, one study found that a key obstacle to success among FGS is that college coursework by its very nature demands independence and individualism, two traits often at odds with the culture of working-class students socialized in environments that fostered collaborative learning (Stephens et al. 2012). A related study found that cocurricular involvement by FGS is important to success (Garcia 2015), yet indications suggest they are less likely to be involved in cocurricular activities. Pratt and Skaggs (1989) found that FGS are more likely to live and work off campus and have generally lower degrees of social integration into campus life. Terenzini and colleagues (1996) likewise found that first-generation students spent less time socializing with friends.

Another area of the literature finds various researchers trying to isolate the role of family in the pathways taken by college students. Using multivariate regression techniques, Graziella McCarron and Karen Inkelas (2006) found that parental involvement strongly predicted a host of outcomes for all college students, but the role of parents increased if the parents had completed college. Both Terenzini (1996) and Pratt and Skaggs (1989) found that first-generation students perceived their parents to be less supportive of their efforts to complete college.

METHODOLOGICAL NOTES

We started our analysis by looking at a variety of metrics for student success. We examined high school GPA, SAT scores and their equivalencies, English and math placement test scores, freshman GPA, cumulative GPA, and terminal GPA, among other metrics for our LH students. Because we were focused on analyzing the role of PEA, we were keen to examine the effects on performance metrics of having a parent with a bachelor's degree, as well as the students' choice of major and study habits. We also hoped to find any other evidence that would help us understand how best to assist students in our academic setting. Of course, we assumed that PEA does not function independently of gender, ethnicity, language, immigration status, siblings, and other variables, so we attempted to observe and analyze those effects as well. Our methodology was mixed, evolving as results forced us to reconsider our original approach. We began by doing a largely quantitative analysis of nearly 80 variables, using performance metrics and major as dependent indicators of student success and disposition.

Our initial, cursory inventory of traditionally defined first-generation students (TFGS) was disappointing, if not puzzling. We thought we might have to scrap this part of our study because first-generation students *as the federal government defines them* (TFGS) were generally indistinguishable on a host of metrics from their peers from families with a parent with a bachelor's degree (TBDF). These trends held true when we accounted for gender and ethnicity as well. We began to think that California's robust two-year community college system created a significant third category of parental educational attainment. We experimented with several different typologies, eventually settling on a three-category system. Students who reported their parents had never attended college were considered truly first-generation students (FGS). Students whose parents took some college classes or earned a two-year degree were found to share many traits and were placed in the category some college parents (SCP). Students with at least one parent holding a baccalaureate degree (SBDP) constituted our remaining category.

BASIC CHARACTERISTICS

Although LH students cannot be said to be typical of the larger fresh-man cohorts at CSUN from which they are drawn, they are representative enough to provide insight into the conditions and characteristics of FGS in the university at large. Tables 3.2–3.4 detail the differences and similarities between our cohort and the groups from which they were recruited. Our discussion focuses on the two extremes: the first-generation students (FGS) and students with baccalaureate degree parents (SBDP). The students whose parents have completed some college, while distinct in their own right, consistently fall between these two extremes, in keeping with their parents' midlevel educational attainment.

The data summarized in table 3.2 indicate that, with the exception of gender, there are clear differences in background among the three groups of LH students being considered.[2] As is the case with the larger body, FGS in our group were more likely to be poorer and from traditionally underserved backgrounds.[3] Whites and Asians make up less than 5 percent of the FGS in our group, leaving Latina/o students as the overwhelming majority. Conversely, there are a more robust number of students from the major ethnic groups from families with more exposure to college.

Table 3.2. Background characteristics of LH participants and all first-time freshmen in their entry cohorts by parental education

Background Characteristic	Learning Habits Participants			All Entering Freshmen		
	Both parents: High school or less	One or both parents with		Both parents: High school or less	One or both parents with	
		Some College	Four-Year College Degree		Some College	Four-Year College Degree
Gender						
Women	67.5	67.9	62.8	59.3	58.6	51.1
Men	32.5	32.1	37.2	40.7	41.4	48.9
Total	100.0	100.0	100.0	100.0	100.0	100.0
(No. of participants)	(163)	(168)	(387)	(7,179)	(4,507)	(6,045)
	Chi square = 1.88 (NS); df = 2; Cramer's V = .051			Chi square = 102.29 (.001); df = 2; Cramer's V = .076		
Racial and Ethnic Background*						
Traditionally Underserved	78.4	41.6	21.2	85.1	61.8	32.0

Background Characteristic	Learning Habits Participants			All Entering Freshmen		
	Both parents: High school or less	One or both parents with Some College	One or both parents with Four-Year College Degree	Both parents: High school or less	One or both parents with Some College	One or both parents with Four-Year College Degree
American Indian	0.0	0.6	0.0	0.1	0.4	0.4
Pacific Islander	0.0	0.0	0.0	0.1	0.5	0.4
African American	4.9	6.6	3.9	7.9	19.6	11.5
Latina/o	72.8	32.5	15.0	76.3	39.4	18.0
Multirace	0.6	1.8	2.3	0.7	2.0	1.7
Better Served	21.6	58.4	78.8	14.9	38.2	68.0
Asian	3.1	7.2	20.7	6.4	9.6	20.0
White	0.6	1.2	2.9	0.2	0.7	1.6
Multirace (i.e., Asian and white)	13.6	44.0	47.9	5.9	22.1	38.9
Decline to state	4.3	6.0	7.3	2.5	5.8	7.5
Total	100.0	100.0	100.0	100.0	100.0	100.0
(No. of participants)	(162)	(166)	(386)	(7,003)	(4,433)	(5,739)

Chi square = 157.39 (.001); df = 2; Cramer's V = .470   Chi square = 3741.64 (.001); df = 2; Cramer's V = .467

Pell Grant Status (proxy for low income)

	Both parents: High school or less	One or both parents with Some College	One or both parents with Four-Year College Degree	Both parents: High school or less	One or both parents with Some College	One or both parents with Four-Year College Degree
Pell Grant recipient	73.0	35.1	18.6	78.6	52.7	23.2
No grant received	27.0	64.9	81.4	21.4	47.3	76.8
Total	100.0	100.0	100.0	100.0	100.0	100.0
(No. of participants)	(163)	(168)	(387)	(7,179)	(4,507)	(6,045)

Chi square = 149.57 (.001); df = 2; Cramer's V = .456   Chi square = 4043.99 (.001); df = 2; Cramer's V = .478

Entry Term

	Both parents: High school or less	One or both parents with Some College	One or both parents with Four-Year College Degree	Both parents: High school or less	One or both parents with Some College	One or both parents with Four-Year College Degree
Fall 2007	7.4	14.3	11.6	17.1	24.3	23.9
Fall 2008	17.8	18.5	22.7	22.2	24.3	24.2
Fall 2010	32.5	29.8	26.4	27.5	26.7	25.8
Fall 2011	42.3	37.5	39.3	33.2	24.8	26.1
Total	100.0	100.0	100.0	100.0	100.0	100.0
(No. of participants)	(163)	(168)	(387)	(7,179)	(4,507)	(6,045)

Chi square = 7.60 (NS); df = 6; Cramer's V = .073   Chi square = 198.72 (.001); df = 6; Cramer's V = .075

*International students have been excluded from consideration in these breakdowns by racial and ethnic background.

Table 3.3. Entry characteristics of LH participants and all first-time freshmen in their entry cohorts by parental education

Entry Characteristic	Learning Habits Participants			All Entering Freshmen		
	Both parents:	One or both parents with		Both parents:	One or both parents with	
	High school or less	Some College	Four-Year College Degree	High school or less	Some College	Four-Year College Degree
Participation Criteria						
High School GPA of 3.5 or higher and Proficient at entry	26.4	34.5	37.5	—	—	—
but Needed remediation	40.5	24.4	12.1	—	—	—
High School GPA below 3.5 but Proficient at entry	33.1	41.1	50.4	—	—	—
Total	100.0	100.0	100.0			
(No. of participants)	(163)	(168)	(387)			

Chi square = 56.21 (.001); df = 4; Cramer's V = .198

High School GPA						
2.74 or less	4.9	3.6	5.2	16.9	19.0	17.2
2.75–2.99	3.1	5.4	10.9	20.5	20.2	18.2
3.00–3.24	14.7	14.9	17.6	27.9	25.0	26.5
3.25–3.49	10.4	17.3	16.8	17.2	18.0	17.5
3.50–3.74	34.4	26.2	25.3	11.0	10.8	12.3
3.75 or higher	32.5	32.7	24.3	6.6	7.0	8.4
Total	100.0	100.0	100.0	100.0	100.0	100.0
(No. of participants)	(163)	(168)	(387)	(7,179)	(4,507)	(6,045)
Mean	3.54	3.53	3.42	3.10	3.10	3.13
Median	3.60	3.55	3.48	3.09	3.07	3.11
Interquartile range	3.3–3.8	3.3–3.8	3.1–3.7	2.8–3.4	2.8–3.4	2.9–3.4

F = 6.14 (.002); df = 2; Eta = .130   F = 8.49 (.001); df = 21; Eta = .031

Proficiency at Entry						
Fully Proficient	59.5	75.0	87.9	16.0	28.2	40.2
Needs remediation in:	40.5	25.0	12.1	84.0	71.8	59.8
English only	*14.1*	*6.6*	*4.9*	*16.9*	*16.4*	*18.1*

Entry Characteristic	Learning Habits Participants			All Entering Freshmen		
	Both parents: High school or less	One or both parents with		Both parents: High school or less	One or both parents with	
		Some College	Four-Year College Degree		Some College	Four-Year College Degree
Mathematics only	6.1	14.9	4.4	9.9	13.6	12.7
Both subjects	20.3	3.6	2.8	57.2	41.9	29.1
Total	100.0	100.0	100.0	100.0	100.0	100.0
(No. of participants)	(163)	(168)	(387)	(7,179)	(4,507)	(6,045)

Chi square = 55.95 (.001); df = 2; Cramer's V = .279   Chi square = 968.73 (.001); df = 2; Cramer's V = .234

SAT Composite Scores

Below 700	7.4	10.7	7.0	23.1	17.1	14.8
700–799	4.3	1.2	0.8	18.3	11.9	5.6
800–899	16.6	6.6	2.6	23.4	19.7	14.3
900–999	20.9	14.9	10.9	19.6	21.9	20.5
1000–1099	20.9	33.3	28.2	10.0	16.7	20.7
1100–1199	20.9	19.6	29.7	4.2	8.5	15.0
1200 or higher	9.2	13.7	20.9	1.4	4.2	9.1
Total	100.0	100.0	100.0	100.0	100.0	100.0
(No. of participants)	(163)	(168)	(387)	(7,179)	(4,507)	(6,045)
Mean	943.7	957.4	1034.1	754.0	819.7	876.5
Median	1000.0	1050.0	1100.0	830.0	900.0	970.0
Interquartile range	880–1120	955–1120	1010–1180	710–940	770–1020	840–1090

F = 6.44 (.002); df = 2; Eta = .133   F = 216.07 (.001); df = 2; Eta = .154

College Housing Planned Major

Arts, Media, and Communication	9.8	17.9	18.9	9.0	14.4	20.1
Business and Economics	16.6	13.1	12.4	12.5	15.0	16.9
Education	1.2	2.4	1.6	0.5	1.2	0.9
Engineering and Computer Science	6.1	3.6	8.8	7.8	7.5	9.2
Health and Human Development	13.5	10.7	10.9	10.3	11.9	11.8
Humanities	3.7	4.2	7.0	4.6	5.2	4.0

(continued)

Table 3.3. *Continued*

Entry Characteristic	Learning Habits Participants			All Entering Freshmen		
	Both parents: High school or less	One or both parents with		Both parents: High school or less	One or both parents with	
		Some College	Four-Year College Degree		Some College	Four-Year College Degree
Science and Mathematics	9.2	15.5	16.5	9.2	9.4	9.0
Social and Behavioral Sciences	18.4	13.1	7.5	17.8	14.0	10.2
Undeclared	21.5	19.6	16.5	28.4	21.5	18.0
Total	100.0	100.0	100.0	100.0	100.0	100.0
(No. of participants)	(163)	(168)	(387)	(7,179)	(4,507)	(6,045)
	Chi square = 35.49 (.003); df = 16; Cramer's V = .157			Chi square = 675.32 (.001); df = 16; Cramer's V = .138		

Table 3.4. **Persistence and academic success of LH participants and all first-time freshmen in their entry cohorts by parental education**

Persistence Measure	Learning Habits Participants			All Entering Freshmen		
	Both parents: High school or less	One or both parents with		Both parents: High school or less	One or both parents with	
		Some College	Four-Year College Degree		Some College	Four-Year College Degree
One-Year Continuation Rate						
Enrolled at beginning of second year	92.0	91.7	94.3	69.6	72.9	77.1
Not enrolled at beginning of second year	8.0	8.3	5.7	30.4	27.1	22.9
Total	100.0	100.0	100.0	100.0	100.0	100.0
(No. of participants)	(163)	(168)	(387)	(7,179)	(4,507)	(6,045)
	Chi square = 1.73 (NS); df = 2; Cramer's V = .049			Chi square = 94.86 (.001); df = 2; Cramer's V = .073		
Academic Standing at End of First Year						
In good standing	94.5	96.4	96.4	67.6	72.3	79.7
On probation	3.7	3.0	2.6	15.4	14.0	10.7
Disqualified	1.8	0.6	1.0	17.0	13.7	9.6

Persistence Measure	Learning Habits Participants			All Entering Freshmen		
	Both parents: High school or less	One or both parents with Some College	One or both parents with Four-Year College Degree	Both parents: High school or less	One or both parents with Some College	One or both parents with Four-Year College Degree
Total	100.0	100.0	100.0	100.0	100.0	100.0
(No. of participants)	(163)	(168)	(387)	(7,154)	(4,486)	(6,006)

Chi square = 1.72 (NS); df = 4; Cramer's V = .035   Chi square = 255.05 (.001); df = 4; Cramer's V = .085

CSUN GPA at End of First Year

1.99 or less	4.9	3.6	3.6	29.1	25.1	17.7
2.00–2.49	4.9	5.4	6.5	19.1	18.6	15.1
2.50–2.99	17.2	11.3	18.6	23.7	23.8	25.0
3.00–3.49	39.3	36.3	31.5	20.0	21.2	26.1
3.50–3.74	18.4	20.8	19.9	5.1	7.1	10.1
3.75 or higher	15.3	22.6	19.9	3.0	4.3	6.0
Total	100.0	100.0	100.0	100.0	100.0	100.0
(No. of participants)	(163)	(168)	(387)	(6,912)	(4,370)	(5,867)
Mean	3.19	3.32	3.26	2.40	2.51	2.71
Median	3.26	3.42	3.35	2.53	2.64	2.86
Interquartile range	3.0–3.6	3.1–3.7	2.9–3.7	1.8–3.1	2.0–3.2	2.3–3.3

$F = 1.51$ (NS); df = 3; Eta = .080 $F = 187.85$ (.001); df = 21; Eta = .144

Cumulative CSUN Units Earned at End of First Year

15 or fewer units	1.2	2.4	1.8	19.8	18.2	15.5
16–24 units	22.7	17.9	17.8	38.1	34.4	30.2
25–30 units	66.3	64.3	63.1	35.7	40.6	46.1
31 or more units	9.8	15.5	17.3	6.3	6.7	8.1
Total	100.0	100.0	100.0	100.0	100.0	100.0
(No. of participants)	(163)	(168)	(387)	(7,179)	(4,507)	(6,045)
Mean	26.4	26.7	27.1	21.4	22.1	23.0
Median	27.0	27.0	27.0	24.0	24.0	25.0
Interquartile range	25–28	25–29	25–30	18–26	19–27	20–28

$F = 1.46$ (.03); df = 3; Eta = .079 $F = 122.85$ (.001); df = 2; Eta = .090

Degree Status (at end of 2015–2016)

Baccalaureate Degree completed	69.9	79.2	76.5	41.1	48.9	54.8

(continued)

Table 3.4. *Continued*

Persistence Measure	Learning Habits Participants			All Entering Freshmen		
	Both parents: High school or less	One or both parents with		Both parents: High school or less	One or both parents with	
		Some College	Four-Year College Degree		Some College	Four-Year College Degree
Degree not completed	30.1	20.8	23.5	58.9	51.1	45.2
but still enrolled at CSUN	*3.1*	*1.2*	*1.3*	*3.5*	*3.0*	*2.5*
and no longer enrolled at CSUN	27.0	19.6	22.2	55.5	48.1	42.7
Total	100.0	100.0	100.0	100.0	100.0	100.0
(No. of participants)	(163)	(168)	(387)	(7,179)	(4,507)	(6,045)
	Chi square = 4.16 (NS); df = 2; Cramer's V = .076			Chi square = 252.11 (.001); df = 2; Cramer's V = .119		
Four-Year Graduation Rate						
Graduated in Four Years or Less	32.5	36.9	40.3	8.5	11.0	16.4
Did Not Graduate within Four Years	67.5	63.1	59.7	91.5	89.0	83.6
Total	100.0	100.0	100.0	100.0	100.0	100.0
(No. of participants)	(163)	(168)	(387)	(7,179)	(4,507)	(6,045)
	Chi square = 3.03 (NS); df = 2; Cramer's V = .065			Chi square = 200.25 (.001); df = 2; Cramer's V = .106		
Five-Year Graduation Rate						
Graduated in Five Years or Less	62.0	70.2	69.5	30.3	35.7	42.8
Did Not Graduate within Five Years	38.0	29.8	30.5	69.7	64.3	57.2
Total	100.0	100.0	100.0	100.0	100.0	100.0
(No. of participants)	(163)	(168)	(387)	(7,179)	(4,507)	(6,045)
	Chi square = 3.52 (NS); df = 2; Cramer's V = .070			Chi square = 216.16 (.001); df = 2; Cramer's V = .110		
Likely Graduation Rate						
Graduated or Enrolled in Fall 2016	73.0	80.4	77.8	44.6	51.9	57.3
No Longer Enrolled at CSUN	27.0	19.6	22.2	55.5	48.1	42.7

Persistence Measure	Learning Habits Participants			All Entering Freshmen		
	Both parents: High school or less	One or both parents with Some College	One or both parents with Four-Year College Degree	Both parents: High school or less	One or both parents with Some College	One or both parents with Four-Year College Degree
Total	100.0	100.0	100.0	100.0	100.0	100.0
(No. of participants)	(163)	(168)	(387)	(7,179)	(4,507)	(6,045)

Chi square = 2.66 (NS); df = 2; Cramer's V = .061   Chi square = 205.03 (.001); df = 2; Cramer's V = .108

Baccalaureate Degree Recipients

CSUN GPA at Graduation

Persistence Measure	LHP: HS or less	LHP: Some College	LHP: Four-Year	AEF: HS or less	AEF: Some College	AEF: Four-Year
1.99 or less	0.0	0.0	0.3	0.2	0.1	0.2
2.00–2.49	2.6	3.0	5.1	14.7	13.7	9.6
2.50–2.99	22.8	10.5	15.9	38.4	35.0	32.0
3.00–3.49	36.0	42.9	37.8	33.5	34.9	37.6
3.50–3.74	21.9	22.6	23.0	9.4	10.9	13.8
3.75 or higher	16.7	21.1	17.9	3.8	5.5	6.9
Total	100.0	100.0	100.0	100.0	100.0	100.0
(No. of participants)	(114)	(133)	(296)	(2,948)	(2,203)	(3,314)
Mean	3.29	3.39	3.33	2.97	3.02	3.09
Median	3.27	3.38	3.38	2.96	3.01	3.10
Interquartile range	3.0–3.6	3.2–3.7	3.1–3.7	2.7–3.3	2.7–3.4	2.8–3.4

F = 1.55 (NS); df = 2; Eta = .076   F – 56.64 (.001); df = 2; Eta = .115

Cumulative CSUN Units Earned

Persistence Measure	LHP: HS or less	LHP: Some College	LHP: Four-Year	AEF: HS or less	AEF: Some College	AEF: Four-Year
110 or fewer units	0.0	0.0	0.0	0.1	0.1	0.2
111–120 units	7.9	11.3	13.2	3.0	5.0	7.3
121–130 units	37.7	42.9	41.2	34.9	38.8	41.5
131 or more units	54.4	45.9	45.6	62.0	56.1	51.1
Total	100.0	100.0	100.0	100.0	100.0	100.0
(No. of participants)	(114)	(133)	(296)	(2,948)	(2,203)	(3,314)
Mean	135.4	133.0	132.7	135.0	134.2	133.6
Median	132.0	129.0	128.0	133.0	132.0	131.0
Interquartile range	125–145	123–141	122–140	128–140	126–140	125–140

F = 1.75 (NS); df = 2; Eta = .080   F =11.88 (.001); df = 2; Eta = .053

(continued)

Table 3.4. *Continued*

	Learning Habits Participants			All Entering Freshmen		
	Both parents: High school or less	One or both parents with		Both parents: High school or less	One or both parents with	
Persistence Measure		Some College	Four-Year College Degree		Some College	Four-Year College Degree
Time to Degree						
Four years or less	46.5	46.6	52.7	20.6	22.5	29.8
Four to six years	50.9	48.1	46.3	72.2	70.2	63.9
More than six years	2.6	5.3	1.0	7.2	7.3	6.3
Total	100.0	100.0	100.0	100.0	100.0	100.0
(No. of participants)	(114)	(133)	(296)	(2,948)	(2,203)	(3,314)
Mean	4.6	4.6	4.4	5.0	5.0	4.9
Median	4.5	4.5	4.0	5.0	5.0	5.0
Interquartile range	4.0–5.0	4.0–5.0	4.0–5.0	4.5–5.5	4.5–5.5	4.0–5.0
	$F = 2.14$ (NS); df = 2; Eta = .089			$F = 31.93$ (.001); df = 2; Eta = .087		

We found the differences in entry-level preparation by PEA intriguing. Among all students, the students with higher levels of PEA generally arrive apparently better prepared for college than their counterparts, especially in terms of SAT scores. Among LH students, however, we find that FGS students arrive with much better high school GPAs than students whose parents finished a bachelor's degree, contradicting the findings noted in Lee Ward, Michael Siegal, and Zebulun Davenport's work (2012). For the other two entry characteristics considered, stronger differences are evident: FGS are less likely than SBDP to be fully proficient at entry (60 vs. 88 percent) and to score 1,000 or higher on the SAT (51 vs. 79 percent).

FGS in our study group also tended to differ from SBDP students. They are nearly half as likely as students from SBDP to declare majors from the colleges of humanities; arts, media, and communication; or science and mathematics. Instead, FGS pick majors in social and behavioral sciences (especially sociology and psychology), or they are undeclared upon entry. These findings partially contradict earlier research that suggests that FGS are more likely to be certain about their major than their counterparts (Terenzini et al. 1996).

Several notable trends caught our attention in terms of the academic performance of FGS. The good news, at least for students in our group, is that PEA makes little difference. To be sure, it is still advantageous to come from families where parents have gone to college, but for the most part, LH FGS students graduated in a timely fashion and with a healthy GPA. The picture is not as rosy among the student population at large; less than half of our FGS are likely to leave CSUN with a diploma.

A lot of that dropout rate can be traced to an unsuccessful first year, so we were particularly interested in learning how student coping mechanisms are used by freshmen. At first glance, it appears that LH FGS were doing just as well as their counterparts. After all, over 90 percent were still enrolled after one year on campus, and their collective year-one GPAs averaged 3.19, just below what their counterparts were averaging. However, because GPA held such an outsized grasp on the self-assessment of success among FGS (see discussion below), it was interesting to note that the drop in GPA between high school and the freshman year was most exaggerated among FGS. This "freshman slump" would seem to be one indicator of preparation for college, and it was muted among SBDP, suggesting a far smoother transition to college for students whose parents had gone to or finished college. Among the general population, the freshman slump was more extreme, especially among FGS.

In sum, the above discussion revealed typical differences in both the background and college preparedness of FGS and SBDP LH students. FGS are more likely than SBDP to be Pell Grant recipients and stem from traditionally underserved backgrounds. They enter college more likely to need developmental work in at least one subject and to have composite SAT scores below 1,000. However, despite these clear differences in background and preparation, differences in achievement among LH students with differently educated parents are remarkably small, with many no longer statistically significant. Given the academic success of first-generation students in the Learning Habits Project, their views of beneficial campus and in-class practices should be of particular importance to faculty and staff interested in enhancing the success of the many similar students currently enrolled in diverse, urban institutions such as ours. These are reviewed in the remainder of this chapter.

BASIC FINDINGS AND THEIR IMPLICATIONS

The most basic finding of our analysis of LH students found that overall, first-generation students perform as well, and occasionally better, on several metrics of college success than their peers from bachelor's degree families. The data also suggest that neither standardized test scores nor high school GPA is a consistent marker for success in college. In general, we found that among our LH students, high school GPA was a better indicator of college GPA than SAT score and that high school GPA was higher among first-generation students than their counterparts whose parents had some college or a four-year degree.

Perhaps the most interesting trend made obvious by our expansion of PEA to three categories was the inverse relationship between high school GPA and PEA scores. LH students from families with the lowest levels of PEA had the best high school GPAs; increases in PEA level (from no high school to graduate school parents) resulted in progressively lower average high school GPAs. SAT scores were exactly the opposite. Students from families with greater educational attainment did much better on SATs. It is evident that FGS are worse test takers than their peers, and their SAT scores are significantly worse than SBDP peers (1,034 vs. 943). When we observed this phenomenon through the lens of ethnicity, the trend holds for high school GPA. For African American and Latina/o students, SAT scores are much higher for those from families with parents that had at least some college. The trend is less clear with whites and Asians, but it appears that SAT scores for these groups are less correlated with PEA.

THE FRESHMAN SLUMP

Of great concern to our research group was how students adjust to academic roadblocks. Transitioning from high school to college is in itself a challenge, and the adjustment from being a high school superstar to being merely "above average" very likely compounds the difficulty of freshman year. Almost all LH students saw their GPAs drop from high school to college. We call this the "freshman slump," and it is evident for every PEA category, both genders and all ethnicities. However, the freshman slump is greatest for students from the lowest PEA categories, especially for Latina/o and African American students, many of whom come to CSUN with sterling high school GPAs. SAT scores and their equivalents exhibit nearly a perfectly inverse relationship with high school GPA.

It seems plausible that students from underperforming high schools are not as well prepared for the strictly academic elements of college as are their peers from more competitive high schools, from which most of our SBDP come. We also speculate that students who are the first in their families to attend college have fewer *tangible* resources to draw upon as they encounter challenges in and out of the classroom. It's clear that students whose parents have advanced degrees have the smoothest transition to college. Those students often have less impressive high school GPAs, but it appears that the competitiveness of their high school experiences and familial resources they have to draw upon keep their college GPAs more in line with what they earned in high school.

The reason for the mismatch between high school GPA and SAT score may lie in the nature of the high schools that many of our students with low PEA attend. Many FGS come from large, urban high schools where few students are college bound. Within that context, students planning to go to college often find themselves consistently at the top of their class and without many peers with whom to both compete and cooperate. This is not to say that such students are unworthy of their lofty GPAs, but attending schools with fewer college-bound peers may present unique challenges to the graduates who do manage to go to college.[4] After a few semesters of college, the differences between these two student groups gradually disappear. By the time students in our group graduate from CSUN, both FGS and their SBDP peers have nearly the same GPA.

QUALITATIVE ASSESSMENT

Exactly how and why LH students, regardless of the level of PEA, wind up more or less indistinguishable on several performance indicators remains unclear, but the hundreds of interviews conducted with project participants do shed light on the impact of family on student trajectories. One persistent theme that caught our attention was how parental expectations shape student attitudes toward grades. Several surprising trends emerged that we suspect partly explain the curious relationship between high school GPA and college GPA. Parental attitudes toward grades and learning were one of the areas where we noticed divergence among students from different backgrounds. We noted that many FGS were subject to a wider variety of familial stressors. These stressors often appeared to be almost at odds with each other and more extreme than those faced by students whose parents went to college.

For example, it's not uncommon to hear students at our university lament a lack of family (community) emotional support. Students have told us that people in their family and community are dismissive of—or even hostile to—the value of higher education. Men, particularly from working-class Latina/o families, report a kind of emasculating harassment from other male community/family members who consider schooling, and even some career paths, as less than manly options. Women from some immigrant backgrounds also report that being the first to attend college represents a significant departure from traditional gender roles in their families, one that some parents find troubling, confusing, or insulting. While such statements were not common among our LH students, several interviews did reveal how parents from educationally limited backgrounds can offer less than helpful advice to a struggling student. One sociology major told us that her mother encouraged her to drop out after she earned a couple of poor grades. Her mother, perhaps not realizing the difficulty of getting straight As, asked, "Why are you [even] going to college?" and then advised her, "Just go work." The student did not take the suggestion to heart, but it's reasonably clear that many others in similar situations do exactly that.

Another sociology major reported a very similar exchange with his parents, who were lukewarm about the idea of college and a bit baffled about his participation in a campus club recommended by one of his professors:

> Casually, they said, "Yeah, don't be like us. Go to college," but they . . . don't really know what college is about. If I tell them about extracurricular [activities], they'll [say], "Why are you doing this? What is the point?" They don't really understand, and it gets frustrating. But eventually after long talks they eventually get it.

These two experiences stand in stark contrast to a kinesiology junior whose college-educated parents consider college a standard rite of passage, little different from attending high school:

> We're not the kind of family that [doesn't] go to college. Like it's kind of expected of everybody in my family to go to college. And so far, we all [siblings] are in college. So, the primary . . . motivation [for doing well] is the fact that . . . I have to be there. But I mean, I also really want to do well. . . . I'm constantly thinking ahead in my life . . . where do I see myself in five years, in 10 years.

Grades, rather than learning or the "collegiate" experience, also seem to garner an outsized emphasis among FGS and their parents. Consider one Latino engineering student who was exceptionally successful in high school, both as a student and an athlete. He was clear about how self-flagellation could become an issue when he failed to live up to his own exceptionally high standards. He told us about breaking the news to his parents (who did not attend college):

> My father and my mother, I always talk to them about my grades. But then when I refer to my family, it means my whole entire family. For some reason, they all look at me as this star person, this star athlete, this star student. I have to always excel. Anytime I fail, it feels like a burden because they all look at me differently.

He noted that many members of his extended family in rural Mexico also closely follow his grades and athletic accomplishments.

A business major from a similar background understands those expectations. His parents immigrated to the United States and his father works seven days a week, rising at 5:00 a.m. to clean properties. His mother is unable to work because of ill health. Along with our student, two siblings, and a dog, they live in a garage near East LA. His parents, despite their lack of educational background, expect straight As:

> They have the highest of the highest expectations for me. So if I get an A minus, it's like, well, you know, some people call it an "Asian F." So, you know, they have that kind of expectation.

Students whose parents did go to college seem to be generally less interested in GPA and instead impart a more holistic understanding of the value of education and how to manage unhealthy stress. A number of students in this SBDP group told us one of the most helpful things their college-educated parents provided was perspective. A chemistry major who called her parents her biggest supporters said they thought she worked too hard:

> They kind of want me to take it easy, not stress. So they, sometimes, kind of close my books and say, "You know you should go out and do something different." Yeah, so that's how they kind of remind me that I have a life.

Another pair of college-educated parents had similar advice for their finance major daughter, who was struggling with an economics course:

> Well, they have given me advice when I've been telling them that I've been . . . discouraged. . . . My mom told me to . . . make sure that at least one day a week I don't do any homework, so that helped.

One mother, who had also been through college, helped her daughter, an African American journalism major, to worry less about her GPA by staying focused on the learning process. She quoted her mother:

> I don't care about the grades you get. What I care about is you understanding, you gaining that knowledge because you're going to apply that later on in life, you know, and you're going to use these things that you're learning now in your profession.

Dealing with the stress of grades is only one of the ways LH students reported college-going parents as helpful. One of the most traumatic junctures in college is deciding on a major. It is pretty clear from our data that FGS consider fewer options for majors, in general. First-generation students tend to pursue degrees in highly practical fields (engineering, business, etc.) or where they experienced early success in their general education sequence (sociology, psychology, child development, etc.). Those from multigenerational college families tend to branch out a good bit more, and some of the interviews helped shed light on how these decisions might be made.

Two very good examples came from women majoring in theater, one of the majors least likely to attract first-generation students. One student said that telling her parents she wanted to major in theater was "like coming out of the closet," but still her parents supported her because, "no matter what it is I choose to do, they seem to like being a part of that, and [to] hear as much about it as they can so that they can see what's up with me, which is really nice." Another theater major noted that her family's happy acquiescence to her choice of major was partly rooted in her father's unhappiness with his decision to become an engineer and his subsequent career trajectory. She said,

> And because he never [majored in performing arts] . . . he regretted it. I think that I showed . . . a little bit of talent singing-wise, and then I said, "I love musical theater. I love singing musical theater songs; that's what I want to do." My dad was like, "If that's what you want to do, then that's what you want to do. And I will support you and whatever we can do to make that happen for you, we will." So, I think my parents are the most supportive people in the world. I've been extraordinarily lucky 'cause I know some theater majors, their parents are like, "Why are you a theater major? That's never going to get you anywhere in life."

Recognizing that the challenges presented by college are surmountable was another simple but effective advantage that students accrue if a parent, or a sibling, has gone to college. A computer science major explained that knowing her mother overcame great challenges in the classroom gave her confidence that she could also face down difficult odds:

> My mom has a master's degree. So it's kind of just like, this is what you have to do. My mom had me when she was 19 [and] she got her master's degree with me, so . . . it's to the point . . . where I'm just, like, need to get over it, need to get there. I don't even have a kid, so what am I shouting about?

Our quantitative analysis of our data suggests that siblings have a substantial impact on collegiate success. They seem to have a variety of influences on the academic and social trajectories of college students. For some, siblings are a burden, but on the whole brothers and sisters seem more often to be a help rather than a hindrance. For example, at CSUN and other campuses with large commuter populations, there are thousands of students shouldering responsibilities for the care of siblings. Babysitting and shuttling younger brothers and sisters to lessons, practices, and school are part of a daily routine. Students in our group, many of whom could have gone elsewhere for college, chose CSUN because of familial obligations. Frequently these obligations are more impactful on first-generation students, especially among working-class students and cultural groups where familial obligations take precedence over individual aspirations. Yet even the burdensome responsibilities borne by many of our students appear to motivate them to do well in the classroom, as we discuss below.

Some of the influences mentioned during student interviews were predictable. Several students noted sibling rivalries as an element in their success. One young woman said she's weighed down a bit by thoughts of having to compete with an older sister but also conceded,

> She's actually helped me a lot. . . . She . . . warns me about things, like how [organic chemistry] is going to be. She's, like, "Just wait until you get into [organic chemistry]" and I'm, like . . . "[this is going to be tough]" . . . so I mentally prepare myself.

The learning can be vicarious as well. One Latina, whose older sister was attending CSUN at the same time, found her sister to be both an unanticipated friend on campus (they had "not been really close until college") and a source of knowledge about hard-won lessons:

> I learn a lot from her mistakes, so a lot of things that she did, I make sure not to do that, and I think that that's another reason why I am so successful because—she's successful too, but she was the first one to go through everything. So she made the mistakes [and] I saw how mad my parents would get, or how much she would dig herself in a hole [and] I did not want to go there, you know? So I think that's also why I really do try hard because I know what it's like for someone to fall behind, I guess. I've seen it.

Perhaps the most common challenges faced by college students are financial. A significant number of students talked about how attending college creates cross-cutting burdens and obligations within the family. We were surprised by the number of students with well-educated parents who reported having to work to help out with making ends meet. Mortgages were mentioned on several occasions. Indeed, many of the interviews were conducted in the midst of the Great Recession (2007–2010) that acutely affected housing values in the San Fernando Valley. For first-generation students, burdensome mortgage payments and making car payments were often replaced with worries over unreasonably high rents, sibling care, and the time costs associated with using public transportation in Los Angeles. The differences between FGS and SBDP were not as clear-cut as one would imagine on this front.

Lucky were the students without some concern about finances. There were several in our group who discussed their blessings. One accounting major whose parents had some college was able to quit her job at her parents' urging so she could focus on school:

> I feel lucky. I feel like a lot of kids don't have that, but I mean, I feel like I have a very traditional kind of home life. My parents are married, you know, my brother is out of school now, but before that, we all lived you know, in the house and everything. So my mom, even back when I was in first grade, she volunteered in the class. It's very typical, but it's very helpful. I always feel like I can fall back on them, and there's just the support level that I definitely feel. Yeah, it sounds cheesy, I know.

An engineering major whose parents have four-year degrees but were divorced had to keep his job to help out at home. His success remained at the top of his family's priority list, and the whole family appeared to factor into how he understood his situation:

> My mom told me, "We're here to help you get through—get you through college. If you can't afford it, you know, we'll find a way. We'll ask family members, you know, this, this, and that." There's a strong desire for me to succeed and hopefully there will be that strong of a desire for my siblings to succeed. I don't want to see them not go to college.

Many students are similarly pinched between their familial aspirations and the financial onus of realizing those dreams. The sacrifices required over a period of years are real for families, and students express both guilt at being a drain and a determination not to squander the sacrifices made by those around them. For first-generation students, this dynamic is often greatly magnified. For example, a daughter of high school–educated, immigrant parents with younger siblings said it was hard for her to complete school tasks in a timely fashion because her mother expected her to help the younger ones with homework and to run errands. To her parents, it hardly seems a burden, compared to their duties when they were her age. But the student knows that similar chores are less common for middle-class students whose parents help with homework, hire tutors, and run errands themselves.

One undecided major who held jobs both on campus and off also joined a fraternity. He talked about how, despite trying his best to have a full collegiate experience, he still had many responsibilities at home: "I work this many hours because I pay bills at my house as well. . . . I help pay bills, rent; I help with groceries. And then my younger brother, I help babysit him when I have time."

Not all first-generation students have to work two jobs and keep the family from falling into financial ruin. For example, a sociology major whose parents held only high school degrees said she had to work very few hours and had limited responsibilities in caring for her three younger sisters. Another young woman, an engineering major whose parents could not afford to go to college in Vietnam, also felt blessed to be able to focus on her studies. She was particularly grateful for the ample scholarship funding she was able to secure that paid for most of her fees.

Despite their sometimes inadequate financial help and their inability to provide tutoring, proofreading, or experiential advice, parents of first-generation students who have made immense sacrifices for their children often provide powerful motivation. One student, whose parents work so she didn't have to, noted as much: "The sacrifices that . . . my parents make . . . that also motivates me to get my stuff done."

A consistent theme from the interviews, especially among FGS, was how parents worked hard to afford their children opportunities denied them. Immigrant parents perhaps present this lesson most vividly. Here are the words of a student whose parents emigrated here from two different Central American countries; their personal history is an important source of motivation to do well:

> Well, my parents . . . they come from poorer countries, and they came here to the U.S., and my mom never, she wasn't able [to go to school] because she had to take care of her brothers and sisters when she got here. But she—they've been a [positive] influence on me, like telling me, "It's good to go to college. You want to do a better life than what we had." And I think it's true. I really appreciate [that] my parents have pushed me, and my dad has been able to—because he's the only one that works now. . . . Mom's at home, always. . . . We—with my dad's work—have been able to pay for school and, and be here.

The sacrifices made by parents can be so great that first-generation students are saddled with expectations beyond what children from more established families face. An undecided freshman reported that in many ways, she's in college to fulfill her father's aspirations: "This whole thing, it has always been my dad's dream for me to go to college," adding that beyond that, her father could help her little in terms of schoolwork. A first-generation business major felt compelled to meet those expectations:

> They do support me, but they also have, like, this tremendous pressure on me to do well. And if I don't do well, I get . . . reminded of, you know, all the people and, like, everything that's depending on me doing well. So that's, like, an extra motivation for me to just keep powering through. I look at them and I see that

they're hard workers, but it's, like, the product of their hard work that inspires me to keep working hard . . . to get into university, like, my mom had to sell her wedding bands. So, my parents are willing to give up that much so that I can keep studying. It's heavy motivation.

POLICY AND PEDAGOGY

Our data analysis and discussions with students have been compelling and useful as we seek to learn from the learners. Perhaps the most important finding is that, at least among the more promising students entering college, family matters. But how family matters varies wildly. It is left to us as professors, counselors, administrators, and others to try to identify the strengths students bring from home in order to help them leverage familial strengths productively.

We found that LH students, regardless of the nature of their familial educational attainment, were largely able to navigate their way through our huge, comprehensive, urban university, completing a wide variety of degrees, largely on time and with respectable grade point averages. Within our group, very few students got into the kind of academic trouble that resulted in academic probation or disqualification, and for the few who did, parental educational attainment did not seem to matter much. The small number of students in our group who found themselves in serious academic trouble were just as likely to have parents with graduate degrees as they were to have parents without high school degrees.

Universities and faculties must do a better job of monitoring early signs of trouble among students. Big data and statistical modeling of student outcomes have vastly expanded our ability to predict when and how any student is likely to struggle or drop out, often before students have even stepped a foot on campus. Admissions offices could consider sending, alongside the joyous news of acceptance to the university, friendly reminders that college is not simply an extension of high school and that the tasks that lie ahead require an upgraded commitment to academic work. Overburdened faculty members, especially those teaching large-section courses, can likewise take advantage of the data capabilities of course management software to identify students in trouble, contact them with offers of help, and refer them to tutors or other help sources provided by the college or university. The university in turn must work with the faculty to offer *appropriate* help to struggling students. It can't simply be math tutoring and writing advice. Faculty, students, and administration have to work together to identify the root causes of student struggles and seek to find solutions for those, rather than focus on academic issues that are often only symptomatic of larger problems.

The university and its academic subdivisions should also consider experimenting with a number of programs focused on alleviating the very real psychological challenges faced by FGS. One reasonably simple programmatic offering would be parents' night. Some may scoff at the notion, but our interviews suggest that even among the least at-risk FGS at CSUN, many parents have little idea what transpires on campus. At some traditional colleges, many parents are involved at least in the "drop-off" day, leaving the student at the dorm and attending a sort of parental orientation. Parents often also visit campus before enrollment with their high school student as part of the campus evaluation process. Neither of these rituals characterizes the experience for many students at CSUN, although the university does offer similar daytime events to freshmen and transfer students. Our FGS largely pick CSUN because it fits their budget, their geographical constraints, and helps them meet familial obligations. It would seem that few working-class parents, struggling to send their children to large, urban campuses like our own, have time for daytime visits to campus, or for old-school homecoming events, and so forth. A nighttime parents' event, not completely unlike what grade schools do, might help provide students a forum to explain the importance of higher education to parents who have never stepped foot on a campus. Anyone who has attended a commencement ceremony at a campus like ours can sense the wonderment, and even bewilderment, among many parents and grandparents visiting campus for the first and only time during their child or grandchild's years in college. Campuses should not be terra incognita for parents who pay, often dearly, to provide students with a crack at a better life.

Another reasonable program suggested by our research is an FGS buddy program, where FGS freshmen are paired with successful FGS who are juniors or seniors. This would be especially important for those students without older, college-going siblings. Campuses could offer priority registration or other inducements for peer mentors to help freshmen cope with the myriad problems navigating college life, both inside and outside the classroom. Support groups, faculty mentors, and other options for FGS that provide students with a sort of lifeline would also seem reasonable courses of action for schools with large FGS populations.

The freshman year is critical, especially for students whose families provide little in the way of tangible support in navigating the pitfalls of that first year. Students from all backgrounds tend to see their grades go down as workloads and expectations increase. As doubts and frustrations creep into students' minds, where can they turn for guidance? It seems that for students with parents or siblings who went to college, a reassuring chat on the phone is a common and powerful antidote to a possibly poisonous attitude.

For FGS, that reassurance must come from the university community itself. It is critical for the faculty to remind students who are struggling that learning is difficult and that disappointment is okay if it motivates them toward growth. Straight As are great, but Bs and the occasional C are acceptable. Students who have simplistic metrics for gauging their own intellectual growth need reminders that a B is not the end of the world and that grades are often a blunt instrument for gauging real growth. These assurances may be of particular importance for students at risk of suffering from the so-called imposter syndrome. Students from such backgrounds need to understand that most students, even those from families where both parents have postgraduate degrees, experience a drop in GPA from high school to college and that it is quite normal and a product of increased competition as well as elevated expectations for excellence.

The good news for confused, stressed, or depressed students unaccustomed to grades other than As is that the transition period is reasonably short and that the work ethic that helped them succeed in high school tends to provide them with the resiliency they need to succeed.

NOTES

1. Los Angeles is home to the largest community of people of Armenian descent outside of Armenia itself. Many Armenians live in Glendale, a community well within the geographic footprint of CSUN. CSUN very likely has the largest number of Armenian American college students in the United States.

2. The summary figures appearing in the last section of table 3.2 are shown to document that students in the various subgroups are not disproportionately drawn from different entry cohorts. The small differences that appear among the LH students are not statistically significant. Those for all freshmen are statistically significant, primarily because of the disproportionate representation of the FGS within the fall 2011 entry cohort.

3. Five subgroups make up the larger set of students stemming from traditionally underserved backgrounds: American Indians, Pacific Islanders, African Americans, Latina/o, and multirace. Others are referred to as stemming from better-served backgrounds.

4. Among the few LH students who attended a high school with at least 10 FGS and 10 students from families with some college, the FGS had consistently lower high school GPA versus their counterparts.

REFERENCES

California State University, Northridge (CSUN), Office of Institutional Research. 2017. "All Student Headcount by Ethnicity." February 22. http://irqry.csun.edu :8080/openweb/csun_btn/currentstudata.jsp?d=4&c=12.

Garcia, Valerie. 2015. "First-Generation College Students: How Co-curricular Involvement Can Assist with Success." *Vermont Connection* 31 (1): 6.

Horn, Laura, and Anne-Marie Nuñez. 2000. *Mapping the Road to College First-Generation Students' Math Track, Planning Strategies, and Context of Support.* Collingdale, PA: Diane Publishing.

Hsiao, Karin P. 1992. "First-Generation College Students." ERIC Digest. http://files.eric.ed.gov/fulltext/ED351079.pdf.

Los Angeles Times. 1998. "The Early Years: San Fernando Valley State College." September 21. Accessed February 22, 2017. http://articles.latimes.com/.

McCarron, Graziella P., and Karen K. Inkelas. 2006. "The Gap between Educational Aspirations and Attainment for First-Generation College Students and the Role of Parental Involvement." *Journal of College Student Development* 47 (5): 534–49.

McConnell, Penny J. 2000. "ERIC Review: What Community Colleges Should Do to Assist First-Generation Students." *Community College Review* 28 (3): 75–87.

National Center for Educational Statistics. 1998. *First-Generation Students: Undergraduates Whose Parents Never Enrolled in Postsecondary Education.* Washington, DC: U.S. Department of Education.

Pratt, Phillip A., and Thomas C. Skaggs. 1989. "First-Generation College Students: Are They at Greater Risk for Attrition Than Their Peers?" *Research in Rural Education* 6 (2): 31–34.

Reyes, Nicole, and Nora Amaury. 2012. "Lost among the Data: A Review of Latino First Generation College Students." White paper prepared for the Hispanic Association of Colleges and Universities.

Stephens, Nicole M., Stephanie A. Fryberg, Hazel Rose Markus, Camille S. Johnson, and Rebecca Covarrubius. 2012. "Unseen Disadvantage: How American Universities' Focus on Independence Undermines the Academic Performance of First-Generation College Students." *Journal of Personality and Social Psychology* 102 (6): 1178–97.

Terenzini, Patrick T., Leonard Springer, Patricia M. Yaeger, Ernest T. Pascarella, and Amaury Nora. 1996. "First-Generation College Students: Characteristics, Experiences, and Cognitive Development." *Research in Higher Education* 37 (1): 1–22.

Vuong, Mui, Sharon Brown-Welty, and Susan Tracz. 2010. "The Effects of Self-Efficacy on Academic Success of First-Generation College Sophomore Students." *Journal of College Development* 51 (1): 50–64.

Ward, Lee, Michael J. Siegal, and Zebulun Davenport. 2012. *First-Generation College Students: Understanding and Improving the Experience from Recruitment to Commencement.* San Francisco: Wiley.

4

The Role of Gender in Fostering Persistence and Effective Learning Habits

Bettina J. Huber

With the aid of data from both the Learning Habits Project (LHP) and the widely administered freshman survey TFS (The Freshman Survey), this chapter examines possible reasons that young men entering California State University, Northridge (CSUN) during the 2007–2011 period were less likely to persist than their female counterparts, despite their better preparation for college work at entry. Initial discussion traces these gender differences in preparation and persistence for both the learning habits (LH) students and freshmen within the entry cohorts from which they are drawn.

The lag in performance may reflect, at least in part, men's preference for the math-heavy majors that CSUN students typically find challenging. However, it also appears to reflect differences in high school experience not normally considered in assessing readiness for college, a possibility that is explored in the following pages with the aid of data from TFS, which has been administered at CSUN since 2007. These data point to differing activity patterns, suggesting that LHP women formed habits in high school that put them in a better position to handle the increased academic demands of college. CSUN's incoming freshmen men, in contrast, devote less effort than their female counterparts to schoolwork and have less experience with the types of social interaction that foster learning. As a result, men may have fewer resources at their disposal if they run into trouble in college, especially since LH data suggest their behavior during their early college years tends to mimic their high school practices.

The initial college success of newly enrolled men may also be inhibited by their remarkably high levels of confidence in the excellence of their intellectual and other abilities, a confidence they carry over into their initial college work. Although self-confidence is generally considered a virtue, entering college with too much self-confidence is not advantageous. The danger lies in the complacency it engenders, perhaps blinding entering freshmen to the increased effort that college success requires. The detrimental effects of such overconfidence are especially great when coupled with poorly developed study skills.

How this combination plays out during the first years of college is outlined with the aid of the LH data reviewed in the last sections of this chapter. This review indicates that men, who enter so confident of their college success, are also the ones disproportionately likely to believe that reliance on their high school skills will enable them to master college assignments. LH women, in contrast, are more realistic about the challenges of college work and better able to build on the study skills and interactive strengths developed in high school.

RECENT EVOLUTION IN UNDERSTANDINGS OF GENDER

During the 1980s and 1990s, research on the college student experience grew apace. Despite the great proliferation, most empirical work did not consider variation by key background characteristics (Pascarella and Terenzini 2005). In keeping with this, widely used models developed during this period to assess how college affects students did not pay much attention to the differentiating impact of gender or other key background factors (Astin 1993; Pascarella 1985; Tinto 1987). In the case of gender, in particular, this pattern prevailed through the early 2000s. With few exceptions, empirical research on college student development and growth was undertaken in the absence of any attention to developmental differences by gender. This was as true of more recent work on student engagement (e.g., Kuh 2001) as it had been of earlier work.

It is important to note that the prevailing research emphases remained unchanged, despite the appearance of important critiques by feminist scholars of the unconscious male bias underlying dominant theories of psychosocial development. Work by Nancy Chodorow (1978) and Carol Gilligan (1982), in particular, argued that prevailing theories ignored the importance of interpersonal relationships in young women's development during late adolescence and early adulthood.

Thus, as Linda Sax stresses (2008), by the early 2000s, we knew surprisingly little about the distinct effects of college on different types of students. She attempted to begin remedying this situation in the case of gender with the aid of two large data sets: TFS responses provided by students entering college in fall 2006 and all students enrolled at coeducational four-year institutions who completed TFS in 1994 and the 1998 college student survey. Both of these surveys are administered by the University of California at

Los Angeles's (UCLA) Cooperative Institutional Research Program (CIRP). Given the large data sets on which Sax relied, with their wide array of specific responses, she isolated a range of gender-specific patterns, some of which overlapped and conflicted. Although men's advantage in self-confidence remained clear-cut, the benefits of interaction with the faculty proved to be complex and sometimes more beneficial to men than women. This is not to deny that young men continue to arrive at college with less well-developed academic engagement skills.

Sax's (2008) work on gender differences among college students provides particularly helpful background to discussion in this chapter because of its reliance on the large repository of CIRP data. Since such data also are available for the LH students considered here, Sax's discussion provides important context, suggesting that, by and large, the attitudes and characteristics of CSUN's entering freshmen are typical of those enrolling at other four-year institutions in fall 2006. Nonetheless, it should be noted that Sax's highly quantitative approach contrasts with the largely qualitative approach adopted here, in part because our data set is so much smaller and in part because, perforce, it focuses on a single institutional context, albeit a rarely studied one.

Analysis of subgroup differences, more generally, received increasing attention through the 2000s. Much of it has focused on differential outcomes by racial and ethnic background and low income status, with many programs and initiatives proving particularly beneficial for such students (Mayhew et al. 2016, 559–64). Here, the availability of financial aid and the campus racial climate are of particular importance to student persistence. This shift in research focus undoubtedly reflects the increasing presence on college campuses of students from minority backgrounds.[1]

Since Sax's 2008 examination, one other study of the gender gap relying on a large-scale data set has appeared. With the aid of a 1988 National Education Longitudinal Study (NELS) data set of high school graduates entering college during the 1990s, Stephanie Ewart (2012) examines factors contributing to differing male and female graduation rates. She finds that two sorts of divergent college experiences contribute to the gender gap. First, women perform better in college than men and thus are more likely to graduate. Second, men are more likely than women to drop out for one or more semesters, which depresses their graduation rate. Like Sax, Ewart finds that both men and women benefit from social integration (e.g., participation in clubs). She also points to the importance, for men in particular, of participation in various kinds of sports teams.

In addition to the large-scale studies of recent years, there have been a good many more restricted examinations of differences by gender in postcollege earnings and the evolution of key attitudes during the college years. Among other things, these include perceptions of appropriate women's roles and the development of religiously based worldviews (e.g., Bryant 2003, 2011). Sax, along with many other researchers, has turned her attention of late to the STEM (science, technology, engineering, and mathematics) disciplines (Kanny, Sax, and Riggers-Piehl 2014), presumably because it is within some of them that women have remained severely underrepresented (DiPrete and Buchmann 2013, 1–3). Some studies of smaller subgroups have appeared as well, such as college success among black males or females (Patton and Croom 2017; Wood and Palmer 2015) and the role of men and women's friendship networks in college success (McCabe 2016). Finally, studies of gender-specific performance in various types of courses make a frequent appearance in the literature, with online learning receiving increasing attention.

STUDENT CHARACTERISTICS AND PERSISTENCE

Although some gender differences in persistence to graduation are evident among LH students, differences in background and preparation at entry are minimal. To keep such differences in perspective, comparable figures appear in tables 4.1–4.3 for all freshmen entering the university in the four fall terms during which LH students were recruited.

Table 4.1. Background characteristics of LH participants and all first-time freshmen in their entry cohorts by gender

Background Characteristic	Learning Habits Participants		All Entering Freshmen	
	Women	*Men*	*Women*	*Men*
1. Racial and Ethnic Background				
Traditionally Underserved	41.3	31.2	63.9	55.6
American Indian	*0.0*	*0.4*	*0.3*	*0.3*
Pacific Islander	*0.0*	*0.0*	*0.3*	*0.4*
African American	*5.3*	*3.3*	*13.9*	*9.8*
Latina/o	*33.7*	*25.7*	*48.1*	*43.9*
Multirace	*2.1*	*1.5*	*1.4*	*1.2*
Better Served	58.7	68.8	36.1	44.4
Asian	*12.9*	*14.3*	*10.2*	*14.7*
White	*36.8*	*43.4*	*19.3*	*23.3*
Multirace (i.e., Asian and white)	*1.4*	*2.6*	*0.7*	*0.9*
Decline to state	*7.2*	*7.7*	*5.9*	*5.6*
Total	100.0	100.0	100.0	100.0
(No. of participants)	(484)	(269)	(10,435)	(8,018)
	Chi square = 8.02 (.018); df = 2 Cramer's V = .103		Chi square = 132.50 (.001); df = 1 Cramer's V = .085	

Background Characteristic	Learning Habits Participants		All Entering Freshmen	
	Women	Men	Women	Men
2. Pell Grant Status (proxy for low income)				
Pell Grant recipient	36.6	30.5	56.1	47.5
No grant received	63.4	69.5	43.9	52.5
Total	100.0	100.0	100.0	100.0
(No. of participants)	(487)	(272)	(10,714)	(8,472)
	Chi square = 2.82 (.009); df = 1 Cramer's V = .061		Chi square = 142.24 (.001); df = 1 Cramer's V = .086	
3. Parental Education (Indicator of First-Generation College Status)				
Both parents: high school or less	22.6	19.5	39.7	34.5
One/both parents: some college	23.4	19.9	24.7	22.0
One/both parents: four-year degree	49.9	52.9	28.8	34.9
Unknown	4.1	7.7	6.8	8.6
Total	100.0	100.0	100.0	100.0
(No. of participants)	(487)	(272)	(10,714)	(8,472)
	Chi square = 1.88 (NS); df = 2 Cramer's V = .051		Chi square = 102.29 (.001); df = 2 Cramer's V = .076	
4. Entry Term				
Fall 2007	11.7	9.2	21.8	21.1
Fall 2008	22.4	20.2	24.4	23.6
Fall 2010	29.4	29.8	27.0	27.1
Fall 2011	36.6	40.8	26.8	28.3
Total	100.0	100.0	100.0	100.0
(No. of participants)	(487)	(272)	(10,714)	(8,472)
	Chi square = 2.24 (NS); df = 3 Cramer's V = .054		Chi square = 6.10 (NS); df = 3 Cramer's V = .018	

Entry Characteristics and Background

The data in table 4.1 summarize key background characteristics of the men and women participating in the project.[2] Some modest differences by racial and ethnic background are evident, as the first section of table 4.1 indicates. Although the majority of participants stem from better-served racial and ethnic backgrounds, the men are more likely to do so than the women, two-fifths of whom stem from traditionally underserved backgrounds. Students from Latina/o backgrounds predominate within both gender groups. A similar pattern of gender differences is evident in the larger freshman group, as the right side of the table indicates, although the proportion of students from traditionally underserved backgrounds is far larger (56–64 percent).[3]

The second and third sections of table 4.1 show that close to a third of both men and women in the Learning Habits Project were Pell Grant recipients at entry, indicating that they are low income, while just over half have parents with four-year college degrees. Differences by gender on these two characteristics are also minimal for the larger freshman group. The percentage of Pell Grant recipients is considerably higher, however, while the percentage of students whose parents have four-year degrees is considerably lower, hovering around two-fifths.

In terms of the formal criteria generally used to assess college preparedness, men enter CSUN better prepared than women, a difference that is as evident among the LH students as among their freshman counterparts. Thus, the men participating in LH are somewhat more likely than the women to be fully proficient at entry (85 vs. 76 percent) and therefore well prepared for college work (see section 1 of table 4.2). They also tend to have higher composite SAT scores: 53 percent of men report scores exceeding 1100 compared to 36 percent of women. Although similar gender differences are evident for the larger freshman group, entry-level preparation is considerably lower (23–32 percent fully prepared), as are students' SAT scores (10–19 percent with scores of 1100 or higher).

Table 4.2. Entry characteristics of LH participants and all first-time freshmen in their entry cohorts by gender

Entry Characteristic	Learning Habits Participants		All Entering Freshmen	
	Women	Men	Women	Men
1. Proficiency at Entry				
Fully Proficient	75.8	84.9	22.9	32.4
Needs remediation in:	24.2	15.1	77.1	67.6
English only	*7.6*	*6.6*	*13.6*	*22.2*
Mathematics only	*8.6*	*4.4*	*14.3*	*8.3*
Both subjects	*8.0*	*4.0*	*49.3*	*37.0*
Total	100.0	100.0	100.0	100.0
(No. of participants)	(487)	(272)	(10,714)	(8,472)
	Chi square = 8.84 (.003); df = 1 Cramer's V = .108		Chi square = 218.86 (.001); df = 1 Cramer's V = .107	
2. SAT Composite Scores				
Below 700	8.4	7.0	20.8	17.9
700–799	1.8	1.5	14.4	9.2
800–899	8.4	3.7	21.0	16.8
900–999	15.8	9.6	20.3	20.5
1000–1099	29.4	25.4	13.9	16.8

Entry Characteristic	Learning Habits Participants		All Entering Freshmen	
	Women	Men	Women	Men
1100–1199	23.0	29.4	6.8	11.5
1200 or higher	13.1	23.5	2.9	7.2
Total	100.0	100.0	100.0	100.0
(No. of participants)	(487)	(272)	(10,714)	(8,472)
Mean	974.4	1037.1	782.8	833.1
Median	1050.0	1100.0	870.0	920.0
Interquartile range	940–1140	1020–1190	740–990	780–1060
	F = 6.99 (.001); df = 1; Eta = .096		F = 97.95 (.001); df = 1; Eta = .071	
3. High School GPA				
2.74 or less	3.5	7.7	14.2	22.2
2.75–2.99	5.7	11.0	18.9	20.5
3.00–3.24	12.3	24.6	27.0	26.2
3.25–3.49	16.0	15.1	18.7	15.4
3.50–3.74	30.0	22.8	12.6	10.0
3.75 or higher	32.4	18.8	8.5	5.7
Total	100.0	100.0	100.0	100.0
(No. of participants)	(487)	(272)	(10,714)	(8,472)
Mean	3.53	3.35	3.15	3.05
Median	3.58	3.37	3.14	3.04
Interquartile range	3.3–3.8	3.1–3.6	2.9–3.4	2.8–3.3
	F = 29.04 (NS); df = 1; Eta = .192		F = 253.09 (.001); df = 1; Eta = .114	
4. Participation Criteria				
High School GPA of 3.5 or Higher				
and Proficient at Entry	38.4	26.5	—	—
but Needed remediation	24.0	15.1	—	—
High School GPA below 3.5 but				
Proficient at Entry	37.6	58.5	—	—
Total	100.0	100.0		
(No. of participants)	(487)	(272)		
	Chi square =30.88 (.001); df = 2 Cramer's V = .202			

(continued)

Table 4.2. *Continued*

Entry Characteristic	Learning Habits Participants		All Entering Freshmen	
	Women	Men	Women	Men
5. College Housing Planned Major				
Arts, Media, and Communication	16.2	16.9	13.8	14.5
Business and Economics	11.7	16.5	11.5	19.2
Education	2.1	0.7	1.2	0.2
Engineering and Computer Science	2.5	15.1	1.7	16.6
Health and Human Development	14.2	5.9	14.0	7.1
Humanities	6.4	3.3	6.6	2.1
Science and Mathematics	14.8	15.1	10.0	8.2
Social and Behavioral Sciences	12.7	8.1	17.6	9.4
Undeclared	19.5	18.4	23.5	22.7
Total	100.0	100.0	100.0	100.0
(No. of participants)	(487)	(272)	(10,714)	(8,472)
	Chi square = 62.07 (.001); df = 8 Cramer's V = .286		Chi square = 2175.26 (.001); df = 8 Cramer's V = .337	

At entry, women outperform men in one respect: they tend to have higher high school GPAs. As seen in the third section of table 4.2, 62 percent of LH women entered CSUN with high school GPAs exceeding 3.50 as compared to 42 percent of the men. Such a large gender gap in GPA is atypical. In the larger freshman group, the gap in the percentage with GPAs of 3.50 or higher is only 6 percent, although women still outperform men (21 vs. 16 percent). As a result of the differences in GPA and proficiency at entry, 60 percent of men qualified for LH thanks to their proficiency in mathematics and English at entry, while 25 percent of the women qualified thanks to their high school GPAs (see section 4 of table 4.2).

While most of the differences in preparation just outlined are modest, they are in keeping with clear differences in students' anticipated majors.[4] As the fifth section of table 4.2 indicates, LH men are much more likely than women to expect to pursue fields housed in engineering and computer science (15 vs. 2.5 percent) and somewhat more likely to favor business majors (17 vs.

12 percent). LH women, in contrast, are more likely to plan majors in two other colleges: health and human development (14 vs. 6 percent) and social and behavioral sciences (13 vs. 8 percent). As figures for the larger freshman group shown in the fifth section of table 4.2 make clear, these gender differences by major are not unique to LH students. Rather, they reflect preferences that are evident among all of CSUN's freshmen. In both the LH and larger freshman cohorts, majors preferred by men are in keeping with their strength in mathematics and their comparatively high SAT scores.

Academic Achievement

Given that the men in LH entered CSUN better prepared for college work than the women, at least by the formal indicators generally relied on, one would expect them to be more likely to succeed in college. This is not the case, however, as table 4.3 indicates. By and large, the two groups perform similarly, with women outdistancing men in several areas. A similar pattern is evident among all freshman entrants, albeit with greater gender gaps in performance.

Table 4.3. Persistence and academic success of LH participants and all first-time freshmen in their entry cohorts by gender

Persistence Measure	Learning Habits Participants		All Entering Freshmen	
	Women	Men	Women	Men
1. One-Year Continuation Rate				
Enrolled at beginning of second year	93.2	93.4	74.4	71.3
Not enrolled at beginning of second year	6.8	6.6	25.6	28.7
Total	100.0	100.0	100.0	100.0
(No. of participants)	(487)	(272)	(10,714)	(8,472)
	Chi square = 0.007 (NS); df = 1 Cramer's V = .003		Chi square = 22.55 (.001); df = 1 Cramer's V = .056	
2. Academic Standing at End of First Year				
In good standing	96.7	94.1	75.9	68.7
On probation	2.5	3.7	11.8	15.5
Disqualified	0.8	2.2	12.3	15.8
Total	100.0	100.0	100.0	100.0
(No. of participants)	(487)	(272)	(10,673)	(8,422)
	Chi square = 3.55 (NS); df = 2 Cramer's V = .068		Chi square = 100.03 (.001); df = 2 Cramer's V = .117	

(*continued*)

Table 4.3. *Continued*

Persistence Measure	Learning Habits Participants		All Entering Freshmen	
	Women	*Men*	*Women*	*Men*
3. CSUN GPA at End of First Year				
1.99 or less	2.9	6.3	21.6	27.9
2.00–2.49	4.5	8.1	16.3	19.3
2.50–2.99	14.6	19.9	24.8	23.5
3.00–3.49	33.5	36.0	24.3	19.7
3.50–3.74	21.6	15.8	8.1	6.3
3.75 or higher	23.0	14.0	5.0	3.4
Total	100.0	100.0	100.0	100.0
(No. of participants)	(487)	(272)	(10,407)	(8,155)
Mean	3.32	3.13	2.6	2.44
Median	3.42	3.25	2.75	2.55
Interquartile range	3.0–3.7	2.9–3.6	2.1–3.2	1.9–3.1
	$F = 20.75$ (.001); df = 1; Eta = .163		$F = 182.90$ (.001); df = 1; Eta = .097	
4. Cumulative CSUN Units Earned at End of First Year				
15 or fewer units	1.9	1.8	15.8	20.9
16–24 units	17.7	22.1	33.4	35.9
25–30 units	63.9	62.9	42.9	37.0
31 or more units	16.6	13.2	7.9	6.2
Total	100.0	100.0	100.0	100.0
(No. of participants)	(487)	(272)	(10,714)	(8,472)
Mean	27.2	26.4	22.7	21.3
Median	27.0	27.0	25.0	24.0
Interquartile range	25–29	25–29	20–27	17–27
	$F = 6.20$ (.013); df = 1; Eta = .090		$F = 142.03$ (.001); df = 1; Eta = .086	
5. Degree Status (at end of 2015–2016)				
Baccalaureate Degree Completed	77.4	73.2	53.1	41.5
Degree Not Completed	22.6	26.8	46.9	58.5
but still enrolled at CSUN (13th term after entry)	*0.8*	*2.9*	*3.2*	*5.2*
and no longer enrolled at CSUN	*21.8*	*23.9*	*43.7*	*53.3*
Total	100.0	100.0	100.0	100.0
(No. of participants)	(487)	(272)	(10,714)	(8,472)
	Chi square = 1.72 (NS); df = 1		Chi square = 256.10 (.001); df = 1	
	Cramer's V = .048		Cramer's V = .116	

Persistence Measure	Learning Habits Participants		All Entering Freshmen	
	Women	Men	Women	Men
6. Four-Year Graduation Rate				
Graduated in Four Years or Less	41.9	29.8	14.4	8.5
Did Not Graduate within Four Years	58.1	70.2	85.6	91.5
Total	100.0	100.0	100.0	100.0
(No. of participants)	(487)	(272)	(10,714)	(8,472)
	Chi square = 10.91 (.001); df = 1 Cramer's V = .120		Chi square = 52.48 (.001); df = 1 Cramer's V = .076	
7. Five-Year Graduation Rate				
Graduated in Five Years or Less	70.4	62.9	41.4	28.9
Did Not Graduate within Five Years	29.6	37.1	58.6	71.1
Total	100.0	100.0	100.0	100.0
(No. of participants)	(487)	(272)	(10,714)	(8,472)
	Chi square = 4.57 (.035); df = 1 Cramer's V = .078		Chi square = 79.82(.001); df = 1 Cramer's V = .093	
8. Likely Graduation Rate				
Graduated or Enrolled in 13th Term after Entry	78.2	76.1	55.6	45.4
No Longer Enrolled at CSUN	21.8	23.9	44.4	54.6
Total	100.0	100.0	100.0	100.0
(No. of participants)	(487)	(272)	(10,714)	(8,472)
	Chi square = 0.45 (NS); df = 1 Cramer's V = .024		Chi square = 198.49 (.001); df = 1 Cramer's V = .102	

At the end of their first year, almost all LH students persisted into a second year of college in good academic standing (sections 1 and 2 of table 4.3). The number of units earned was comparable—25 or more for at least three-quarters of them—but women finished their initial college year with higher cumulative GPAs, according to the third section of table 4.3 (3.42, on average, compared to 3.25 for men). A similar pattern is evident for all freshmen, although the performance levels are lower: close to seven-tenths of the students in this larger grouping were in good standing at the end of their first college year and persisted into a second year of study (69–76 percent). Between two-fifths and one-half had earned at least 25 units by the end of this first year, although very few had cumulative GPAs as high as

3.00 (10–13 percent). A modest difference in average GPA is evident: 2.75 for women versus 2.55 for men.

Turning to graduation, some clear-cut gender differences appear. LH women are more likely than men to have graduated within four or five years, as is evident from sections 6–7 of table 4.3 (42 and 70 percent vs. 30 and 63 percent). The eighth section of the table, however, indicates that the proportion of likely graduates is equivalent.[5] Further, by the end of the 2015/2016 academic year, the proportion of LH students who had earned baccalaureate degrees was largely equivalent (see section 5 of table 4.3). As one might expect, graduation rates among all freshmen are considerably lower than for the LH students, but the gender gap tends to be larger. The freshmen women in question are more likely than the freshman men to graduate within five years (41 vs. 30 percent) or to be likely graduates (56 vs. 45 percent). They were also more likely than men to have baccalaureate degrees in hand by the end of 2015/2016.

These findings suggest that although gender gaps in performance are evident among LH students, they tend to be more modest than those evident for the larger freshman cohorts. And as discussion in the last section indicated, it is these larger gaps in graduation rates that are typical on a national level. The equivalence in likely graduates among the LH students, therefore, is unusual and represents a higher level of performance than found among the larger freshman group.[6] As noted earlier, it is surprising that LH men do not outperform the women, given their better preparation at entry, at least in terms of the formal test scores on which such expectations tend to be based (e.g., SAT). Their failure to do so may reflect, at least in part, their preference for difficult, math-heavy majors. It also may reflect differences in high school experience, however, that are not normally considered in assessing readiness for college, despite their importance.

THE CIRP FRESHMAN SURVEY

In addition to data from LH interviews and end-of-term surveys, another source of information was available to us: TFS, which is administered annually on participating campuses as part of the Cooperative Institutional Research Program (CIRP) at UCLA; the survey has been administered at CSUN to all incoming freshmen since summer 2007. Although not all of the LH responses could be reliably identified, thanks to the flawed campus IDs some students provided, those of three-quarters (76 percent) could be.[7] A selection of LH responses is presented in tables 4.4–4.7, alongside equivalent responses for the larger entry cohorts. By and large, the gender differences within the larger freshman group are similar to those seen among the LH respondents. Thus, wherever possible, discussion below is confined to the latter.[8] Also, unless otherwise noted, the gender-specific patterns described are typical of those seen in the much larger national samples (Sax 2008, 25–35, 42–44). The value of these supplementary data is that TFS includes a wide array of questions about various aspects of students' experiences and attitudes during their last year of high school, a number of which seem likely to affect college performance.

Differences in High School Activities

The freshman survey includes several questions that ask respondents to indicate how frequently they engaged in a wide range of activities during their last year of high school. Table 4.4 displays one such list, with the percentages indicating how many respondents spent at least five hours per week on a range of activities. The first—socializing with friends—is the most frequently cited activity for both sexes, although men are somewhat more likely to report spending significant time socializing with friends (60 vs. 53 percent of women). Men clearly predominate when it comes to time spent on exercise or sports (44 vs. 32 percent for women) and watching TV (29 vs. 21 percent for women), while women are significantly more likely than men to report devoting at least five hours per week to studying and doing homework (47 vs. 30 percent).[9] The women also predominate when it comes to two other less frequently pursued activities: regular weekly participation in student clubs or groups (22 vs. 12 percent) and volunteer work (22 vs. 12 percent). Thus, we see the first evidence of women's greater academic engagement.

In keeping with widespread reliance on electronic media among today's students, close to one-fifth of the LH students reported spending five or more hours per week using online social networks such as Facebook, with no real difference by gender, according to table 4.4, for either the LH or other freshmen. Interestingly, the adjacent row shows a very different pattern for video gaming: one-fifth of men, whether LH participants or not, reported spending five or more hours per week on the activity, compared to only 3–4 percent of women. It seems that participation in social networking is gender neutral, while spending significant time on video gaming is almost exclusively male.

The six activities shown in the top part of table 4.5 constitute class-related activities that students might undertake on a regular basis during their last year of high school. And, in fact, at least two-fifths of the LH students report frequently engaging in such activities.

Strikingly, only one of the items shown—seeking alternative solutions to a problem—is more frequently engaged in by LH men than by women (54 vs.

Table 4.4. Percentage of LH participants and all first-time freshmen in their entry cohorts spending more than five hours per week on selected activities during their last year of high school by gender

Activity	Learning Habits Participants		All Entering Freshmen	
	Women	Men	Women	Men
Socializing with friends	53.4	60.3	55.6	59.6
(no. of responses on which percentages based)	(365)	(194)	(8,260)	(6,103)
	Cramer's V = .066		***Cramer's V = .040	
Exercise or sports	32.0	44.0	33.3	45.5
(no. of responses on which percentages based)	(366)	(193)	(8,255)	(6,119)
	**Cramer's V = .120		***Cramer's V = .124	
Watching TV	21.0	29.1	21.6	27.5
(no. of responses on which percentages based)	(367)	(196)	(8,234)	(6,096)
	*Cramer's V = .091		***Cramer's V = .069	
Partying	6.3	11.8	16.0	20.1
(no. of responses on which percentages based)	(365)	(195)	(8,231)	(6,092)
	*Cramer's V = .095		***Cramer's V = .053	
Playing video/computer games	3.3	20.9	3.9	22.8
(no. of responses on which percentages based)	(367)	(196)	(8,232)	(6,103)
	***Cramer's V = .288		***Cramer's V = .290	
Online social networks (MySpace, Facebook, etc.)	19.3	17.4	22.5	22.2
(no. of responses on which percentages based)	(367)	(195)	(8,254)	(6,098)
	Cramer's V = .023		Cramer's V = .004	
Working (for pay)	25.6	31.6	31.3	32.2
(no. of responses on which percentages based)	(367)	(196)	(8,242)	(6,107)
	Cramer's V = .064		Cramer's V = .009	
Studying/homework	46.9	29.5	28.3	22.8
(no. of responses on which percentages based)	(367)	(193)	(8,285)	(6,133)
	***Cramer's V = .168		***Cramer's V = .062	
Student clubs/groups	21.6	11.9	18.5	11.5
(no. of responses on which percentages based)	(365)	(194)	(8,215)	(6,067)
	**Cramer's V = .121		***Cramer's V = .095	

Activity	Learning Habits Participants		All Entering Freshmen	
	Women	*Men*	*Women*	*Men*
Volunteer work	15.8	8.3	16.7	11.0
(no. of responses on which percentages based)	(367)	(193)	(8,216)	(6,084)
	**Cramer's V = .105		***Cramer's V = .081	
Household/child-care duties	11.8	8.2	18.0	10.2
(no. of responses on which percentages based)	(364)	(195)	(8,239)	(6,085)
	Cramer's V = .056			
Reading for pleasure	13.6	9.2	12.5	6.4
(no. of responses on which percentages based)	(367)	(195)	(8,221)	(6,091)
	Cramer's V = .064		***Cramer's V = .101	

* = Accompanying Chi square significant at the .05 level
** = Accompanying Chi square significant at .01 level
*** = Accompanying Chi square significant at .001 level

44 percent). In contrast, women are significantly more likely to do the following frequently during their last year of high school: take notes in class (80 vs. 53 percent), revise papers to improve their writing (53 vs. 42 percent), and work with other students on class assignments (56 vs. 45 percent).

The six activities shown in the second and third sections of table 4.5 are related to students' academic work in high school, but not as closely related to class activities as those appearing in the first section. Still, half or more of the respondents report engaging in the first four frequently or occasionally during their last year of high school (i.e., performing volunteer work, using the Internet to complete homework, engaging in community service, and studying with other students). Although women more frequently report engaging in any one of these activities, only the volunteer work item shows a difference of 10 percent between the genders (86 percent for women vs. 75 percent for men). A more modest difference is evident for a related item: engaging in community service (59 percent vs. 51 percent).

Finally, rather high percentages of respondents report frequently or occasionally being overwhelmed by all they have to do. A smaller, but still significant, percentage report feeling depressed, at least occasionally. In each case, women are more likely than men to report either feeling (90 and 53 percent vs. 78 and 41 percent), although to some degree the differences may just reflect women's greater willingness to discuss such issues.

Taken as a whole, the CIRP data just reviewed suggest that LH women, like their freshman counterparts at CSUN and a wide range of other colleges

Table 4.5. Percentage of LH participants and all first-time freshmen in their entry cohorts having selected experiences during the last year of high school by gender

Experience	Learning Habits Participants		All Entering Freshmen	
	Women	*Men*	*Women*	*Men*
During the past year, respondents frequently^				
Took notes during class	79.6	52.6	72.1	51.1
(no. of responses on which percentages based)	(348)	(194)	(7,030)	(5,297)
	***Cramer's V = .282		***Cramer's V = .216	
Revised papers to improve their writing	53.1	42.3	46.5	32.9
(no. of responses on which percentages based)	(371)	(201)	(8,461)	(6,284)
	**Cramer's V = .103		***Cramer's V = .137	
Worked with other students on class assignments	55.7	45.1	59.8	47.6
(no. of responses on which percentages based)	(280)	(153)	(5,126)	(3,790)
	*Cramer's V = .102		***Cramer's V = .122	
Sought feedback on academic work	49.6	44.8	47.7	38.4
(no. of responses on which percentages based)	(371)	(201)	(8,438)	(6,259)
	Cramer's V = .046		***Cramer's V = .093	
Asked questions in class	52.3	54.5	50.7	43.6
(no. of responses on which percentages based)	(371)	(202)	(8,479)	(6,294)
	Cramer's V = .021		***Cramer's V = .070	
Sought alternative solutions to a problem^^	44.4	54.0	44.0	44.6
(no. of responses on which percentages based)	(369)	(202)	(8,400)	(6,244)
	*Cramer's V = .091		Cramer's V = .006	
During the past year, respondents frequently or occasionally^^^				
Performed volunteer work	85.9	75.4	83.5	73.7
(no. of responses on which percentages based)	(369)	(203)	(8,449)	(6,229)
	***Cramer's V = .132		***Cramer's V = .119	
Used the Internet for research or homework	86.4	82.3	79.7	71.7
(no. of responses on which percentages based)	(368)	(203)	(8,449)	(6,259)
	Cramer's V = .055		***Cramer's V = .093	

Experience	Learning Habits Participants		All Entering Freshmen	
	Women	Men	Women	Men
Performed community service as part of a class	59.2	51.2	64.2	57.4
(no. of responses on which percentages based)	(370)	(201)	(8,461)	(6,238)
	Cramer's V = .077		***Cramer's V = .069	
Studied with other students	90.5	88.2	90.6	86.3
(no. of responses on which percentages based)	(370)	(203)	(8,458)	(6,259)
	Cramer's V = .037		***Cramer's V = .067	
Demonstrated for or against a cause	43.5	34.0	39.4	36.5
(no. of responses on which percentages based)	(370)	(203)	(8,411)	(6,215)
	*Cramer's V = .093		***Cramer's V = .029	
During the past year, respondents frequently^^^				
Asked a teacher for advice after class	33.1	26.1	34.2	28.7
(no. of responses on which percentages based)	(369)	(203)	(8,461)	(6,261)
	Cramer's V = .072		***Cramer's V = .058	
During the past year, respondents frequently or occasionally^^^				
Felt overwhelmed by all they had to do	89.5	77.8	88.9	74.5
(no. of responses on which percentages based)	(370)	(203)	(8,453)	(6,253)
	***Cramer's V = .157		***Cramer's V = .188	
Felt depressed	53.1	40.8	52.8	41.8
(no. of responses on which percentages based)	(369)	(201)	(8,446)	(6,247)
	**Cramer's V = .118		***Cramer's V = .109	

^ Of the 14 habits of mind considered in the CIRP survey, those shown in the top part of the table had Cramer's V values of at least 0.05 and were significant at the .001 level. The one exception is shown because the learning habits Cramer's V value is statistically significant.

^^ A related item—seek solutions to problems and explain them to others—shows no differences by gender.

^^^ Of the 21 items considered in the relevant section of the CIRP survey, those shown in the bottom sections of the table had Cramer's V values of at least 0.05 and were significant at the .001 level. The one exception is shown because the learning habits Cramer's V value is statistically significant.

* = Accompanying Chi square significant at the .05 level
** = Accompanying Chi square significant at .01 level
*** = Accompanying Chi square significant at .001 level

and universities, may have formed habits in high school that make them better able to handle the increased academic demands of college, their periodic feelings of being overwhelmed notwithstanding. Viewed more broadly, such beneficial academic engagement seems to have two components. The first component is commitment to doing well in school; women are more likely to spend significant time on homework and studying. They are also more likely to report frequently taking notes in class or revising their papers to improve their writing. The second component of academic engagement concerns interaction with others in relation to classwork and school-related activities. Women's advantage in this area is seen in their more frequent participation in student clubs and volunteering for community service. This initial impression of female advantage is strengthened by TFS data on expectations about college.

Expectations for College

Table 4.6 lists a range of expectations that entering college students might have, usually about their first year. The percentages in the body of the table indicate the relative number of LH or freshman respondents who consider the chances "very good" that they will engage in any of the activities shown. Within this group, four expectations are expressed by at least two-fifths of the respondents: socialize with someone of a differing racial and ethnic background (60 percent), make at least a B average (57 percent), get a job to help pay for college expenses (51 percent), and be satisfied at CSUN (44 percent).[10]

Within the first "academic" grouping at the top of table 4.6, LH women are consistently more likely than men to consider it very likely that they will engage in or achieve the matters listed. Thus, women are more likely than men to expect to discuss course content with other students outside of class (49 vs. 38 percent), communicate regularly with their professors (39 vs. 31 percent), and participate in a study-abroad program (28 vs. 15 percent). The bottom section of the table indicates that LH women are also disproportionately likely to anticipate participating in student clubs or community service (48 and 34 percent vs. 31 and 15 percent for men). These are all activities that build on women's greater academic engagement in high school, especially their commitment to the types of interpersonal interaction that can be effective in facilitating learning. They are also in keeping with feminist thinking that women's psychosocial development fosters reliance on such interpersonal interaction.

Put a bit differently, the findings suggest that CSUN's incoming male students are less committed than their female counterparts to interpersonal inter-

Table 4.6. Percentage of LH participants and all first-time freshmen in their entry cohorts who consider the chances very good that they will engage in selected college activities by gender^

Activity	Learning Habits Participants		All Entering Freshmen	
	Women	Men	Women	Men
Do the following academically:				
Discuss course content with students outside class	48.7	38.1	41.2	30.5
(no. of responses on which percentages based)	(337)	(189)	(6,797)	(5,094)
	*Cramer's V = .102		***Cramer's V = .109	
Communicate regularly with your professors	39.3	30.8	37.0	27.1
(no. of responses on which percentages based)	(359)	(198)	(8,138)	(6,024)
	*Cramer's V = .084		***Cramer's V = .103	
Work on a professor's research project	30.6	27.0	35.8	28.6
(no. of responses on which percentages based)	(333)	(189)	(6,802)	(5,088)
	Cramer's V = .039		***Cramer's V = .075	
Participate in a study-abroad program	28.1	15.2	29.8	16.6
(no. of responses on which percentages based)	(359)	(198)	(8,148)	(6,026)
	***Cramer's V = .147		***Cramer's V = .152	
Be satisfied with CSUN^^	48.8	40.9	47.0	40.2
(no. of responses on which percentages based)	(361)	(198)	(8,146)	(6,026)
	Cramer's V = .075		***Cramer's V = .068	
Make at least a B average	67.8	67.5	57.7	55.6
(no. of responses on which percentages based)	(363)	(197)	(8,177)	(6,046)
	Cramer's V = .003		**Cramer's V = .056	
Make the following personal decisions:				
Socialize with someone of another racial/ethnic group	73.5	68.5	64.4	54.2
(no. of responses on which percentages based)	(362)	(197)	(8,148)	(6,024)
	Cramer's V = .053		***Cramer's V = .103	
Get a job to help pay for college expenses	58.2	49.5	55.4	44.7
(no. of responses on which percentages based)	(359)	(198)	(8,153)	(6,054)
	*Cramer's V = .084		***Cramer's V = .106	

(continued)

Table 4.6.   *Continued*

Activity	Learning Habits Participants		All Entering Freshmen	
	Women	Men	Women	Men
Have a roommate of different race/ethnicity	32.6	27.3	37.4	27.5
(no. of responses on which percentages based)	(356)	(198)	(8,122)	(6,010)
	Cramer's V = .055		***Cramer's V = .104	
Engage in the following extracurricular activities:				
Participate in student clubs/groups	47.8	30.5	45.1	29.1
(no. of responses on which percentages based)	(360)	(197)	(8,162)	(6,030)
	***Cramer's V = .168		***Cramer's V = .163	
Participate in volunteer or community service work	33.9	14.7	27.2	13.2
(no. of responses on which percentages based)	(360)	(197)	(8,151)	(6,025)
	***Cramer's V = .206		***Cramer's V = .169	

^ Of the 21 likely college activities considered in the CIRP survey, those shown in the table had Cramer's V values of at least 0.05 and were significant at the .001 level. Activities considered likely by fewer than 15 percent of all freshman respondents are also excluded (i.e., change career choice, seek personal counseling, join a fraternity or sorority, play intercollegiate sports, or participate in student government).

^^ Although expectations of persistence at CSUN are relatively low, no more than one-tenth of the freshmen respondents consider it very likely that they will transfer to another college; differences by gender are minimal.

* = Accompanying Chi square significant at the .05 level
** = Accompanying Chi square significant at .01 level
*** = Accompanying Chi square significant at .001 level

action in a variety of guises. Insofar as this interaction involves academically relevant pursuits (e.g., volunteer work or community service, participating in campus clubs, communicating with professors, and discussing course content with classmates), men may have fewer resources at their disposal should they encounter difficulties in college.[11]

In addition to the differing experiences and expectations just reviewed, men and women bring differing self-perceptions with them to college. As seen in table 4.7, men generally arrive at CSUN more confident of their outstanding abilities in a range of areas. Despite such divergent perceptions at the outset, it should be noted that men participating in the Learning Habits Project are no more likely than their female counterparts to consider it very likely they will make at least a B average; two-thirds of the students express such a view. The same applies to the larger freshman cohorts of which they are a part, as the bottom row in the first section of table 4.6 indicates.

Differing Self-Perceptions

Table 4.7 lists a range of intellectual and other traits, some more global than others, on which TFS respondents are asked to rate themselves. The percentages shown indicate the proportion of respondents who consider themselves "outstanding" on any given trait, which means they rated themselves as "above average" or among the top 10 percent of their age group for the trait in question. Given this rather high bar, it is worth noting that the majority of freshmen entering CSUN during the fall 2007–2011 period consider themselves "outstanding" on four of the eleven intellectual traits shown: intellectual self-confidence, academic ability, leadership ability, and creativity.[12] LH participants express similarly positive views of their abilities in these areas, with the majority also considering their writing skills outstanding. Such views are by no means atypical, as a glance at any given year's freshman survey report reveals (e.g., Eagan et al. 2016).

LH men consistently rate their intellectual skills more highly than do the women. The gap between the sexes is most marked on four of the nine traits shown in table 4.7: intellectual self-confidence (75 vs. 53 percent), mathematical ability (60 vs. 36 percent), computer skills (46 vs. 37 percent), and public speaking ability (43 vs. 33 percent).

A similar picture emerges for the other traits shown at the bottom of table 4.7, although here LH women are at least somewhat more likely to rate themselves as outstanding on the last three traits shown: understanding of others, drive to achieve, and cooperativeness. In contrast, the gender differences for the six traits on which men view themselves more positively than women range from 9 points for social self-confidence to 16 points for emotional health and 21 points for physical health. All are statistically significant at the .05 level or higher.

In short, both LH men and all male freshman entrants display remarkably high levels of confidence in their outstanding intellectual and other abilities. Although some of this greater self-confidence may be justified, given their stronger quantitative skills at entry, there are other traits where such disproportionate confidence does not appear warranted (e.g., public speaking ability, physical health, and self-understanding). The danger of such views is that they may engender complacency among entering men, thereby initially blinding them to the increased effort that college success requires. How this plays out during the first years of college emerges from the LH data reviewed below.

Table 4.7. Percentage of LH participants and all first-time freshmen in their entry cohorts who considered themselves outstanding^ on selected traits by gender

Traits	Learning Habits Participants		All Entering Freshmen	
	Women	Men	Women	Men
Intellectual Traits				
Self-confidence (intellectual)	53.1	75.0	46.2	60.8
(no. of responses on which percentages based)	(369)	(204)	(8,451)	(6,262)
	***Cramer's V = .215		***Cramer's V = .145	
Academic ability	80.5	84.2	48.3	60.0
(no. of responses on which percentages based)	(370)	(203)	(8,466)	(6,286)
	Cramer's V = .046		***Cramer's V = .116	
Mathematical ability	36.3	59.8	22.3	41.9
(no. of responses on which percentages based)	(369)	(204)	(8,456)	(6,269)
	***Cramer's V = .226		***Cramer's V = .211	
Computer skills	36.7	46.3	31.7	48.8
(no. of responses on which percentages based)	(371)	(203)	(8,463)	(6,283)
	*Cramer's V = .094		***Cramer's V = .174	
Public speaking ability	33.3	42.9	29.6	33.9
(no. of responses on which percentages based)	(369)	(203)	(8,441)	(6,259)
	*Cramer's V = .095		***Cramer's V = .047	
Leadership ability	51.5	58.1	49.9	53.3
(no. of responses on which percentages based)	(371)	(203)	(8,453)	(6,266)
	Cramer's V = .064		***Cramer's V = .034	
Artistic ability	37.6	37.7	30.8	33.4
(no. of responses on which percentages based)	(370)	(204)	(8,467)	(6,284)
	Cramer's V = .002		***Cramer's V = .028	
Creativity	59.8	62.3	52.7	55.1
(no. of responses on which percentages based)	(371)	(204)	(8,479)	(6,286)
	Cramer's V = .024		**Cramer's V = .023	
Writing ability	52.7	52.0	37.5	38.5
(no. of responses on which percentages based)	(370)	(204)	(8,441)	(6,254)
	Cramer's V = .007		Cramer's V = .010	

Traits	Learning Habits Participants		All Entering Freshmen	
	Women	Men	Women	Men
Other				
Physical health	38.5	59.6	37.0	57.4
(no. of responses on which percentages based)	(371)	(203)	(8,446)	(6,273)
	***Cramer's V = .202		***Cramer's V = .203	
Competitiveness	48.8	58.9	43.6	61.3
(no. of responses on which percentages based)	(303)	(163)	(6,748)	(4,983)
	*Cramer's V = .096		***Cramer's V = .175	
Emotional health	45.8	61.4	41.1	53.0
(no. of responses on which percentages based)	(371)	(202)	(8,435)	(6,255)
	***Cramer's V = .149		***Cramer's V = .118	
Self-understanding	53.1	64.2	49.7	58.8
(no. of responses on which percentages based)	(369)	(201)	(8,441)	(6,241)
	**Cramer's V = .107		***Cramer's V = .091	
Popularity	20.8	32.5	28.1	36.6
(no. of responses on which percentages based)	(346)	(194)	(7,074)	(5,304)
	*Cramer's V = .129		***Cramer's V = .091	
Self-confidence (social)	43.8	52.7	47.8	53.7
(no. of responses on which percentages based)	(370)	(203)	(8,460)	(6,260)
	*Cramer's V = .086		***Cramer's V = .059	
Understanding of others	72.2	63.7	67.6	63.1
(no. of responses on which percentages based)	(371)	(204)	(8,430)	(6,247)
	*Cramer's V = .088		***Cramer's V = .047	
Drive to achieve	83.3	76.4	72.4	69.4
(no. of responses on which percentages based)	(371)	(203)	(8,458)	(6,276)
	*Cramer's V = .084		***Cramer's V = .033	
Cooperativeness	75.7	73.4	67.7	66.9
(no. of responses on which percentages based)	(370)	(203)	(8,448)	(6,262)
	Cramer's V = .025		Cramer's V = .009	

^ The percentages shown include students who said they were "above average" on a given trait, along with those who said they were among the top 10 percent of their age group on the trait in question.

* = Accompanying Chi square significant at the .05 level
** = Accompanying Chi square significant at .01 level
*** = Accompanying Chi square significant at .001 level

THE EVOLUTION OF NEW AND STRENGTHENED STUDY HABITS

We now examine selected end-of-term and interview responses that cast light on how the LH men and women build on strengths they bring from high school in order to negotiate the first years of college. Special attention is given to elucidating factors that inhibit or enhance their performance during those years.

Mastering College Assignments

Over time, the LH students were asked whether their approach to several types of assignments had changed since coming to CSUN. Initial questions of this sort, asked in the students' first year, concerned reading and writing assignments. The next set, posed in the second year, focused on critical thinking and quantitative reasoning skills, while a third set, asked toward the end of the third year, dealt with information competence.[13] Responses were grouped within two common categories: changed my approach to assignments of a given type or did *not* change my approach. Within each, reasons for change or the lack thereof were enumerated.

Table 4.8 summarizes major subcategories within the "no change" category. The size of the broader category varies, with almost no one asserting that they had *not* adapted their approaches to assignments focusing on critical thinking or information competence, presumably because such matters received relatively little attention in their high schools.[14] In contrast, responses to questions about approaches to writing, reading, and quantitative reasoning assignments quite frequently fell within the "no change" category. In all instances, consistent gender differences are evident, with those for writing and quantitative reasoning statistically significant. The figures indicate that men are more likely than women to claim there is no need to change their approach to the assignment in question—they know what works for them! A few examples convey the tone, first about writing, followed by comments on math:

> I have always considered myself a somewhat above satisfactory writer, even before I entered CSUN. The way I approach my writing assignments has not changed because I do not need to change it.

> I think I have found what works for me, and if it works I won't mess with it.

> I have always done well with mathematics so I did not need to alter any of my approaches.

> Because the only way I get through mathematics is by hard work and many, many hours of tears and comfort food. That has been the same since middle school. Ha ha.

Table 4.8.   Reasons students have *not* changed their approaches to different types of assignments since arriving at CSUN by gender

Characteristic	Women	Men
Approach to Writing Assignments		
I. No Need for Change: I Know What Works for Me[1]	12.3	22.3
II. Approach Developed in High School Continues to Work	12.5	11.6
III. Don't Do Much Writing at CSUN	6.5	9.8
(Number of excerpts on which percentages based)	(463)	(224)
Approach to Reading Assignments		
I. No Need for Change: I Know What Works for Me[2]	18.6	22.2
II. Approach Developed in High School Continues to Work	3.4	5.6
III. No Courses Have Focused on Reading	3.0	6.0
(Number of excerpts on which percentages based)	(472)	(234)
Approach to Assignments Focusing on Critical Thinking		
I. No Need for Change: I Know What Works for Me	1.2	0.9
II. Approach Developed in High School Continues to Work	1.2	1.4
(Number of excerpts on which percentages based)	(416)	(217)
Approach to Assignments Focusing on Quantitative Reasoning		
I. No Need for Change: I Know What Works for Me[3]	18.6	32.4
II. Adequate quantitative reasoning skills developed before came to CSUN	7.6	7.4
(Number of excerpts on which percentages based)	(397)	(204)
Approach to Assignments Relying on Ability to Find and Use Information		
I. Already Knew How to Research Information	0.5	0.9
(Number of excerpts on which percentages based)	(412)	(220)

1. Chi square = 11.51 (.001); df = 1; Cramer's V = .129
2. Chi square = 1.26 (NS); df = 1; Cramer's V = .042
3. Chi square = 14.18 (.001); df = 1; Cramer's V = .154

What I have been doing has been working well for me so far, so I see no reason to change it.

Such views are of a piece with men's greater self-confidence at entry.

Quantitative Reasoning

Among students who reported changing their approaches to quantitative reasoning assignments, additional gender differences are evident. Women were more likely than men to articulate two relatively infrequent responses: the importance of seeking help when needed and striving for a better understanding of assignments (13 vs. 7 percent). A difference in emphasis is also evident in a subsequent question focused on reasons why courses were particularly helpful in strengthening students' quantitative reasoning skills. Here, women were more likely than men to discuss the importance of the instructor's approach to class content (16 vs. 9 percent), with an emphasis on the ability to explain mathematical content or logic (8 vs. 4 percent). The examples below are illustrative of the women's responses.

> The most important part of learning math for me has been having a good professor. . . . At CSUN, all of my math professors have been passionate about the subject and had a positive attitude. They are encouraging, communicate well, and are organized. Also, if we had any questions, we could ask during lecture and during office hours, which of course helped a great deal.

> One of my engineering professors gave us homework from the book. He went over the material but gave us problems that required us to think more [not just copy]. That forced me to understand better what was going on in each problem.

> I believe the professor's method and pace played a large role in my progress with quantitative reasoning. She allows enough time in lecture and lab for students to ask questions because she does not present an overwhelming amount of information at once.

Reading

A set of questions equivalent to those just reviewed for quantitative reasoning was asked with regard to assigned readings. Since these revealed clear struggles among both men and women, students' comments about successful changes to their approaches to reading assignments during their face-to-face interviews were isolated. Some differences by gender emerged, especially during the junior interviews. Women were significantly more likely than men to mention having changed their approaches to reading assignments during the first years of college (60 vs. 46 percent), giving special attention in their comments to improvement in note-taking and reading with care.[15] The following responses are typical:

> The teacher tells you to read before class, but for me I'll try to skim it and then take [the instructor's] notes, and then I'll read afterwards because [during class] he actually talks about what's probably going to be on the test. So that's what I try to emphasize the most when I'm reading.

> But in regards to the past, I realize I would just scan because there's so many pages to read that you're just trying to get through them and you're not really paying attention. I've gotten better about that. Now I actually try to read, and if

I don't understand it I go back. . . . The outlines help. I break them down to say, okay, this I what I need to do, and I'll do a summary about every point I learn or something like that. So now I think I'm better about organizing the way I study.

In contrast, men were somewhat more likely than women to note the importance of doing the assigned readings (58 vs. 49 percent), with disproportionate attention to the importance of increasing their reading speed and matching their procedures to individual class expectations. This last, which is also described by some of the women, is of particular interest because it reveals the importance of being able to balance competing demands and of understanding what you need to do to match your effort to individual instructor expectations. As one young man commented,

I skim through [reading assignments] right before class. And then listen to the lecture. And it depends on what they say. And, well, most professors are really good at letting you know if what they say in a lecture is going to be covered, or what they say and what's in the book is going to be covered, like, on the test. I pay attention . . . because it saves time. I mean, if they're just going to go off their lecture, I usually rent books or buy them really cheap. It's just saving time and helps me with my time management.

Said another,

I don't really read the text unless it's required. It's helpful for me to talk to the professor or pay attention in class. . . . If you can catch the drift that the teacher goes off on their own kind of style, than you are probably safe without reading the book.

The following examples provide the flavor of comments related to improved reading speed.

On advice to incoming freshmen: Probably just to make sure to pay attention in class especially, and also read the text. Because at times during my freshman year I wouldn't read the text and I'd be able to get by. But if I had read the text I probably would have done better. . . . I've had a lot more reading this year. Like . . . I've had at least around 100 or so pages a week to read . . . in some classes.

The only thing that is a little bit difficult with the reading is something that I realized a little later. A lot of the books are really dense and so normally what I'll do is if I see a section that was covered in class and the notes, I'll just skim over it. I mean I'll skim over the whole chapter so that I don't have to waste time reading every single word. But if it's something I say okay I know this very well, then I'll just skip over it and I'll go to the next thing.

If Only I'd Known

Additional insight into students' differing approaches in college emerged from responses to an end-of-term question posed in both the third and seventh semesters after entry. It asked students to specify what they knew now that they wished they had known at entry. Gender differences are more evident for the rising seniors than for the rising sophomores, so discussion focuses on the former. Even here, gender differences are not overwhelming, although some difference in emphasis is evident. Thus, men were somewhat more likely than women to report they wished they had had a better sense of effective study habits (16 vs. 13 percent) and strategies for college success (25 vs. 19 percent) as freshmen. As several men noted,

> You will eventually need to apply yourself and cannot coast through a [discipline] degree. I understand how to study now but wish I had learned sooner.

> I would tell new freshman to focus on their grades early. In addition, I would say that they should choose to learn the material rather than memorizing it. It is so much more effective to really understand material, for any class . . . as it will benefit you extremely in the future.

> I would advise any new freshman to work on developing better study habits. As my classes have progressed, I have noticed that my workload has greatly increased. If I developed better study habits as a freshman, I feel that I would have had an easier time adjusting. I would also advise against procrastination.

In contrast, women were somewhat more likely than men to regret not entering with greater awareness of campus resources (14 vs. 8 percent), the importance of course planning (34 vs. 25 percent), the value of faculty support (16 vs. 12 percent), or involvement in campus activities (13 vs. 9 percent). As several students noted,

> I would also advise students to remain on top of scheduling for classes as well as establishing relationships with professors, as both of these factors are vital for a smooth and successful college experience.

> The advice that I would give freshmen would be to get involved in school activities and to take advantage of the resources that CSUN has to offer its students.

> I wish I would have known more about studying abroad and other programs out there that help enhance and create a better learning experience and academics. I would advise freshmen to join one club and stick with them for a year.

BENEFICIAL PRACTICES IN AND OUT OF THE CLASSROOM

Two of the broad themes in the face-to-face interviews provide further detail about LH participants' distinctive approaches to college life. The differences by gender, enumerated below, focus on effective teaching practices and rewarding campus activities.

Effective Teaching Practices

Although teaching practices that benefit student learning were relatively infrequently discussed during the first-year interviews, they were described with some frequency during the second round of interviews in students' third year. Within the relevant set of responses, gender differences of two sorts are evident, as table 4.9 indicates. First, and most importantly, men were more

Table 4.9. Interview excerpts relating to LH participants' comments on effective teaching practices encountered at CSUN by gender (percentages; junior-year responses)

Excerpt Topic			Women	Men
I.		The Way Instructor Approached the Course Benefited My Learning	42.1	46.9
	I.A.	Instructor's focus on student learning was beneficial[1]	23.7	13.6
		1. *Conveyed the desire to foster student learning*	*12.1*	*8.6*
		2. *Approachability (e.g., available to answer questions, supportive)*	*11.1*	*3.7*
		3. *Articulated clear expectations for student performance*	*3.2*	*2.5*
		4. Other beneficial aspects of instructor's focus on learning	0.0	1.2
	I.B.	Expressed enthusiasm and passion for subject	7.9	12.3
	I.C.	Course content linked to current events and students' daily lives	7.4	6.2
	I.D.	Clear, well-organized class presentations and materials	2.6	3.7
	I.E.	Instructor's knowledge of subject	3.2	4.9
	I.F.	Balance between lecture and discussion during class sessions	5.3	2.5
	I.G.	Instructor's style of presentation facilitated my learning[2]	6.3	18.5
		1. *Instructor made the course interesting*	*3.2*	*7.4*
		2. *Draws students into class discussion or lecture*	*1.6*	*6.2*
		3. Uses humor to liven discussion	2.6	4.9
		4. Other aspects of instructor's style	0.5	2.5
All relevant excerpts (N for percentages shown above)			190	81
Junior Interviewees			351	178
Percent of interviewees responding			54.1%	45.5%

1. Chi square = 3.54 (.04); df = 1; Cramer's V = .114
2. Chi square = 9.43 (.003); df = 1; Cramer's V = .187

likely than women to discuss their appreciation of instructors' efforts to present course material in a way that facilitated their learning (see I.G. in table
4.9). Judging by their responses, efforts to make the course interesting were
particularly welcome, as were efforts to draw students into class discussion.
The examples below are illustrative:

> It's a phenomenal class. What has made it phenomenal is the professor, I would
> say. . . . Not to step on anyone's toes, but a history class, in my opinion, is
> quite worthless in terms of, you know, my major . . . and the kind of focus that
> I want. . . . I'm required by the school to take a history class. Okay, I'm just
> going to take it, whatever, you know? However, the professor is engaging. He's
> loud. He's really just one of those people that loves what he knows, and he just
> lays down history like it's a story. It's quite a difficult class. . . . We have essay
> examinations. . . . You know, we really have to keep on top of the reading, but
> it's not difficult because it's engaging. It's interesting.

> I can read the book, and reading the book sometimes is just really boring, and
> just reading through it, like, yeah, I want this to be over with, you know? But
> when teacher[s] actually take the time, instead of just reading from the book,
> they actually explain it to you and know interesting facts, and [don't] just stick
> to the curriculum but tell you things that will actually spark an interest—it's
> those little things that want to pull me in and just listen a little bit more.

Women, in contrast, more frequently mentioned the value of faculty members focusing on student learning, expressing particular appreciation for their
evident desire to foster learning and ready availability to answer questions
(see I.A. in table 4.9). The following student comments make this clear:

> I've had teachers that make you feel dumb for asking questions. But teachers
> here, they try to make you feel comfortable asking questions, and I guess they
> all say no question is a stupid question, but they actually make you feel that
> way. And they see if you're struggling, like, they'll try to help you, they'll try to
> explain it to you again, you know. Just things like that.

> Well, having cool professors, a lot of times they're more willing to help you out.
> They're not there because they have tenure. They're there because they want to
> be there, and they want to help you, they want to see you succeed.

Enriching Campus Activities

In addition to having modestly different views of effective classroom practices, the LH men and women varied in their assessment of the value of
campus support systems and activities. Some noteworthy shifts in emphasis

emerged between the first- and third-year interviews. In both, as table 4.10 indicates, everyone was more likely to mention one or more of the following activities when identifying those that were helpful: campus facilities such as the library or the learning resource center, study groups, and student clubs and other groups. The order of frequency changed, however, with participation in student clubs moving from third to first place between the first and second interviews.

Table 4.10. Interview excerpts relating to LH participants' views of beneficial campus activities by gender (percentages)

Excerpt Topic	First-Year Interviews		Third-Year Interviews	
	Women	Men	Women	Men
Campus Activities That Contributed to Learning				
I.A. Campus facilities (e.g., Library, Learning Resource Centers, Athletics)[1]	47.0	58.0	29.7	22.9
I.B. Participation in study groups[1]	21.7	31.0	22.6	19.8
I.C. Participation in student clubs, Greek societies, etc.[1]	16.6	25.0	41.4	44.8
I.D. Dorm Life	6.7	0.0	1.7	3.1
I.E. Cocurricular or volunteer activities (except internship)	5.9	0.0	6.3	5.2
I.F. Campus diversity (e.g., students, activities offered)	4.0	3.0	1.7	2.1
I.G. Internship	0.4	0.0	4.2	7.3
I.H. Involvement in campus activities (no detail provided)	1.6	0.0	2.1	1.0
I.I. Other	0.8	0.0	2.5	1.0
Gains Provided by Participation				
II.A. Strengthened academic skills[2]	63.2	82.0	53.1	49.0
II.B. Participated in activity (no further explanation)	19.0	16.0	13.4	12.5
II.C. Established or strengthened friendships	10.7	11.0	15.9	18.8
II.D. Provided sense of community	5.9	6.0	7.5	6.3
II.E. Provided career direction	3.6	1.0	16.7	17.7
II.F. Service to others	2.4	0.0	5.4	6.3
II.G. Other	2.0	3.0	7.9	13.5
All relevant excerpts (N for percentages shown above)	253	100	239	96
Freshman interviewees	415	210	351	178
Percent of interviewees responding	61.0%	47.6%	68.1%	53.9%

1. First Year: Combination of first three activities shown above: Chi square = 13.31 (.001); df = 1; Cramer's V = .192
2. First Year: Chi square = 3.35 (.043); df = 1; Cramer's V = .096

In terms of why participation in various campus activities was beneficial, one reason stands out for both sexes and in both interview periods: strengthening academic skills. It is less dominant during the third-year interviews, however, where the benefits of career guidance assume considerably more importance. By the third-year interviews, men and women expressed rather similar views about the value of differing campus activities. However, during the initial interview period, some gender differences were evident. As table 4.10 indicates, the men are disproportionately likely to say that one or more of the three most frequently mentioned activities contributed to their learning. The examples below are typical of their responses:

> And for math we always—I always make sure I have a study group. And the library, those study rooms are really helpful. Last semester, my main study was showing other people how to do [problems]. So I would show them and it would enforce my knowledge.

> I actually attended the writing labs at the [discipline] class. At first, my teacher recommended it and then I began to become a regular because I realized that it helps my writing so much. They just sort of evaluate whatever it may be you're writing about and tell you about your content.

> I spend a lot of hours [in the library]. I mean, you know, just sort of studying, and I feel like it's a great place for me to study because at home I don't always have, you know, like a quiet space or like Internet access or something, you know?

> Yeah, I just joined [a fraternity] this semester. I do like it so far. You have to earn certain grades in order to stay at a fraternity, and they have like a chair for education, so if you have any questions they'll help you out, take you to tutoring, that kind of stuff.

> Being in a social club that's actually been official with a strong community behind you is very helpful when it comes to studying.

Women also made most frequent mention of the three most dominant responses but additionally were often the only ones to mention the other activities listed (e.g., dorm life and cocurricular/volunteer activities). Examples of their more wide-ranging responses include the following:

> I would say living in the dorms has helped a lot, too, because I am on campus and I'm, like, close to everything here. I can just, like, if I need to go to the library, I can walk down here or . . . even the small things like free printing up in the dorms. And so, like, that's helped a lot, I mean, those resources.

I volunteer for CSUN Helpline, which is usually at night and I do that. I answer phone calls from CSUN students or actually anyone can call. It's anonymous and they just talk about their problems. . . . I'm trying to do a little bit now, just to see if it's really what I want to do [in the future].

In terms of why participation in various campus activities was beneficial, men were more likely than women to focus exclusively on the value of strengthening academic skills:

I think it's great. I am like living in the computer room and the library a lot, doing homework and stuff because it's so much easier, and then being in an academic environment it's easier to focus on that instead of being at home and having video games and food and all that.

I'm not just saying that our fraternity is the only one, but our fraternity, if you have below a certain GPA, we have mandatory study hall every Sunday night. And we put education before the fraternity, really.

I have study partners in my math class. Certainly. I always make sure that if there is a subject that I feel is going to be difficult, I always try to create a study group to, you know, because there's always going to be that one person that will know more than you. And that will only help you.

Other benefits of participating in campus activities are evident in the women's comments shown above (e.g., friendships and service to others).

Preceding discussion has indicated that men about to enter CSUN express remarkable confidence in their skills and abilities, while women express greater commitment to key elements of academic engagement: seriousness about schoolwork and experience with the types of social interaction that fosters learning. Once in college, the data suggest, LH students build on these entering strengths during their first years of college. The men, who entered so confident of their college success, are disproportionately likely to believe that reliance on their high school skills will enable them to master college assignments. They also tend to be more likely to expect instructors to make course material engaging. Although some men were more strategic than their female counterparts in approaching their studies, when asked to look back on their initial years, they were the ones most likely to wish they had known more about effective study habits and strategies for success.

The women, in contrast, were likely to wish they had known more about existing campus resources and opportunities for campus involvement, building on the interactive strengths developed during high school. Such strength comes to the fore in other ways as well: women are more likely than men to talk about seeking the help of others when they struggle with coursework (in the case of quantitative reasoning assignments, in particular), and to value instructors who were both committed to fostering student learning and readily available to clarify assignments or course material.

IMPLICATIONS OF DIFFERING STRENGTHS AND WEAKNESSES AMONG ENTERING STUDENTS

Initial discussion in this chapter indicated that LH men entered CSUN better prepared for college work than women, at least by the formal indicators generally relied upon. It was unexpected, therefore, that the data also indicated that the two groups perform similarly, with women outdistancing men in several areas. (A similar pattern is seen among all freshman entrants, with greater gender gaps in performance often evident.)

The lag in the performance of the men—in effect allowing the women to "catch up"—reflected differences in high school experience that are not normally considered in assessing readiness for college. This possibility was explored with the aid of data drawn from the CIRP freshman survey, which documented differing activity patterns. The women among the project participants, it emerged, formed habits in high school that made them better able to handle the increased academic demands of college. Such beneficial patterns of behavior include devoting considerable time and effort to schoolwork and interacting with others in relation to classwork or school-related activities. Insofar as the latter involves academically relevant pursuits, men may have fewer resources at their disposal should they encounter trouble in college, especially since the relevant LH data reviewed indicated that students' behavior during their early college years often mirrored their high school practices.

Men outpace women—among both LH students and all freshman entrants—in one important respect: they display remarkably high levels of confidence in their outstanding intellectual and other abilities, a confidence that the LH data suggest they carry over into their initial college work. Although some of this greater self-confidence may be justified given their stronger quantitative skills at entry, this is not the case in other areas.

As earlier discussion has noted, the high self-confidence of first-year men appears to be quite typical of most male college students. This difference in confidence has generally been interpreted as a male strength and a female weakness by previous researchers. That is, it is lack of sufficient self-confidence that consistently leads young women to underestimate their capabilities (Sax 2008, 25–35). In fact, however, they may be the realistic ones, with young men overestimating their abilities.

Entering college with such overarching self-confidence, therefore, may be a liability, engendering complacency and possibly initially blinding new students to the increased effort that college success requires. Such slowness to recognize the greater demands of their new setting, when coupled with the men's less well-developed academic engagement, is likely to jeopardize their successful persistence. As Marcus Weaver-Hightower (2010) has pointed out, many men come to college unprepared to deal with the higher expectations and freedoms of the college setting.

Women, in contrast, thanks to their "lower" self-confidence, may be quicker to recognize the new challenges that the transition to college brings with it and can build on the study habits developed in high school to master them. The notion that women's college success rests on their more realistic confidence levels, coupled with their stronger study habits at entry, also has the advantage of explaining their better performance. The notion that women lack academic self-confidence, in contrast, as most other researchers have posited, simply leaves one puzzled about their greater persistence and success.

Although a good many of the differences by gender highlighted above are modest and should not be overstated, they do have a number of implications for prevailing practice. First and foremost, they suggest that conventional measures of college preparedness (e.g., high scores on the SAT or other objective tests) are not necessarily good indicators of the differing levels of academic engagement that students bring with them to college. And these, the data indicate, are at least as important as incoming students' objective test scores. This suggests that courses designed to introduce entering freshmen to college resources and effective study habits, such as freshman seminars, may be just as important for apparently well-prepared students as they are for those entering with deficiencies in preparation. For example, offering such courses to all students hoping to pursue engineering or other STEM majors, in which apparently well-prepared young men frequently predominate, may be particularly worthwhile. Equally important, the data suggest, is to stress to new students that college work is likely to be more challenging than high school was, with the result that false confidence in one's abilities can quickly lead to trouble.

Of course, not all students enter college with the toxic combination of high self-confidence and weak study skills, as preceding discussion has shown. These students—who enter with less confidence about their abilities but good study habits—are likely to need more than courses about the rigors of college work, although they are likely to benefit from them. For these students, assurances from a supportive faculty and staff that their skills and talents are sufficient to excel may be key. Such a message may be particularly appropriate for majors in which women predominate (e.g., humanities).

The above recommendations appear to contradict one another but only if one assumes that entering students bring the same skills and abilities with them. Clearly, they don't, and finding ways of effectively serving various types of students, especially in universities that are home to both men and women, remains a challenge.

NOTES

1. The percentage of Latina/o and African American students among all baccalaureate degree recipients increased by half between 2000–2001 and 2014–2015, rising from 16 to 23 percent. During this period, the total number of degree recipients grew by just over 400,000 (National Center for Education Statistics 2016, tabs. 323.20 and 324.20).

2. The summary figures appearing at the bottom of table 4.1 are shown to document that the young men and young women participating in the Learning Habits Project are not disproportionately drawn from different entry cohorts. The small differences that appear are not statistically significant.

3. Such gender differences in racial and ethnic background are relatively typical nationally. By mid-2000s, according to Sax (2008, 16–19), women were more likely than men to stem from traditionally underserved and low-income backgrounds. They are were also less likely to have college-educated parents. Nonetheless, in contrast to CSUN, the majority of entering freshmen nationwide continued to be white and have college-educated parents.

4. It is worth noting that a good many LH students enter CSUN without a declared major. And here there are no gender differences, with approximately one-fifth of the young men and young women entering undeclared. The same is true for the larger freshman grouping, although the percentage undeclared is a bit higher (23–24 percent).

5. "Likely graduates" are those who have graduated within a given period of time (five or six years in this instance) or are still enrolled in the following fall term.

6. Among the students who were invited to join the project but did not, a statistically significant gender gap also remains evident for likely graduates, with 64 percent of the women projected to be likely graduates compared to 51 percent of the men.

7. The identification rate varies by cohort, however, with 80–90 percent of the two most recent LH cohorts identifiable compared to two-fifths for the 2007 entrants and two-thirds for the 2008 entrants.

8. Because of the number of respondents in the larger freshman grouping, even small gender differences yield statistically significant differences, making the statistics shown less meaningful than those for the much smaller LH subset.

9. Although relatively few students report spending significant time partying, young men are clearly more likely to do so than are young women.

10. It is worth noting that even though this last percentage is relatively low, the percentage of freshmen expecting to be dissatisfied enough to transfer to another institution is considerably lower (12 percent). This suggests that many students enter-

ing CSUN may simply be uncertain about how college in general will work for them, with men more likely than women to express such uncertainty.

11. The second section of table 4.6 also indicates that the young women participating in the LH project are significantly more likely than their male counterparts to expect to get a job to help pay for college expenses (58 vs. 50 percent).

12. Of the other traits shown in table 4.7, the majority of the full set of freshman respondents see themselves as outstanding on two-thirds of the nine traits shown: competitiveness, self-understanding, self-confidence (social), understanding of others, drive to achieve, and cooperativeness.

13. This last was assumed to deal with information found on the Internet, but the question wording did not make this entirely clear. Thus, some students interpreted the question more broadly and discussed other types of information (e.g., quantitative survey data). Such differences in interpretation were distinguished during the coding process.

14. Note that these questions were generally posed around 2010, when reliance on electronic media was less widespread than it is today.

15. Although areas of emphasis were similar for comments made during the first-year interviews, no differences by gender were evident at this early stage.

REFERENCES

Astin, Alexander W. 1993. *Assessment for Excellence: The Philosophy and Practice of Assessment and Evaluation in Higher Education*. Westport, CT: Oryx.

Baxter Magolda, Marcia B. 1992. *Knowing and Reasoning in College: Gender-Related Patterns in Students' Intellectual Development*. San Francisco: Jossey-Bass.

Bryant, Alyssa N. 2003. "Changes in Attitudes toward Women's Roles: Predicting Gender-Role Traditionalism among College Students." *Sex Roles* 48 (3): 131–42.

———. 2011. "The Impact of Campus Context, College Encounters, and Religious/Spiritual Struggle on Ecumenical Worldview Development." *Research in Higher Education* 52 (August): 441–59.

Chodorow, Nancy. 1978. *The Reproduction of Mothering*. Berkeley: University of California Press.

DiPrete, Thomas A., and Claudia Buchmann. 2013. *The Rise of Women: The Growing Gender Gap in Education and What It Means for American Schools*. New York: Russell Sage Foundation.

Eagan, Kevin, Ellen B. Stolzenberg, Abigail K. Bates, Melissa C. Aragon, Maria R. Suchard, and Cecilia Rios-Aguilar. 2016. *The American Freshman: National Norms Fall 2015*. Los Angeles: Higher Education Research Institute, UCLA.

Ewart, Stephanie. 2012. "Fewer Diplomas for Men: The Influence of College Experiences on the Gender Gap in College Graduation." *Journal of Higher Education* 83 (6): 824–50.

Gilligan, Carol. 1982. *In a Different Voice: Psychological Theory and Women's Development*. Cambridge, MA: Harvard University Press.

Kanny, Mary A., Linda J. Sax, and Tiffani A. Riggers-Piehl. 2014. "Investigating Forty Years of STEM Research: How Explanations for the Gender Gap Have Evolved over Time." *Journal of Women and Minorities in Science and Engineering* 20 (2): 127–48.

Kuh, George. 2001. "Assessing What Really Matters in Student Learning: Inside the National Survey of Student Engagement." *Change* 33 (3): 10–17.

Mayhew, Matthew J., Alyssa N. Rockenbach, Nicholas A. Bowman, Tricia A. Seifert, and Gregory C. Wolniak, eds. 2016. *How College Affects Students: 21st Century Evidence that College Works*. San Francisco: Jossey-Bass.

McCabe, Janis M. 2016. *Connecting in College: How Friendship Networks Matter for Academic and Social Success*. Chicago: University of Chicago Press.

National Center for Education Statistics. 2016. *Digest of Education Statistics 2016*. Washington, DC: U.S. Government Printing Office.

Pascarella, Ernest T. 1985. "College Environmental Influences on Learning and Cognitive Development: A Critical Review and Synthesis." In *Higher Education: Handbook of Theory and Research*, edited by C. Smart, vol. 1, 1–61. New York: Agathon.

Pascarella, Ernest T., and Patrick T. Terenzini. 2005. *How College Affects Students: A Third Decade of Research*. San Francisco: Jossey-Bass.

Patton, Lori D., and Natasha N. Croom, eds. 2017. *Critical Perspectives on Black Women and College Success*. New York: Routledge.

Sax, Linda J. 2008. *The Gender Gap in College: Maximizing the Developmental Potential of Women and Men*. San Francisco: Jossey-Bass.

Tinto, Vincent. 1987. *Leaving College: Rethinking the Causes and Cures of Student Attrition*. Chicago: University of Chicago Press.

Weaver-Hightower, Marcus B. 2010. "Where the Guys Are: Males in Higher Education." *Change: The Magazine of Higher Learning* 42 (3): 29–35.

Wood, J. Luke, and Robert T. Palmer. 2015. *Black Men in Higher Education: A Guide to Ensuring Student Success*. New York: Routledge.

5

Campus Diversity and College Learning through the Eyes of Learning Habits Students

Bettina J. Huber

As discussion elsewhere has indicated, California State University, Northridge (CSUN) is one of the most diverse campuses within the state system of higher education. This is evident in the socioeconomic composition of the four freshman cohorts from which the learning habits (LH) students were drawn. Among them, close to three-fifths of the students stemmed from traditionally underserved racial and ethnic groups, with Latina/o students accounting for 44 percent of the larger freshman group.[1] Just over half of the students in the four cohorts were Pell Grant recipients, and close to two-fifths (37 percent) have parents with no more than a high school education. The diversity of CSUN's incoming freshman classes increased steadily during the 2000s. For example, 52 percent of the 2007 entry cohort, from which the first LH students were drawn, stemmed from traditionally underserved backgrounds, while 41 percent were Pell Grant recipients. By the time the fall 2011 freshman cohort entered, these percentages had risen to 63 and 61 percent respectively.

Given this rapid shift in student demographics and the past decade's steadily increasing national attention to ensuring the success of students from all backgrounds, CSUN has participated in several national initiatives that focus on issues of diversity and equity.[2] Therefore, it seemed quite natural to include a question relating to campus diversity among the end-of-term questions posed to LH students. The multipart question posed at the end of participants' seventh semester after entry focused on how existing campus diversity affected their learning experience at CSUN. The three-part question included two close-ended subquestions and one open-ended subquestion:

A. CSUN, like many other CSU campuses, has a student body that is quite diverse in several respects. Would you say that your high school was

    a. More diverse than CSUN?
    b. Less diverse than CSUN?
    c. Much like CSUN in terms of diversity?

B. Has the diversity of students you encountered at CSUN during the last three years
    a. Enhanced your learning? Y/N
    b. Hindered your learning? Y/N
    c. Made no difference to your learning? Y/N

C. Why do you think the diversity of the student body at CSUN has affected your learning in the way that it has? If it has helped in some cases, but hindered in others, please try to explain the circumstances that gave rise to the different effects.

Responses to these questions, which were unexpected in some respects, are reviewed later in this chapter.

The discussion indicates that student views on the value of campus diversity were generally positive and unaffected by the diversity of the high schools they attended, with very few saying that such diversity hindered their learning. The students' views differed only modestly by racial and ethnic background or first-generation status. Gender, combined with planned major, did differentiate student views, however, with men planning STEM (science, technology, engineering, and mathematics) majors considerably more likely than both other men and their female counterparts to claim their learning was unaffected by campus diversity.

HIGH SCHOOL DIVERSITY

The first row of table 5.1 indicates that approximately three-fifths (61 percent) of LH students responding to the survey in their seventh term reported that their high schools were less diverse than CSUN, while 35 percent said their high schools had much the same mix of students as CSUN. Only 4 percent reported that their high schools were more diverse.

According to the second section of table 5.1, student views of how their learning was affected by the diversity at CSUN did not vary by the diversity of their high schools. Overall, close to two-thirds reported that campus diversity enhanced their learning, while nearly 25 percent said it had no effect. A distinct pattern emerged for the small group of students coming from high schools that were more diverse than CSUN. While the majority reported that campus diversity enhanced their learning, a quarter reported

Table 5.1. Students' views of how CSUN's diversity affected their learning by the reported diversity at their high schools

	My High School Was			
	Less Diverse than CSUN	*As Diverse as CSUN*	*More Diverse than CSUN*	*All Respondents*
All respondents				
Percent	61.2	34.9	3.9	100.0
(Number of respondents)*	(251)	(143)	(16)	(410)
How Learning Was Affected by Diversity at CSUN:				
Diversity Enhanced Learning	68.1	65.0	56.3	66.6
Enhanced only	*67.7*	*62.9*	*56.3*	*65.6*
Hindered as well	*0.4*	*0.7*	*0.0*	*0.5*
Had no effect as well	*0.0*	*1.4*	*0.0*	*0.5*
Diversity Had No Effect on Learning	24.7	21.7	18.8	23.4
Diversity Hindered Learning	5.2	9.8	25.0	7.6
Other	2.0	3.5	0.0	2.4
Total	100.0	100.0	100.0	100.0
(Number of respondents)	(251)	(143)	(16)	(410)

*Excluded from this total are 30 students (6.8 percent of the larger group) who did not respond to this initial question.

that it hindered their learning. The following examples provide a flavor of these infrequent responses.

> I feel like most of CSUN is [nationality]. . . . So they all segregate together in all of my classes and talk in [their language] . . . which separates them and it has also distracted me from learning.

> My learning was hindered when diversity was viewed as unintelligent or misinformed. This was especially true with political diversity.

VARIATION IN VIEWS BY KEY BACKGROUND FACTORS

The degree to which student views of campus diversity differ by three key background factors is shown in table 5.2. The sharpest differences are evident for gender, with women significantly more likely than men to report that campus diversity enhanced their learning (73 vs. 55 percent) and less likely

Table 5.2. **Students' views of how CSUN's diversity affected their learning by selected background characteristics**

	Campus Diversity:			(No. of Excerpts on which Percentages Based)
	Enhanced Students' Learning[1]	Had No Effect[2]	Hindered Students' Learning	
All Responding Students	67.0	23.9	7.7	(439)
Gender				
Men	54.6	34.0	9.2	(141)
Women	72.8	19.1	7.0	(298)
Racial and Ethnic Background				
Traditionally Underserved	73.1	21.6	5.3	(171)
Better Served	62.8	25.6	9.4	(266)
Parental Education (proxy for first-generation college student)				
High school or less—both parents	81.3	17.6	2.2	(91)
Some college—one or both	68.9	25.6	3.3	(90)
Four-year degree—one or both	60.3	26.5	11.1	(234)

1. Gender: Chi square = 14.35 (.001); df = 1; Cramer's V = .181
1. Race Groups: Chi square = 5.00 (.03); df = 1; Cramer's V = .107
1. First Generation: Chi square = 3.90 (NS); df = 2; Cramer's V = .138

2. Gender: Chi square = 11.70 (.001); df = 1; Cramer's V = .163
2. Race Groups: Chi square = 0.88 (NS); df = 1; Cramer's V = .045
2. First Generation: Chi square = 2.04 (NS); df = 2; Cramer's V = .100

to say it had no effect on their learning (19 vs. 34 percent). Similar gender differences have been reported by Linda Sax (2008, 147–51, 233–35). She points out, however, that, regardless of their views, men are more strongly affected than women by discussions of diversity issues in the classroom and by interaction with diverse peers during the college years.

Like women participating in LH, first-generation students and those from traditionally underserved backgrounds are more likely than other participants to report that campus diversity enhanced their learning (73–81 percent vs. 60–69 percent). According to the statistics at the bottom of the table, however, the difference by first-generation status is not statistically significant.[3] Similarly, the difference by racial and ethnic background is significant in only one respect, with traditionally underserved students more likely than the better served to say that campus diversity enhanced their learning (73 vs. 63 percent); the percentages saying that it had no effect are equivalent.

On the face of it, the similarity of views across racial and ethnic boundaries, in particular, is surprising. And, to some degree, the most unexpected finding is that one-quarter of the students from traditionally underserved backgrounds did not report that campus diversity benefited their learning. (This may just reflect the fact that campus diversity can also breed animosity and resentment, thereby complicating the views of traditionally underserved students, its frequent targets.) In addition, the largely similar views of the two major racial and ethnic groupings on this issue are in keeping with the similarity of views expressed by LH students when questioned about their study habits and faculty teaching practices. It may, therefore, simply reflect a widespread similarity of approach among well-prepared college students in the Southern California context. Further, a campus as diverse as CSUN is likely to attract freshmen who are comfortable with this attribute.

Differences by gender, which are statistically significant for both of the dimensions considered, are amplified by attention to students' open-ended comments and, interestingly, by differences in planned major, as table 5.3 shows. The first column indicates that both women and men often justified their initial responses in two ways: by saying that campus diversity enhanced their educational experience and increased their personal growth and interaction with others. Women were more likely to focus on the first, often specifying that campus diversity enhanced their learning by providing interaction with people of other cultures, broadly defined (20 vs. 8 percent). These examples are typical of these survey responses:

> The diversity of the student body at CSUN has affected my learning in a positive way because I have gotten to know people of different races and cultures. For instance, I have learned to interact with different kinds of people in group work assignments.

> It helps to broaden my knowledge of society in general. It gives me a taste of reality because in the "real world" diversity is all we'll see. CSUN has diversity varying from students, educators, employees, etc.

> I think that in class discussions everyone is subjected to so many different kinds of opinions from people with different backgrounds. I took a world music class that had students from all around. They were able to discuss their culture and how the music tied in with their life. I think it helps everyone become more cultured and understanding.

> It's cool . . . you learn about different cultures and see different viewpoints.

Table 5.3. Reasons the diversity of the CSUN student body did or did not affect students' learning by gender and planned entry major

			All Students	STEM Majors*	Other Majors	Business Majors
WOMEN						
Diversity Enhanced Learning[1]			72.8	68.0	73.0	78.4
I.	Enhanced educational experience		33.2	28.0	34.6	32.4
	I.A.	Provided exposure to differing perspectives	5.4	0.0	6.6	5.4
	I.B.	Provided interaction with people from other cultures	19.5	18.0	20.4	16.2
	I.C.	Opened my mind to new ideas and ways of doing things	6.7	10.0	6.2	5.4
	I.D.	Other	2.3	0.0	2.4	5.4
II.	Increased personal growth and interactions with others		30.2	26.0	29.4	40.5
III.	III. Lack of campus diversity would have adversely affected learning experience.		2.0	6.0	1.4	0.0
IV.	Other		10.4	8.0	11.4	8.1
Diversity Had No Effect on Learning[2]			19.1	20.0	19.0	18.9
Diversity Hindered Learning			7.0	12.0	5.7	8.1
	(Number of excerpts on which percentages based)		(298)	(50)	(211)	(37)
MEN						
Diversity Enhanced Learning[1]			54.6	38.3	56.9	75.9
I.	Enhanced educational experience		21.3	10.6	24.6	31.0
	I.A.	Provided exposure to differing perspectives	4.3	0.0	6.2	6.9
	I.B.	Provided interaction with people from other cultures	7.8	4.3	7.7	13.8
	I.C.	Opened my mind to new ideas and ways of doing things	4.3	2.1	4.6	6.9
	I.D.	Other	5.7	4.3	6.2	6.9
II.	increased personal growth and interactions with others		28.4	19.1	30.8	37.9
III.	Lack of campus diversity would have adversely affected learning experience.		2.8	0.0	1.5	10.3
IV.	Other		2.8	8.5	0.0	0.0

	All Students	STEM Majors*	Other Majors	Business Majors
Diversity Had No Effect on Learning[2]	34.0	48.9	33.8	10.3
Diversity Hindered Learning	9.2	12.8	9.2	3.4
(Number of excerpts on which percentages based)	(141)	(47)	(65)	(29)

*STEM majors are those housed in two colleges: engineering and computer science, and science and mathematics. All others, with the exception of the majors housed in business and economics, are included in the "other" grouping.

1. *Gender: Chi square = 14.35 (.001); df = 1; Cramer's V = .181*
1. Women and Planned Major: Chi square = 1.17 (NS); df = 2; Cramer's V = .063
1. Men and Planned Major: Chi square = 10.47 (.005); df = 2; Cramer's V = .272

2. *Gender: Chi square = 11.70 (.001); df = 1; Cramer's V = .163*
2. Women and Planned Major: Chi square = 0.03 (NS); df = 2; Cramer's V = .010
2. Men and Planned Major: Chi square = 11.90 (.003); df = 2; Cramer's V = .290

THE INTERPLAY OF GENDER AND MAJOR

Introducing the three major groupings shown in table 5.3 (STEM, business, and other) into the picture makes relatively little difference among LH women. The proportions saying that diversity enhanced their learning or had no effect on it do not differ significantly across major subgroups, although women planning STEM majors are somewhat less likely than others to say that campus diversity benefited their learning (68 vs. 73–78 percent). In addition, female business majors are somewhat more likely than others to mention that campus diversity increased their personal growth and interaction with others. Said one young woman,

> I think that the diversity helped me become accustomed to different people and how to work/network with them. It has enhanced my learning with new viewpoints and opinions, opening the perspective I initially had.

Said another,

> It made me connect with different people in different ways. In addition, it has definitely trained and enhanced my communication skills which I strongly believe will be very helpful for me once I step into the professional world.

Among the men, in contrast, responses are sharply divided by planned major. In particular, men pursuing STEM majors are significantly less likely than those planning business majors to say that campus diversity enhanced their learning (38 vs. 76 percent) and significantly more likely to claim that diversity had no effect on their learning (49 vs. 10 percent). These examples typify the responses of STEM majors:

I haven't paid much attention to it.

People are people; their ethnicity does not affect my learning in the slightest way. It never has and it never will.

The diversity of the student body at CSUN has not affected my learning in any way. I don't think my learning experience would have been any different if CSUN were any less or more diverse.

While I have made friends who are diverse, this does not affect how I learn. I have made friends who are diverse and they have helped me learn; however, it was not their diversity that helped me. I found their diversity interesting to learn about, but that diversity has not helped me learn anything new in the field that I am in.

I don't believe diversity amongst the student body played a role in my learning process. I met some cool people from different countries, but that played no role in my ability to learn.

Such views contrast with those of men planning business majors, who tend to focus on the benefits of personal growth and interaction:

The diversity of the student body has helped me by allowing me to broaden my mind to see how people of different backgrounds and cultures interpret current events and other topics in a way I've never been exposed to.

The diverse student body has helped me to question my preconceived points of view on several issues. . . . The student makeup in my major is not as diverse as is the rest of the university, but I think the diversity—combined with the success of many people in my major—serves to further improve my learning experience.

I loved being able to connect with people with all kinds of background. Especially in the business world it is vital to be able to relate to your customer, which is similar to what I learned from my CSUN experience.

I think that [campus diversity] is helpful because it gives people the ability to see what things will be like after college. Everyone will most likely have to deal with all sorts of people outside of college, and CSUN does a good job of preparing people for this.

In short, student views of the benefits of campus diversity appear to be influenced by the disciplinary perspectives they encounter in their majors, with the views of men particularly strongly affected by the perspectives of STEM disciplines.

Gender differences within the three disciplinary groupings shown in table 5.3 serve to reinforce this conclusion. In particular, the degree to which men and women say that campus diversity enhanced their learning is largely the same for those planning business majors (76 vs. 78 percent) but quite different among those planning STEM majors (38 vs. 68 percent, a 30-point difference). A more modest difference is evident among men and women planning majors combined in the "other" group (57 vs. 73 percent). Compare the examples below, which are limited to women planning STEM majors, to those above for male STEM majors:

I think that the diversity helped my learning and improvement as a person altogether because different people from different cultures often can provide a perspective you haven't considered. This opens your mind to new ideas and possibilities.

The diversity hasn't really affected my academic learning, but it has enhanced my cultural learning and worldviews. You get to see things from a different perspective and broaden your own.

The diversity has enhanced my learning because it has taught me how to work with others. It has helped develop social skills that I can use in my future career. The better I can socialize now with diverse groups of people, the better I will be able to communicate with future coworkers as well as clients.

How could diversity *not* help? Besides teaching us the legitimacy of tolerance, different people have different opinions that are all relevant and important. Having a myriad of people learning together promotes mutual understanding between people who are now able to see each other's points of view.

IMPLICATIONS: THE IMPORTANCE OF DISCIPLINARY PERSPECTIVES FOR VIEWS OF CAMPUS DIVERSITY

Campus diversity is valued by most LH participants, with very few claiming that such diversity hindered their learning. The sharpest differences in view are evident by gender, with women significantly more likely than men to report that campus diversity enhanced their learning. Some differences by racial and ethnic background and first-generation status were also evident, but they were modest, at best.

Examining student views of campus diversity by several disciplinary groupings highlighted strong differences by major among the men but only modest differences among the women. Men planning STEM majors were shown to be at the heart of these differing patterns of response, thanks to their atypical views. Fully half of them said that campus diversity had no effect on their learning, compared to 20 percent of the female STEM majors and 30 percent of the men planning other majors. Judging by the examples provided, the men appear to attribute the unimportance of diversity to their view of learning as something that involves the absorption of facts and figures, which can be equally well accomplished in isolation. As one observed, "My major is not one of diverse opinions, so the learning only comes from the facts and information, not opinion."

In short, the LH data strongly suggest that the disciplinary perspectives to which students are exposed affect their views of the benefits of campus diversity, with men particularly strongly affected by the perspective on learning prevailing within the STEM disciplines. To some degree, the timing of the question may have served to maximize the observed differences in response. That is, by their seventh term at CSUN, a good many of the LH students were seniors and would be focused on completing the courses required for their majors. And here, the technical learning required of STEM majors, especially those in which men predominate, is quite different from the customer- or client-service perspectives of many other majors.[4]

Further, given the relatively small number of students providing the responses reviewed here, one should not exaggerate the differences in perspective that have come to the fore.[5] Still, the findings suggest that campus-wide and cross-disciplinary discussions around the prevailing views of the nature of learning and how it is affected by campus diversity might be fruitful. This is not to suggest that some of the views expressed by the LH students are right and others are wrong or misguided; rather, discussion of these matters by faculty members and administrators might bring greater clarity and consistency to a complicated set of issues.

NOTES

1. Five subgroups make up the larger set of students stemming from traditionally underserved backgrounds: American Indians, Pacific Islanders, African Americans, Latina/o, and multirace. Others are referred to as stemming from better-served backgrounds.

2. By way of example, the campus is currently participating in a project sponsored by the American Association of Colleges and Universities (AAC&U) titled "Committing to Equity and Inclusive Excellence" (http://www.aacu.org/committing -to-equity).

3. To some degree, the lack of statistical significance by first-generation status reflects the small size of two of the subcategories shown.

4. Among the LH students planning STEM majors, women are far more likely than men to be biology majors (48 percent vs. 21 percent), a discipline in which diversity of all kinds is a key consideration.

5. By the time the seventh semester rolled around, those LH students planning to graduate within four years, which many did, had less incentive to complete the end-of-term surveys, since the reward for doing so—early registration—lay a year ahead. Thus, only 410 of the original 750 LH students responded to the multipart question on which this chapter focuses.

REFERENCE

Sax, Linda J. 2008. *The Gender Gap in College: Maximizing the Developmental Potential of Women and Men*. San Francisco: Jossey-Bass.

Part Three

KEY THEMES IN TEACHING AND LEARNING

In both interviews and end-of-term survey responses, learning habits (LH) students reported a wide variety of teaching practices that facilitated their learning. The chapters in this section describe in detail key themes emerging from students' comments about effective teaching practices. These include mastering the challenges of reading at the college level, gains in writing proficiency, and the mixed blessings of the entry of technology into academia and the classroom. This introduction sets the stage for these more focused discussions by providing a brief overview of beneficial teaching practices identified by LH students in their interviews.

EFFECTIVE TEACHING PRACTICES

It is worth noting that during their face-to-face interviews, LH freshmen discussed effective teaching practices far more extensively than did juniors. The likely reason for these differing frequencies is that the freshman interviews included an explicit question about effective teaching, while the junior interviews did not. This difference in format notwithstanding, there is a difference in emphasis: juniors were more likely than freshmen to discuss the importance of instructors providing guidance on how to complete specific tasks (24 vs. 13 percent). Freshmen, in contrast, were more likely than juniors to discuss how an instructor approached a course, with special emphasis on the balance between lecture and discussion (10 vs. 4 percent) or the instructor's style of presentation (19 vs. 10 percent). Use of humor received a special boost in this last category (9 vs. 3 percent). The following student comments illustrate their perceptions of what helps them learn, starting with faculty members who care:

You know, most teachers, luckily, like, the ones that I've had, they want you to pass, they want to help you, they want you to succeed.

INTERVIEWER: How did they convey that to you?

Teachers here, they try to make you feel comfortable asking questions, and I guess they all say no question is a stupid question, but they actually make you feel that way. And they see if you're struggling, like, they'll try to help you, they'll try to explain it to you again, you know. Just things like that.

I'm actually, like, satisfied with the experience because I feel like every professor I've had takes their, you know, their profession like really seriously. And they want everybody to, like, succeed. It's not like they want anybody to fail.

Students appreciate faculty members who learn their names: "She's very interactive. She memorized every single one of our names, for instance, that I haven't had done at CSUN. She memorized every single name the first day." Others noted the use of humor:

And then I was, like, okay he's a really good teacher. He makes the class funny. He jokes around. Like he'll be serious and do problems, but he'll make it an environment where it's not just, like, student/teacher. You do have the respect for your teacher, but you also feel like—they're still above you but they're not kind of looking down on you.

She was really relatable, she was funny in class. You know, humor always works, I think.

Many of the LH students spoke about their most passionate teachers:

For instance, in my business law class, I always pay attention. I don't get distracted in that class because he is so passionate about the subject and he keeps us involved with examples, and keeps asking us questions, so it keeps us engaged and I like that.

We were learning in class, for example, we took a class about American Indian writing. And I've never really been interested in that, but the fact that the professor was so passionate about it, made me want to learn it, you know, and I was, like, "Well, there has to be something to it 'cause they're so passionate about it." Or just making the material that the professor chooses for the class—make it relevant, make it interesting.

Chapters 8 and 9 examine the use of technology by the faculty, both pro and con. Not surprisingly, students like technology—such as PowerPoint and webnotes—when it is used well and hate it when it is done badly. One student said,

> I don't like PowerPoints because I find it hard to keep up with. . . . But I really like it when a teacher just talks and just whips out the board marker and, as they go, kind of write it because I don't bring an iPad to school. So everything that I do is by hand, so I like that better.

Other teaching practices that engender a fair amount of comment include small-group work and course/lecture organization and structure.

6

Reading with Understanding

What Do College Students Say?

Linda S. Bowen and Elizabeth Berry

INTERVIEWER: Do you read the book?

STUDENT: It depends.

INTERVIEWER: It depends on what?

STUDENT: The teacher.

College faculty members almost universally bemoan the fact that their students "just don't do the reading!" They have trouble, however, attributing a reason for students not reading. Part of the problem may be that students are not competent readers and do not know how to "decode the disciplines." Even students who arrive as highly qualified academic freshmen often find they are ill equipped to deal with the volume and complexity of reading required in their classes.

Launched in fall 2007, the Learning Habits Project at California State University, Northridge (CSUN) was designed to track, over seven years, groups of newly enrolled students deemed most likely to succeed based on their superior high school grades and California State University–mandated placement exams. The project generated rich qualitative and quantitative data that reveal significant information about student success at a large, public, mostly commuter, comprehensive master's degree–granting university known for its diverse undergraduate population. The project tracked more than 700 students from 2007 through 2014 to uncover what learning strategies they found helpful. Based on both extensive interviews and end-of-term surveys, the data reveal valuable information that can and has produced innovative solutions. In our study, "Reading with Understanding," our interest was on how students adopt new strategies in their approach to increased and higher-level reading requirements and whether faculty supported these efforts.

Across the seven years, at all course levels and for all subgroups, one of the most repeated comments from students referred to the difficulty of keeping up with their reading. And while they reported having received instruction on writing, students noted that no curriculum specifically addressed challenges in navigating the density of reading required by instructors. As a result, this chapter focuses on when and how students solved the reading issue for themselves and concludes with a discussion of the numerous CSUN faculty-created tactics for helping students become competent college readers. The following are typical of student comments on how they figured it out for themselves:

> I haven't really taken any classes that have been particularly helpful in developing my reading skills. . . . Any development in my reading has come from my own analyzations of what I need to gain from reading. Over time, I've learned by trial and error.

> There has been no course that I have taken that has greatly improved my reading skills. What has improved my reading skills is reading frequently.

Data developed from interviews with both freshmen and juniors in the project show how extensively students changed their approaches to reading assignments out of necessity. About one-third of freshmen and more than half of the juniors cited a variety of strategies they devised to manage the onslaught of reading assignments, not only recognizing the need to perform at a higher level but also taking steps to cope and succeed.

This chapter draws from the students' interviews to uncover what the "learners" say about their reading habits and how they approached their college-level work. We briefly outline the existing literature to examine the contemporary state of reading at the college level. This is followed by a deeper exploration of the study methodology and its significant results. Finally, we suggest workable solutions to the "reading problem," including the Reading Matters Initiative at CSUN. Launched in 2013, the project was designed to address issues raised in an analysis of the learning habits (LH) data and interviews.

REVIEW OF THE LITERATURE

College students' inability to read at an appropriate level of understanding is not a new problem, as seen in an article published in the *New York Times* in

1921: "The question [of] what college students read has perennial interest. One undergraduate of an eastern university sorrowfully answered an inquirer: 'they don't read at all.' . . . No one expects to find many mighty readers in college."

More recent studies show the problems persist. "Whenever faculty get together to talk about student writing or critical thinking, they inevitably turn also to problems of student reading," writes John C. Bean (2011), who addresses helping students read difficult texts in the popular guide *Engaging Ideas: The Professor's Guide to Integrating Writing, Critical Thinking, and Active Learning in the Classroom.*

In dozens of recent articles about college students' reading habits, researchers may be coming closer to one key problem: students never learned to read complex texts. They struggle to understand complicated material as reading assignments mount. For example, Michael Pressley (2011) hypothesized in his research published by the International Reading Association that students need expert instruction in metacognitive reading skills and advocated the teaching of such strategies for reading comprehension. Metacognition is awareness of when text is understood or, conversely, when it is not understood. Skilled reading comprehension is complicated; good readers are active. It is known, however, that many high school graduates and beginning college students have not reached metacognitive maturity with respect to reading. In particular, high school students rarely report active comprehension strategies. The author argues that students need expert instruction in metacognitive reading skills. Pressley's work is supported in two recent studies:

- A 2011 study, reported in "College Students' Textbook Reading, or Not!" As an introduction, Kylie Baier and colleagues reviewed numerous studies citing the low number of students completing their assigned reading before class. Instead, many students read the texts just before the exam. In this study of 395 participants, students reported their reading habits, including time spent, strategies employed, and instructors' role in helping them read more effectively. The most common response to what the instructor could do was "tell me what is important in the reading." Almost 20 percent of students indicated that the instructor should speak regularly about how the readings relate to course content.
- Mary E. Hoeft (2012) assessed reading compliance and comprehension of first-year students at a small two-year liberal arts college. Her results showed less than half reported they read assignments. Of those who reported doing so, only about half comprehended what they had read. Reasons they did not read included lack of interest and the teacher not emphasizing or reminding them to, among others. The study does not address the need to help students understand how to read scholarly articles.

Overcoming that obstacle is addressed in *Decoding the Disciplines: A Model for Helping Students Learn Disciplinary Ways of Thinking*. Joan Middendorf and David Pace (2004) emphasize the importance of recognizing the disciplinary nature of knowledge. They outline steps to identify what students have difficulty learning and what they should know, as well as methods for practicing skills in reading in the disciplines (1–12).

Eric Hobson (2004) challenges the assumptions that reading is fundamental in college courses. He cites research related to both student preparation and compliance with assignments and discusses the "preparation problem" as well as the "compliance problem." Hobson notes research that established compliance with course reading at 20–30 percent for any given day and argues that faculty "misread audience," that is, normative levels of student ability, motivation, and commitment (3). Hobson offers 14 tips for encouraging compliance and concludes, "If high levels of student reading compliance and, by extension, high levels of reading comprehension are end points that truly matter, faculty must accept their role in an inter-dependent process; they are the key agents in making reading fundamental in college" (8).

Of course, reading well goes hand in hand with writing competency. In their article "Reading: A Bridge to Everywhere," Tracy Hallstead and Glenda Pritchett (2013) argue that student writing cannot advance unless student reading improves and therefore reading merits attention. Their analysis of the reading process suggests that students lack metacognitive activity while reading.

These elemental skills are also at the heart of the notion of literacy transition to college, argue Sonya Armstrong and Mary Newman (2011) in "Teaching Textual Conversation: Intertextuality in the College Reading Classroom." They say students need to reconceptualize their views of reading and writing and must recognize the need for active reading or "textual conversation," that is, intertextuality. Students need instruction in how to link course material with supplementary texts that focus on specific topics related to core material. Because few faculty members provide explicit instruction in how to read disciplinary texts, a developmental reading course is one way to help students make a transition to higher education.

Washington University psychologists Peter Brown, Henry Roediger, and Mark McDaniel (2014) suggest reading should be coupled with active learning strategies since their research shows repetitions, such as rereading notes and assignments, are not effective.

Two more general publications also shed light on the issue of students reading with understanding. Richard Light's well-known 2001 book, *Making the Most of College*, uses student stories, gleaned from extensive interviews, to examine certain choices that students make. The subjects of this study are high-achieving students admitted to Harvard in the 1990s. Although the study reflects a select demographic, many of the topics covered can be adapted, as did the Learning Habits Project. The compilation of 11 articles edited by Maryellen Weimer (2010) offers practical suggestions for faculty members from faculty members who have tried various methods in their classrooms.

These publications point out the problem: overall, this brief review suggests that rarely are students instructed on how to read complex texts. Some pick it up; others struggle. Few, however, describe why students do not read or, if they do read, what strategies they employ. Advice given to the faculty does little to help these teachers understand how to approach students' reading deficits.

DIFFERENCES BY GENDER, RACE/ETHNICITY, AND CLASS LEVEL

As LH students pointed out repeatedly, they were on their own. One young man said,

> For you to understand it more, I realize that you have to read everything because they're not going to go over everything that's in the text and that's why they give you the text. So, I've learned that I have to read more . . . in high school, I really didn't. I didn't read a whole lot in high school.

One place we looked was traditionally underserved versus better-served students, as a way to look at race and ethnicity.[1] Sixty percent of traditionally underserved juniors said they changed their approach to reading assignments, compared to 52 percent of better-served juniors, a possible reflection on how well high school prepared them for college (see table 6.1). Juniors reported their main strategy was learning to take better notes. For freshmen, both traditionally underserved and better-served students cited similar experiences in realizing the amount of reading and the need to perform at a higher level. As expected, their strategies were not well formed.

There were differences in the reading experience in terms of gender as well, but primarily at the junior level. For freshmen, little difference was apparent. For example, interview excerpts related to approaches to reading assignments by gender showed that responses from freshmen men and women were essentially the same (see table 6.2). But when students reached their junior year, the disparities were marked: less than half of the men acknowledged having changed their approaches to reading assignments, while three-fifths of women had changed theirs.

Table 6.1. Interview excerpts relating to LH participants' approaches to their reading assignments by racial and ethnic grouping and interview timing (percentages)

Excerpt Topic	First-Year Interviews		Third-Year Interviews	
	Traditionally Underserved	Better Served	Traditionally Underserved	Better Served
I. Required to Do More Reading at CSUN than in High School	20.3	18.1	20.8	12.2
II. Need to Perform at Higher Level than in High School	11.1	10.0	12.7	13.9
III. Importance of Doing Assigned Readings	61.8	58.9	47.0	55.6
III.A. Prioritize readings based on class structure or professor's style	16.1	16.2	15.7	24.0
III.B. Importance of doing assigned reading before class	30.4	23.7	22.5	26.7
III.C. Have learned to skim/ read faster	6.9	9.0	11.4	10.8
III.D. Other	24.9	20.2	2.5	2.4
IV. Have Changed Approach to Reading Assignments	32.7	32.7	60.2	52.4
IV.A. Importance of reading for understanding	10.6	7.2	14.0	8.3
IV.B. Have learned to take better notes	9.7	11.2	35.2	28.1
IV.C. Read more carefully/in depth	6.5	5.6	6.8	5.6
IV.D. Importance of reading and reviewing multiple times	9.7	13.7	12.7	16.0
IV.E. Other	4.1	2.5	16.1	12.2
V. Other	7.4	11.5	5.5	4.5
All relevant excerpts (N for percent)	217	321	236	288
Freshman Interviewees	232	389	203	323

Table 6.2. Interview excerpts relating to LH participants' approaches to their reading assignments by gender and interview timing (percentages)

Excerpt Topic	First-Year Interviews		Third-Year Interviews	
	Men	Women	Men	Women
I. Required to Do More Reading at CSUN than in High School	19.0	19.0	12.2	17.6
II. Need to Perform at Higher Level than in High School	9.5	11.0	14.7	12.7
III. Importance of Doing Assigned Readings	63.1	58.7	57.7	49.3
III.A. Prioritize readings based on class structure or professor's style	*16.7*	*16.1*	*25.0*	*18.2*
III.B. Importance of doing assigned reading before class	*29.2*	*25.2*	*24.4*	*24.9*
III.C. Have learned to skim/read faster	*9.5*	*7.5*	*16.0*	*8.9*
III.D. Other	*20.2*	*22.8*	*1.9*	*3.0*
IV. Have Changed Approach to Reading Assignments	30.4	33.5	45.5	60.2
IV.A. Importance of reading for understanding	*9.5*	*8.0*	*11.5*	*10.6*
IV.B. Have learned to take better notes	*7.1*	*12.1*	*24.4*	*34.1*
IV.C. Read more carefully/in depth	*5.4*	*6.2*	*3.8*	*7.0*
IV.D. Importance of reading and reviewing multiple times	*12.5*	*11.8*	*14.7*	*14.4*
IV.E. Other	*3.6*	*2.9*	*10.3*	*15.4*
V. Other	13.1	8.3	5.8	4.6
All relevant excerpts (N for percent)	168	373	156	369
Freshman Interviewees	210	415	178	351

As would be expected, responses about developing reading understanding were evident in the lower-division students. When LH respondents were asked as freshmen and sophomores about changes in how they approached reading assignments, three-fifths reported they had adopted new strategies. Almost one in three said the change was dictated by the need to do more reading or by the higher level of mastery required in college. At the same time, less than two-fifths of the respondents explicitly identified specific courses that were particularly helpful in strengthening their reading skills. Students' responses suggested they more frequently worked out new approaches to reading assignments on their own than they did for their writing assignments, for which they received guidance.

ADOPTING NEW STRATEGIES

Selections from interview transcripts illuminate, in their own words, how students learned to tackle the texts. Their varied and sometimes surprising answers offer important insights for faculty and students alike that can be applied in the classroom.

> In college, it's more difficult because I have so much reading already. In high school, it was like 20 pages in the textbook. Now it's like 30 pages from this textbook, 30 pages from this textbook, every textbook you have to read. . . . After I've done reading all this, my brain is just like, "No more reading."

> In high school, I was able to skim through my reading. . . . But at CSUN, you have to read your assignments before the next class day.

LH students were asked to indicate, at the end of their third semester at CSUN, whether the way they approached their reading assignments had changed since entering as freshmen. Three-fifths of respondents agreed (see table 6.3).[2] Among those, just over one in three said the adjustment was a consequence of the need to do more reading or to the higher level of mastery required (see sections III and IV in table 6.3).

Particularly interesting among the responses dealing with the importance of doing assigned reading in a timely manner is a subset describing how to use course structure or instructor preferences to determine reading priorities (see section VII.B in table 6.3).

> The trick to reading for five or more classes while you're in college is simply a matter of assessing each professor. Some professors focus entirely on their lectures when creating exams, while others may borrow from the textbooks and lectures collectively, and still others think their textbooks are the sacred text from which all knowledge will flow.

> I feel like the main point that most students miss is that they don't look at what kind of teacher they have. Sometimes a teacher that's strictly from the book, so you say, "OK, well, I don't even have to go to class. I just have to read the book and then I'll be fine. . . ." Or you have a teacher that says straight out, "This is what is going to be on the test." So, I'm going to listen to what you have to say and that's what's going to be on the test.

> So, find out what they want you to know from the reading. You know with history it's hard because they want you to know all the facts but they don't want you to quote the book verbatim. . . . For English, they want you to get a main theme, or a motif, or a symbol or something like that. So, find out what it is. It's hard with English when you're reading novels. I mean, you really have to read the whole thing.

Table 6.3. Reasons students have or have not changed their approaches to reading assignments since arriving at CSUN (percentages)

Reason for Change or Lack of Change	Percentages
My Approach to Reading Has Changed	**60.2**
I. Have Learned New Techniques and Approaches in CSUN Classes	3.5
A. *English Classes Singled Out*	*1.5*
B. *Other Classes Singled Out*	*1.0*
C. *Both Types of Classes or CSUN Classes in General Mentioned*	*0.5*
D. *Other (no CSUN activity mentioned)*	*0.5*
II. Have Changed Approach to Writing Assignments	—
III. Practice Makes Perfect (Required to Do More Reading at CSUN)	13.9
IV. Need to Perform at Higher Level than in High School	8.0
V. Other Writing Comments	—
VI. Have Changed Approach to Reading Assignments	*38.3*
A. *Have learned to take better notes*	*14.4*
B. *Importance of reading for understanding**	*9.5*
C. *Read more carefully/in depth*	*9.5*
D. *Importance of reading and reviewing multiple times*	*6.5*
E. *Other*	*6.0*
VII. Importance of Doing Assigned Readings in a Timely Way	20.4
A. *Have learned to skim/read faster*	*8.5*
B. *Prioritize readings based on class structure or professor's style*	5.5
C. *Importance of doing assigned reading before class*	*4.0*
D. *Other*	*5.0*
VIII. Other Reading Comments	3.0
My Approach to Reading Has NOT Changed	**39.8**
I. No Need for Change: I Know What Works for Me	30.3
A. *Current approach has always worked*	*23.9*
B. *Description of approach to reading; lack of change implied*	*8.0*
II. No Courses Have Focused on Reading	5.5
III. Approach Developed in High School Continues to Work	3.0
A. *Did Extensive Reading in High School*	*1.5*
B. *Other*	*1.5*
IV. Other Writing/Reading Comments	2.0
(Number of respondents on which the percentages are based)	(201)

*Reading for understanding involves gaining a better understanding of an assignment or the necessary basis for critical analysis.

As noted in table 6.3, close to one in ten students who have changed their approaches to reading report doing so because the procedures that worked for them in high school proved inadequate to the demands of college work. In contrast, a similar question focusing on changes in approaches to writing assignments since college entry yielded almost no comments about the increased amount of writing required in college. It is only in the case of reading, therefore, that a significant number of respondents mention how much more is required at CSUN than in high school. This differing response pattern suggests that the big change between high school and college is not the amount of *writing* required but the volume of *reading*.

> And the teacher, thankfully, understood that, yes, this is a hard book. And so, he had us, for each section, we would write, we'd have to either write five questions about anything we didn't understand or just to show that we had read it.

Closely related to the comments about the amount of reading required is a set of responses focusing on the importance of efficiently managing one's assigned readings (see section VII of table 6.3). The examples below illustrate the tenor of the responses.

> It is always important to keep up with the reading that is assigned, even when it seems like it may be impossible to read so much and retain the information.

> Instead of reading every word of the text, I skim through the paragraphs and summarize the main points.

> Sometimes it's a simple matter of skimming through the book to find the sections you're not too sure about, reading those sections, and then moving on through the rest of it.

> I try and make sure I do the reading before class. I didn't for one class and found that I struggled to catch up all semester.

> I now read material before it is lectured on. This way, even if a concept is foggy when I read it, it solidifies when covered in lecture. Consequently, I retain information, having only to have read the material once.

> I do the reading after [the class session]. . . . To me it helps me hear it in the classroom and have a brief introduction to it and so when I go to the book I kind of know what to expect.

> I'd go through Spark notes and look up the book and read the key points, read the quotes at the end, and then I'd speed read through the books.

Over half of the respondents described their new practices in meeting the challenges of dealing with the volume of reading required (see section VI in table 6.3). As one student noted, "I have learned since coming to CSUN how to dissect a reading assignment and how to pull out the important information for comprehension."

The most frequently mentioned new reading practices involved mastering the art of taking notes and appreciating the importance of reading for understanding (see sections VI.A and B of table 6.3). Comments related to note-taking suggest a variety of tactics, including highlighting:

I take a lot of notes. I need to have the notes because a lot of my tests have been online or it is open book, or if it's not, I make flash cards for it. And I've noticed that if I don't take notes, I don't comprehend it as well. I kind of glaze over, so I take a lot of notes.

INTERVIEWER: And are you taking those in handwriting?

It depends. If it's an online book, then I type it just because I can have the book there, and I can have a Word document to the side, and I can type and read at the same time. But if it's a book that's open, then I take the notes handwritten.

I definitely recommend highlighting and annotating when you're reading, trying to connect things to lectures and things you're talking about in class.

I highlight a lot of things, a lot of bold terms. I highlight things I don't understand. I usually do the ones I don't understand in brighter colors as opposed to ones that need to be on the test. I'll do those in lighter colors, not as bright, but you can still obviously see it when you open up the page, mainly because it's like, "Yes, I need to know that but let me understand this first kind of thing."

Data suggest that respondents have more frequently worked out new approaches to their *reading* assignments on their own than is the case for their *writing* assignments (46 vs. 29 percent). In part, this may stem from differences in course content: one-quarter of the writing comments deal with new techniques and approaches discussed in respondents' college classrooms. In contrast, as section I in table 6.4 indicates, very few responses point to similarly useful classes in relation to reading (3.5 vs. 25 percent for writing).[3] Instead, close to a quarter of the reading responses deal with the importance of keeping up with assigned readings (see section VI in table 6.4), a concern that is virtually absent in the writing responses. This difference may well be another reflection of the challenge posed by the volume of reading required in college. One student described her approach:

Every time I go to school, I go home and I study for at least three or four hours, because we have so much reading. For a class, we have 40 pages to read, so I read that. And then I can highlight the book now, so it's much easier for me. I also still take notes on my laptop. I bring it everywhere, so if I don't read my book, I can just go over my notes. And I always go over the teachers' lectures on the slides and their PowerPoint presentations. And I test myself. I look online for practice tests . . .

INTERVIEWER: For what subjects?

I did it for sociology; I did it for English class. Now I'm doing it for poli sci, anthropology, and biology.

Table 6.4. Percentage of LH students indicating whether and why their approach to reading or writing assignments has changed by type of response

Reason	Writing Responses	Reading Responses
My Approach to Writing/Reading Has Changed	**67.7**	**60.2**
I. Have Learned New Techniques and Approaches in CSUN Classes	24.9	3.5
II. Have Changed Approach to Writing Assignments	29.4	—
III. Required to Do More Writing/Reading at CSUN (Practice Makes Perfect)	1.5	13.9
IV. Need to Perform at Higher Level than in High School	9.0	8.0
V. Other Writing Comments	5.5	—
VI. Importance of Doing Assigned Readings in a Timely Way	—	20.4
VII. Have Changed Approach to Reading Assignments	—	38.3
VIII. Other Reading Comments	—	3.0
My Approach to Writing/Reading Has NOT Changed	**33.8**	**39.8**
I. No Need for Change: I Know What Works for Me	19.4	30.3
II. Don't Do Much Writing at CSUN/No Courses Have Focused on Reading	3.5	5.5
III. Approach Developed in High School Continues to Work	10.4	3.0
IV. Other Writing/Reading Comments	1.5	2.0
(Number of respondents on which the percentages are based)	(201)	(201)

Asked about courses that were particularly helpful, only half stated that they had taken courses at CSUN that improved their reading skills. Some students discussed changes in their approaches to reading but mentioned no specific courses, as the following illustrate:

I started highlighting and taking notes on my own, because I realized it would help me remember the material much better.

By practicing, I was able to explore what kinds of note-taking strategies worked best for me so I could achieve maximum efficiency. Besides courses, being active in the writing labs helped me learn new ways of reading and examining texts.

Among students explicitly discussing helpful courses, 22 percent echoed an important theme in response to the more general question about changes in approaches to reading: the different amounts of reading assigned in various courses required a different approach (see section I in table 6.5).[4]

[Courses in two disciplines] were some classes that involved testing over massive amounts of information. The difficulty of dedicating a lot of time solely

Table 6.5. Percentage of LH students citing different reasons their initial coursework was particularly helpful in strengthening their reading skills

Reason for Change or Lack of Change	Percentages
I. Amount of Assigned Reading Required Different Approach	22.1
A. *Interesting assignments make requirement easier to meet*	4.4
B. *Other*	17.6
II. Integrating Assigned Reading into Course	14.7
A. *Quizzes and tests focusing on reading*	7.4
B. *In-class discussions based on readings*	4.4
C. *Essay assignments based on readings*	2.9
D. *Instructor expectation that comprehension of assigned readings integral to course*	1.5
III. Providing Guidance on How to Approach Reading Assignments	16.9
A. *Analytic reading skills (i.e., reading for understanding) taught in course*	10.3
B. *Provide review questions on assigned readings that draw out implications*	2.9
C. *Critical reading skills taught in course*	2.2
D. *Subdivide sections of required books (other than text) into multiple assignments*	1.5
IV. Learning about Writing Helps Improve Reading Skills	1.5
V. Other	5.1
VI. No Specific Courses Mentioned as Being Helpful	11.8
A. *Described own techniques for approaching reading*	7.4
B. *Improved skills through trial and error or my own efforts*	1.5
C. *Other*	2.9
VII. Have Not Taken Courses That Improved Reading Skills (no further explanation)	33.1
(Number of respondents on which the percentages are based)	(136)

to reading and note-taking developed a natural strengthening of reading skills, since there was so much to learn.

All of the classes I have taken have a lot of reading assignments. This alone has helped with my reading skills.

According to another 15 percent of respondents, courses with regular class activities focusing on reading assignments ensure that these are completed in a timely way. The vehicles instructors use for this purpose, as section II of table 6.5 indicates, include quizzes, tests, in-class discussions, and essay assignments. In addition, a good many instructors provide explicit guidance about how to approach certain types of reading assignments (e.g., literature and logical arguments).

The following examples are drawn from the subset of responses focusing on instructor guidance about analytic and critical thinking. Such comments account for almost two-thirds of the responses in the larger category (see section III in table 6.5).

> The one class that has helped me strengthen my reading skills was [one in which] the professor would tell us to analyze the key points of the section as well as look for things that stood out and had value to what we were reading. By learning this tool, it has helped me throughout the semester.

> Now when I read anything from a novel to an article, I am able to pick out main points and supporting arguments and analyze them on the basis of strength.

> [An English class] has helped in strengthening my reading skills by analyzing the deep issues authors may be commenting on when it comes to the political, social, and economic contexts in which they were written. Open discussion within the classroom and outside of the classroom moderated and guided by the instructor really helps in understanding reading assignments and finding deeper messages written between the lines.

Judging by LH student responses, courses such as those described above are few and far between. This stands in contrast to the many classes mentioned in students' responses to the question about courses that were particularly helpful in strengthening their writing skills.

Underlying a good many of the reading comments is a sense of crisis: becoming a more efficient reader, they imply, is a necessary response to the mountain of reading required by the four to five college courses so many students attempt each semester.

ONE SOLUTION: READING MATTERS INITIATIVE

One Reading Matters Initiative participant, a university librarian, wrote,

> The critical message that many students need to be directed towards developing successful reading habits remains absent from formal university programming. . . . Discussion on critical reading habits is often missing from curricular or cocurricular student success programming. Formal and informal tutoring and instruction is primarily devoted to assisting students with Mathematics and developing research techniques—while tutorial and information about recommended approaches to college level reading remain seemingly nonexistent. (Berry and Klein 2014, 9)

As the LH study progressed and data mounted, a special task force was established in 2009, in response to students' comments about the challenges of college-level reading, to explore the "reading problem" and provide resources for the campus. The resultant Reading Matters Initiative identified numerous methods for addressing reading challenges in the classroom. Under CSUN's faculty development umbrella, the initiative's work and resources have become a helpful clearinghouse for the faculty, with focused workshops and a website to disseminate interdisciplinary strategies for enhanced student reading.[5]

Initiative members represented a range of disciplines. The faculty met monthly for three semesters to discuss and implement sustainable solutions. The goals were to make explicit (a) the variety of demands that reading in university disciplines presents; (b) the range of purposes reading may have in coursework; (c) the nature of faculty expectations for students' reading; and (d) the challenges to students' comprehension and use of the reading they are asked to do. Faculty members engaged in lively meetings that reinforced their commitments to the importance of dealing with students' reading issues. Cross-disciplinary discussions are always valuable but often not possible at the university level, and this approach of engaging the faculty from the different colleges at CSUN proved extremely worthwhile.

Faculty members were stimulated by what they heard and read and willingly shared their ideas and challenges. In so doing, they discovered common problems, no matter their discipline. The major one was how to get students to complete assigned reading. As important was the question of how to help students become competent readers in their major discipline. To that end, the group read and discussed a number of articles and shared their various approaches. During the initiative's last semester, faculty participants shared their projects with their departmental and college colleagues and asked them for strategies they used for helping students navigate difficult texts. Most reported that their college faculty were well aware of "reading resistance" but employed no specific ways to address the issue.

There were, however, some faculty members who employed strategies to motivate students to complete reading with understanding. Of those who responded to requests for information, most had devised a version of study guides.

One philosophy professor changed her teaching method. She developed reading guides that focus the student on key concepts, passages, and arguments. In the guides, she poses questions to engage the students with the issues. "Share with students the inherent nature of the difficulty of philosophical texts," she suggests. "Some feel 'dumb' for not following what they read without realizing that everyone, even the most experienced, find certain texts very difficult to grasp."

Another professor, from economics, recognized the students' difficulty in understanding academic articles. So, she began by demonstrating how she approaches a journal article in her discipline. She told them that she had to read the article at least three times, which was a surprise to many of her students. One told her, "If *you* have to read it three times, I guess, I should read it at least more than once." This professor's student comments echo key themes that emerged throughout the interviews. The themes range from having to do more reading and to perform at a higher level than in high school to the importance of doing assigned readings and changing their approaches to assignments.

It's important for the faculty to recognize that while students are routinely taught writing skills, the intertwined skill of reading is not taught. Yet, student writing cannot advance unless student reading improves. The need for attention to this issue is deeply supported by the findings in the Learning Habits Project. By asking their colleagues to consider methods of improving reading competence at the college level and offering help and resources, the Reading Matters Initiative faculty promoted further dissemination of practical advice for a university-wide problem.

CONCLUSION

This chapter contributes specifically unique knowledge about reading at the college level because the Learning Habits Project is the only study of its kind to draw on such a breadth and depth of qualitative and quantitative material. LH students represent a highly diverse cross-section of the U.S. population typical of many institutions of higher education. Therefore, project results have applications for other universities.

When we began interviewing LH students, we assumed that because they had been successful in high school they would continue to use the same learning strategies that had previously worked for them. This was true for some students, but for the majority it became clear they needed new approaches. This was especially evident when it came to reading. As freshmen, they were overwhelmed with the amount of reading and later, as upper division students, with the complexity of texts. We learned how resourceful upper-division students became as they navigated various learning contexts.

A most significant result of our analysis was the discovery of students' strategies: how they approached reading assignments, how they determined what they needed to do, and what worked for them or for a particular course or professor. For the most part, although students did not receive specific guidance about how to read, they recognized the importance of creating successful reading habits. This realization often occurred after receiving a failing test or course grade. They figured out for themselves what to do to succeed in their classes.

It is possible that faculty members are incorrect when they complain that their students don't read. It seems, from the interviews and other study results, that students do read but rarely are given any instruction about how to read efficiently and comprehensively. After trial and error, many come to understand that subjects and professors require different learning strategies. It should be noted that LH students are some of the best students enrolled at CSUN; they are motivated and determined to figure out what they need to do. But what about students who are not as well prepared and who never learn what it means to strategize about learning?

Professors cannot assume that simply assigning pages in a book means students actually will read and understand what they have read.

WHAT UNIVERSITY FACULTY CAN DO

To become skilled readers of complicated texts, students need help, and although faculty members are not "reading experts," they can call attention to ways to approach the texts, especially in their particular discipline.

LH students reported that study guides were helpful, especially if faculty members discussed them in class. Such guides can take various forms, but regardless of the form, it is essential that the purpose of each reading assignment be made clear. Before assigning class reading, faculty members should assess the reason for it and how it will be incorporated into the course content.

If students believe the instructor will cover the text material during class and are given no real reason or guidance, they will neglect reading, perhaps forfeiting a deeper understanding of the subject. As noted by participants in the Reading Matters Initiative, simply demonstrating how they, as faculty members, work with a text gives students insight and confidence in approaching reading assignments. In other words, the faculty can model how we read and "say back" what we read in our own language. Sometimes, it could be as simple as encouraging students to bring their books to class so they can follow along. Faculty members need to encourage students to engage actively with the text, pointing out the overall concepts and particulars, if necessary.

Writing about reading assignments also helps students. For example, faculty members can invite students to jot down important points, confusing spots, and places of disagreement, as if talking to the author. Or students can invent questions for the author.

During our interviews, students frequently spoke about the value of reflecting on their own learning habits, which participating in the project made them do. Comments such as, "It made me more aware of what I was doing" and, "Interviews made me reflect" suggest they were engaging in a metacognitive process, although they did not use the term. The faculty can incorporate various strategies to foster this kind of thinking. For example, in CSUN's freshman seminar, students are frequently asked to reflect on how they approach their assignments. They complete a "self-report card," expressing how they are—or are not—applying successful high school learning habits in their college courses.

Successful students are sensitive to rhetorical cues communicated by their professors. One student told an interviewer, "When a professor smiles and spends time on the subject, it will be on the test." They understand that faculty members have individual approaches to teaching. Learning the subject matter may require a changed way of studying. But it is also the role of the individual instructor to make reading requirements clear and elucidate the reasons for them. In other words, it is critical to communicate the purpose to the students.

If a faculty member is going to explain the content of the course with elaborate PowerPoint presentations in class, students may opt out of reading. But if the instructor wants a lively discussion and dialogue, an outline for the discussion with a study guide, for example, will help. If the instructor models an approach to a text with students following along, the class will benefit. Several faculty members have commented on the value of asking students to write out discussion questions in advance, while others have had students meet in small groups to discuss readings and then participate in an all-class exchange of views.

Prequiz reflection or prereading quizzes can provide guidelines for students for reading unfamiliar texts. One method used by the CSUN English faculty is an assignment called "Anticipation Guides." These guides prepare students to read critically by engaging them in the subject addressed in the text and focusing their attention on what they already know and think.

Here is one example of an "Anticipation Guide" for the reading "Needed: A License to Drink," which argues that issuing a special permit will help reduce alcoholism:

1. Rules and laws are necessary to ensure that people will do the right thing:
   Strongly disagree__ Disagree__ Depends __ Agree__ Strongly agree__

2. Alcoholism is a serious problem in the United States:
   Strongly disagree__ Disagree__ Depends __ Agree__ Strongly agree__

Faculty members report these guides usually stimulate lively discussions and allow students to see how their views and prior experiences compare with those of their classmates, as well as with the author.

Campus-wide workshops that provide methods for helping students become competent readers, as well as departmental meetings that focus on disciplinary reading, are well worth the time. Several years ago, a university-wide retreat offered a session on promoting college reading, at which ideas were shared among faculty members of many disciplines. During the session, a math professor demonstrated how she taught students to read math problems, and an education professor explained the reading process and the importance of context. Many departments have devoted faculty meetings to the topic of developing reading competence for students in their majors.

As a result of sharing LH data with the university at large, CSUN faculty members have become more aware of the need to provide students with a variety of approaches to college reading. They recognize how crucial it is to communicate with students the purpose and reason for the assigned reading.

Further, project participants' testimony illustrates the extensive and valuable suggestions that worked for them. Their advice and strategies could yield useful ideas for the faculty to share with other students in helping them to become better readers:

- Treat quizzes like tests and study the readings as suggested by professors.
- Use Post-it notes to organize ideas in readings and class notes.
- Read ahead of the lecture, looking for key points and ideas. (However, some students found digesting the readings easier *after* hearing the lecture.)
- Encourage students to read difficult material aloud.
- Take notes during lectures.
- Highlight key words and phrases in different colors.
- Skim the assignment to get an idea of the content.
- Enroll in "speed" reading tutorials available online.
- Take breaks/time to think about the content and to form questions.
- Participate in class discussions as a way to reinforce the readings.
- Join a study group to enable discussion, especially for difficult material.
- Learn time management in conjunction with these other strategies.
- Recognize differences in professors' styles. (Some professors lecture straight from the text, while others expect students to have an understanding of the readings.)
- Take books to class. With books in hand, students follow along.

As we can see, there is no one-size-fits-all solution for the "reading problem." Diverse populations make for diverse solutions. When one senior was asked what advice he would give to a freshman, he said, "Go to class; always to go class. Read the book even if you don't know if you have to read the book. Always read the book."

NOTES

1. First-generation students are defined as those whose parents have no more than a high school education. This definition is narrower than the one relied on by the federal government; it considers first-generation students those whose parents lack a four-year college degree.

2. These data were derived from end-of-term responses provided by students in the first two LH cohorts only. Percentages based on the full four-cohort response sample yielded similar response patterns, however.

3. The figures in table 6.4 are based on end-of-term responses from the first two LH cohorts only. More comprehensive data for all four entry cohorts yielded similar results, however.

4. The figures in table 6.5 are based on end-of-term responses from the first two LH cohorts only. More comprehensive data for all four entry cohorts yielded similar results, however.

5. These materials can be found at http://www.csun.edu/undergraduate-studies/reading-initiative/resources.

REFERENCES

Armstrong, Sonya L., and Mary Newman. 2011. "Teaching Textual Conversation: Intertextuality in the College Reading Classroom." *Journal of College Reading and Learning* 41 (2): 6–21. http://dx.doi.org/10.1080/10790195.2011.10850339.

Baier, Kylie, Cindy Hendricks, Kiesha Warren Gorden, James E. Hendricks, and Lessie Cochran. 2011. "College Students' Textbook Reading, or Not!" *American Reading Forum Annual Yearbook* 31. http://americanreadingforum.org/.

Bean, John C. 2011. *Engaging Ideas: The Professor's Guide to Integrating Writing, Critical Thinking, and Active Learning in the Classroom*. 2nd ed. San Francisco: Jossey-Bass.

Berry, Elizabeth, and Sharon Klein. 2014. "Reading Matters Report, 2014." Reading Matters Initiative, 1–39. Project repository available at http://www.csun.edu/undergraduate-studies/reading-initiative.

Beyer, Catharine H., Gerald M. Gillmore, and Andrew Fisher. 2007. *Inside the Undergraduate Experience: The University of Washington's Study of Undergraduate Learning*. Bolton, MA: Anker Press.

Brown, Peter C., Henry L. Roediger III, and Mark A. McDaniel. 2014. *Make It Stick: The Science of Successful Learning*. Cambridge, MA: Harvard University Press.

Hallstead, Tracy M., and Glenda Pritchett. 2013. "Reading: A Bridge to Everywhere." *Double Helix: Journal of Critical Thinking and Writing* 1. http://qudoublehelix-journal.org/.

Hobson, Eric H. 2004. "Getting Students to Read: Fourteen Tips." IDEA Paper 40. Georgia Southern University, the Idea Center, Manhattan, KA, 1–10. http://www.ideaedu.org/.

Hoeft, Mary E. 2012. "Why University Students Don't Read: What Professors Can Do to Increase Compliance." *International Journal for the Scholarship of Teaching and Learning* 6 (2), article 12. https://doi.org/10.20429/ijsotl.2012.060212.

Light, Richard J. 2001. *Making the Most of College: Students Speak Their Minds.* Cambridge, MA: Harvard University Press.

Maleki, Razieh B., and Charles E. Heerman. 1992. "Improving Student Reading." IDEA Paper 26, Kansas State University, Center for Faculty Evaluation and Development. IPFW.edu, Center for the Enhancement of Learning and Teaching.

Middendorf, Joan K., and David Pace. 2004. *Decoding the Disciplines: A Model for Helping Students Learn Disciplinary Ways of Thinking.* New Directions for Teaching and Learning 98. San Francisco: Jossey-Bass.

Pressley, Michael. 2011. "Metacognition and Self-Regulated Comprehension." In *What Research Has to Say about Reading Instruction*, edited by S. Jay Samuels and Alan E. Farstrup, 291–309. 4th ed. Newark, DE: International Reading Association.

Weimer, Maryellen. 2010. "11 Strategies for Getting Students to Read What's Assigned." *Faculty Focus Special Report.* https://www.facultyfocus.com/.

7

Gains in Written Communication between the Freshman and Junior Years

Irene L. Clark and Bettina J. Huber

Since the establishment of freshman writing classes at most American colleges and universities, composition scholars have debated a number of issues associated with the course, including its main purpose, the writing genres that it should emphasize, the extent to which it contributes to writing improvement, and how such improvement should (or can) be defined and assessed. Although the course remains firmly entrenched, scholars concerned with writing across the curriculum (WAC) and writing in the disciplines (WID) have argued that because writing is situated within particular disciplines and professions, a stand-alone writing class may not be effective in helping students respond successfully to other academic or professional writing tasks. Joseph Petraglia's 1995 edited collection *Reconceiving Writing, Rethinking Writing Instruction* presents several still relevant arguments referred to as "the abolitionist movement" in composition, characterized by dissatisfaction with a view of writing as a generalizable skill (general writing skills instruction, or GWSI) and by concern with the lack of evidence establishing the effectiveness of such courses. These reservations are epitomized in David Russell's (1995) oft-cited metaphor—that a stand-alone writing course is no more likely to be effective than a course in "general ball handling" would enable students to gain skill in all sports involving a ball. More recently, the issue of "transfer" constitutes another lens through which to evaluate the first-year writing course, raising additional questions about which writing genres and what "knowledge" about writing will most effectively help students approach writing tasks in other academic and professional contexts.

Through discussion of a study of student writing samples submitted by a subset of students enrolled in the Learning Habits Project at California State University, Northridge (CSUN), this chapter engages with some of the concerns associated with the first-year writing course. It describes the study, explains the assessment protocols that inform it, and discusses the assessment results. It also explores the potential impact of assignment prompts on students' ability to complete writing tasks effectively.

THE LEARNING HABITS PROJECT

As noted elsewhere in this volume, learning habits (LH) students responded to several open-ended questions about their learning at the end of each fall and spring term. Two of the electronic surveys to which students responded posed open-ended questions explicitly concerned with writing and reading. In addition, students also were asked to provide examples of essays they had completed during their first and third years, along with the assignment prompts to which these essays responded. The essays and their assignments form the core of the materials included in the LH writing study on which we report here.

Characteristics of Students Participating in the Writing Assessment

Tables 7.1 and 7.2 summarize a range of entry and background characteristics for two groups: LH participants who were either involved or not involved in the writing assessment. Since initial analysis indicated that the essay writers were largely representative of the full LH group, whose characteristics are reviewed in chapter 2, this discussion focuses on summarizing the characteristics of the students whose essay assignments were included in the writing assessment.

As the top row of table 7.1 indicates, the essay writers constitute one-tenth of the larger LH population, with two-fifths of them entering CSUN in fall 2011. As one might expect, given project requirements, three-quarters were proficient in both English and mathematics at entry, while three-fifths (62 percent) had high school GPAs of 3.50 or higher. In addition, the majority (56 percent) planned majors housed in one of three colleges: arts, media, and communication; science and mathematics; or business and economics.

In terms of background (see table 7.2), two-thirds of the essay writers are women, while 70 percent stem from better-served racial and ethnic backgrounds. A third are Pell Grant recipients, while the majority has at least one parent with a four-year college degree (55 percent). Most are native English speakers (70 percent), even though 60 percent heard another language at home while growing up and have at least one parent who was raised outside the United States. The students whose essays are examined here entered

Table 7.1. Entry characteristics of LH students by participation in assessment of written work

Characteristic	Included in Writing Assessment	NOT Included in Writing Assessment	All Learning Habits Participants
All Respondents			
Percent	10.0	90.0	100.0
(No. of participants)	(76)	(683)	(759)
Entry Term			
Chi square = 14.37 (.002); df = 3; Cramer's V = .138			
Fall 2007	21.1	9.7	10.8
Fall 2008	19.7	21.8	21.6
Fall 2010	15.8	31.0	29.5
Fall 2011	43.4	37.5	38.1
Total	100.0	100.0	100.0
(No. of participants)	(76)	(683)	(759)
Participation Criteria			
Chi square = 5.79 (NS); df = 6; Cramer's V = .062			
High School GPA of 3.5 or higher			
and Proficient at Entry	38.2	33.7	34.1
but Needed Remediation	23.7	20.5	20.8
High School GPA below 3.5 but			
Proficient at Entry	38.2	45.8	45.1
Total	100.0	100.0	100.0
(No. of participants)	(76)	(683)	(759)
College Housing Planned Major			
Chi square = 10.50 (NS); df = 8; Cramer's V = .118			
Arts, Media, and Communication	19.7	16.1	16.5
Business and Economics	17.1	13.0	13.4
Education	2.6	1.5	1.6
Engineering and Computer Science	0.0	7.8	7.0
Health and Human Development	11.8	11.1	11.2
Humanities	5.3	5.3	5.3
Science and Mathematics	19.7	14.3	14.9
Social and Behavioral Sciences	7.9	11.4	11.1
Undeclared	15.8	19.5	19.1
Total	100.0	100.0	100.0
(No. of participants)	(76)	(683)	(759)

Table 7.2. Background characteristics of LH students by participation in assessment of written work

Characteristic	Included in Writing Assessment	NOT Included in Writing Assessment	All Learning Habits Participants
Gender			
Chi square = 0.32 (NS); df = 1; Cramer's V = .020			
Women	67.1	63.8	64.2
Men	32.9	36.2	35.8
Total	100.0	100.0	100.0
(No. of participants)	(76)	(683)	(759)
Racial and Ethnic Background			
Chi square = 2.69 (NS); df = 1; Cramer's V = .059			
Traditionally Underserved	30.3	38.2	37.4
American Indian	*0.0*	*0.1*	*0.1*
Pacific Islander	*0.0*	*0.0*	*0.0*
African American	*5.3*	*4.5*	*4.6*
Latina/o	*22.4*	*31.8*	*30.8*
Multirace	*2.6*	*1.8*	*1.8*
Better Served	69.7	60.9	61.8
Asian	*9.2*	*13.9*	*13.4*
White	*44.7*	*38.5*	*39.1*
Multirace (i.e., Asian and white)	*0.0*	*2.0*	*1.8*
Decline to state	*15.8*	*6.4*	*7.4*
International	0.0	0.9	0.8
Total	100.0	100.0	100.0
(No. of participants)	(76)	(683)	(759)
Pell Grant Status (proxy for low income)			
Chi square = 0.001 (NS); df = 1; Cramer's V = .001			
Pell Grant recipient	34.2	34.4	34.4
No grant received	65.8	65.6	65.6
Total	100.0	100.0	100.0
(No. of participants)	(76)	(683)	(759)
Percent Traditionally Underserved	65.4	62.6	62-8
Among Pell Grant Recipients	(26)	(235)	(261)
Parental Education (indicator of first-generation college status)			
Chi square = 2.55 (NS); df = 2; Cramer's V = .060			
Both parents: high school or less	19.7	21.7	21.5
One/both parents: some college	14.5	23.0	22.1
One/both parents: four-year degree	55.3	50.5	51.0
Unknown	10.5	4.8	5.4
Total	100.0	100.0	100.0
(No. of participants)	(76)	(683)	(759)

CSUN well prepared for college work and come from relatively well-to-do backgrounds. They do not differ from most LH students in these respects.[1]

Because of the strong entering skills of these students, most of those involved in the writing assessment performed at high enough levels at entry to display only modest gains in writing proficiency between their freshman and junior years.

THE LEARNING HABITS WRITING STUDY

The Choice of Thesis-Driven Argumentative Essays

The essays discussed in this study were selected from the larger set submitted by the vast majority of LH freshmen. Initially, 12 paired essays were examined in a preliminary exercise, selected for assessment because they constituted representative examples of argumentative, thesis-driven essays. Most, if not all, of the essays were written in this genre, because at that time, the CSUN composition program emphasized the importance of "academic argumentative writing," a type or genre of writing that was—and to a certain extent still is—emphasized in many composition programs across the country. As Gerald Graff (2003) maintained in *Clueless in Academe*, "One of the most closely guarded secrets that academia unwittingly keeps from students and everybody else is that all academics, despite their many differences, play a version of the same game of persuasive argument" (Graff 2003, 22), which he refers to as "arguespeak." This perspective on academic writing is in accord with the work of Susan Peck MacDonald (1987), who argued for the pervasiveness of "problem definition" in multiple academic venues, noting that "the subject of academic writing either already is or is soon turned into a problem before the writer proceeds. No matter how tentative the solutions are, it is problem solving that generates all academic writing" (MacDonald 1987, 316). More recently, Mary Soliday similarly noted the importance of evidence in academic writing. "In the academy," Soliday maintained, "readers highly value evidence" (Soliday 2011, 36), a perspective additionally supported by research on writing across the disciplines conducted by Chris Thaiss and Terry Myers Zawacki (2006) in *Engaged Writers and Dynamic Disciplines*.

Although it is now recognized that academic argument may not be assigned as consistently across the curriculum as originally presumed (Yancey, Robertson, and Tacsak 2014), argumentation and problem definition had a significant influence on the curriculum informing most of the composition courses that LH students had taken. These courses were taught by graduate student teaching associates or part-time lecturers, all of whom had received extensive training in developing assignments that focus on thesis-driven academic argument. However, although project requirements specified that all essays submitted be argument based, many of the junior-level submissions represented varied writing genres, including straightforward reports, responses to specific content questions, and ethnographic observations. To maximize consistency for the paired text assessment, the researchers were careful to choose junior-level essays that were viewed as most similar to those assigned in first-year writing classes.

The selection process was further complicated by the fact that what is viewed as a "thesis" may differ considerably according to discipline. As Rebecca Nowacek (2011) points out in her interdisciplinary study of various writing genres, the history professor with whom she worked had a different concept of a thesis than did the literature professor, although both used the term in their writing prompts and explicitly cautioned their students about the difference between a "topic" and a "thesis," which they viewed as a type of argument (Nowacek 2011). Recognizing these disciplinary differences, we selected junior-level essays that were most like those assigned in the first-year writing course—thesis-driven arguments.

Paired Essays, Similar Genre, Same Students

This use of paired essays written in a similar genre by the same students at comparable points in their college careers constitutes a significant strength of this study because it enabled the researchers to control for two factors that are important in writing assessment—the students and the genre—allowing us to minimize much of the variation that is unavoidable in the more typical cross-sectional approach to the assessment of student learning. Further, a study based on access to paired essays prepared by students attending a comprehensive institution is relatively rare, enabling us to address the requirements outlined in Brian Huot's *(Re)articulating Writing Assessment for Teaching and Learning* (2002)—that assessments should be site based, locally controlled, context sensitive, rhetorically oriented, and accessible (Elliot and Perelman 2012, 65). We were thus able to develop a rubric that was relevant to both freshman and junior essays.

The Development of the Rubric

Work on the assessment exercise began early in summer 2013, when a group of four experienced writing teachers began the process of developing a scoring rubric. Each evaluator had considerable training in grading student work using both holistic and primary trait scoring, and each had developed varied rubrics in response to different courses and writing tasks. In addition, other rubrics that focused on academic argument were also considered; eventually, the group developed a rubric consisting of six dimensions, each of which was evaluated independently:

- Context and purpose for writing and critical thinking
- Organization and cohesion
- Content development and coherence
- Genre and disciplinary conventions
- Appropriate reliance on sources and evidence
- Control of syntax and mechanics

A complete version of the rubric appears in table 7.7 at the end of this chapter. The decision to use analytic or "multiple-trait" scoring (Hamp-Lyons 2007, 2016) was based on our interest in learning which aspects of writing performance had improved. Four summary descriptions of student expertise served to assess each of the dimensions: less than adequate, satisfactory, competent, and superior; these descriptions could be further refined with the addition of pluses and minuses (e.g., competent+ or satisfactory−).

Following initial development of the rubric, its dimensions were further refined during e-mail exchanges and another face-to-face meeting. This second meeting also served as a norming session in which the four assessors compared their understanding of various dimensions with the aid of selected writing samples and further refined the rubric.

In late July 2013, the group assembled for a daylong session during which each of the 12 essay pairs was evaluated by all members of the panel. After analysis of these preliminary data during fall 2013, an additional 31 essay pairs were assessed in mid-January 2014. In June of that same year, after further analysis of the expanded data set, another 33 essay pairs were assessed. Both phases of the project undertaken during 2014 began with a new norming session and used a more conventional approach to the assessment work proper: Individual essays examined were evaluated by two readers, each of whom was randomly assigned the essays she scored. A third reading was undertaken by the project coordinator in the relatively rare instances when the cumulative essay scores diverged by more than was considered acceptable (e.g., by 5 or more out of 25.2 points).

Once the June 2014 phase of the assessment project was complete, scores from the first phase were adjusted so that the three sets of scores were comparable. This was accomplished by dropping the scores of the project coordinator from the larger set and retaining the two closest ratings among the remaining three scores. The scores from the three assessment phases were combined into a single set of 76 paired scores, with the initial qualitative ratings translated into their numerical equivalents for the purposes of more detailed analysis. These numerical equivalents ranged from 0.8 for a score of less than adequate minus to 4.2 for a score of superior plus.

Before the longitudinal gains of interest could be assessed, "resolved scores" were calculated for each of the freshman and junior ratings pairs. This was accomplished by adding them together (O'Neill, Moore, and Hout 2009, 201, 204). Once calculated, the resolved scores were summed across dimensions to yield a new overall summary score for the essay as a whole.

RESULTS OF THE ASSESSMENT

The primary goal of the LH writing study was to learn whether students in the project had improved as writers between their freshman and junior years, with improvement being defined in terms of the rubric developed for the project. A secondary, although less explicitly stated, goal was to consider the extent to which the freshman composition course facilitated that improvement and, if so, to determine which facets of the course were likely to have been most useful. In terms of the first goal, the results of the study, as noted in table 7.3, indicated that most students did make modest gains in their ability to write thesis-driven, argumentative essays between the two assessment points. This improvement was particularly notable in the use of "sources and evidence," a term used in the assessment rubric.

Improvement in the Use of Sources and Evidence

The fact that student writing improved most in the use of sources and evidence constitutes a significant indicator of improvement, in that, as is noted in a recent study of students' use of sources, the ability to use sources effectively "requires students not only to be familiar with defined areas of disciplinary content, but also to be able to represent themselves through their writing as articulate and authoritative authors" (Thompson, Morton, and Storch 2013, 100). The study further suggests that competence in using sources demonstrates students' developing ability to engage effectively with the "rhetorical aspects of academic writing" and "represent their own ideas in relation to those of the authors of the source texts they employ."

In terms of which students improved most in their writing, our study suggests that students receiving higher overall scores on their freshman essays also earned higher scores on their junior essays, hardly an unexpected finding. However, it also indicates that the greatest improvement occurred for students whose freshman essays had been evaluated satisfactory or lower. Thus, students who received low scores on their freshman essays

Table 7.3. Average resolved essay scores by dimension and essay level

	Context and Purpose	Organization and Cohesion	Content Development and Coherence	Genre and Discipline Conventions	Sources and Evidence	Syntax and Mechanics	Total
Freshman	5.80 Comp-/Comp	5.57 Comp-	5.62 Comp-	5.84 Comp-/Comp	5.57 Comp-	5.95 Competent	34.35
Juniors	5.95 Competent	5.68 Comp-	5.78 Comp-/Comp	5.97 Competent	6.07 Competent	6.09 Competent	35.54
T-test^	0.640	0.472	0.647	0.563	2.104	0.656	0.923
(sinif.)	(NS)	(NS)	(NS)	(NS)	(.037)	(NS)	(NS)
Eta	0.052	0.039	0.053	0.046	0.169	0.053	0.075

^The T-test is a measure of statistical significance, appropriate for comparing two interval scores, while Eta measures the degree of relationship between two variables (it ranges from 0 to 1 with higher scores indicating a stronger relationship).

received proportionally higher scores on their junior essays. Correspondingly, students whose freshman essays had been evaluated as competent or superior continued to be evaluated in these terms when they were juniors. The improvement among these students was not as evident, however, an unsurprising result often referred to as the "ceiling effect." Two other variables that are likely to have contributed to improvement were the impact of the first-year writing class and the nature of the junior-level assignments. These factors are discussed below.

The Role of the First-Year Writing Course

The less explicitly stated and less easily "provable" goal of our study concerned the extent to which the first-year writing course contributed to improvement manifested in the junior essays. This is a result that is impossible to realize definitively, since so many factors can influence writing ability and performance on a particular writing task, including students' prior knowledge, growing familiarity with college writing, developing maturity in the intervening years, and motivational variables, such as interest in course content. However, an end-of-term survey distributed to LH students at the end of their second fall term asked them whether they had "taken courses here at CSUN that were particularly helpful in strengthening your writing skills." Those responding in the affirmative were asked to describe what it was about these courses that had proved so helpful. Their responses are summarized in table 7.4, with many affirming that the first-year writing class had indeed contributed to their development as writers.

The table presents two sets of responses: those of students who specifically referenced their first-year writing class—they account for one-fifth of the total—and those of all respondents, many of whom either identified no particular class or dealt with other writing classes.[2] The proportion referencing the value of their composition course is high, although the ubiquity of the course probably plays a role. Other evidence from the project confirms students' unusual appreciation of their freshman writing course, however. Another end-of-term question, which was repeated each term, asked students to name specific courses that had provided particularly good learning experiences during the preceding term. When we compiled a list of the 527 specific courses mentioned by the first two project cohorts during their first four terms at CSUN, the composition course was mentioned by 8 percent of the LH respondents, a larger percentage than for any other course mentioned.[3]

With three exceptions, the two sets of relevant responses shown in table 7.4 are comparable. As one might expect, students in the freshman writing grouping never reported that they did not take a course that was helpful and

Table 7.4. Reasons courses were particularly helpful in strengthening writing skills by type of course discussed

Reasons Why Courses Were Helpful		Freshman Writing	All Courses
I.	Provided Information on How to Approach Academic Writing Tasks	44.4	41.4
	I.A. Learned to View Writing in a Different Way	11.9	11.8
	I.B. Emphasis on Organizing Essay and Thoughts	7.9	6.7
	I.C. Elements of Logical Arguments and How to Construct Them	5.3	5.9
	I.D. Importance of Distinguishing Components of Writing Process (e.g., outline, research)	7.3	5.3
	I.E. Clear Directions for Approaching Assignments	4.0	3.9
	I.F. Preparing Different Types of Essays	4.0	3.8
	I.G. Attention to Audience	2.0	3.5
	I.H. Other	4.6	1.5
II.	Instructor Behavior	20.5	18.4
	II.A. Actively Involved in My Writing Process	8.6	9.7
	II.B. Had High Standards and Pushed Students to Improve	5.3	3.8
	II.C. Instructor Was Exceptional	5.3	3.0
	II.D. Other	2.6	2.3
III.	Writing Practice Required	16.6	19.9
	III.A. Volume of Writing Required Made the Difference	9.9	9.1
	III.B. Multiple Drafts and Revision Helpful	2.0	4.2
	III.C. Essay Topics Interesting; More Engaged as Result	2.0	3.3
	III.D. Peer Editing Exercises Valuable	2.0	3.2
	III.E. Other	2.0	0.6
IV.	Provided Information on Technical Aspects of Writing	7.9	10.6
	IV.B. Provided Guidance on Preparing Specific Documents (e.g., business letters)	0.7	3.8
	IV.C. Provided Guidance on Citing and Evaluating Sources	4.6	3.0
	IV.A. Dealt With Appropriate Use of Grammar	1.3	2.1
	IV.D. Other	2.0	1.4
V.	Did Not Take Such a Course	0.0	4.1
VI.	Benefited from Required Use of Campus Writing Center	2.0	2.4
VII.	Other	9.9	5.5
	(Number of excerpts on which percentages based)	(151)	(659)

almost never mentioned receiving guidance about preparing specific kinds of documents. Finally, the percentage of unclassifiable "other" comments is considerably higher among freshman writing students than within the larger set of comments. The comments in this subcategory are of two sorts: brief general comments saying no more than that the course was helpful, and comments to the effect that high school learning was key to college success with written assignments. Said one respondent, "My freshman year [discipline] 115 class helped reinforce my writing habits." Another commented,

I took [discipline] 155 here at CSUN, but I wouldn't say it was particularly helpful in strengthening my writing skills. In fact, I would say that I rather applied
the writing skills I learned in my high school English and history classes when
doing the writing assignments for [discipline] 155.

One of the comments appropriately housed in this "other" category is fascinating, illustrating how unanticipated, but profound, the benefits derived
from a class can be:

It was not so much what I learned that was helpful but rather that I was forced to
do it and succeeded. That particular writing class was what scared me the most
in high school, as I looked ahead to college. I did not think I could compete at
the same level as other freshman in my writing skills. So this class was helpful
for me, because it showed me I could succeed and be just as good as others in
my age group.

Table 7.4 indicates that close to two-fifths of the respondents noted that their
freshman writing course had provided valuable guidance about how to approach their academic writing tasks, with one-quarter mentioning the value of
thinking about writing in a different "college" way, as the following examples
make clear:

The freshman English class was very helpful in teaching the different styles of
writing which I was unaware of before.

My writing class freshman year was very beneficial because my high school
didn't focus too much on how to write essays.

[Discipline] 115 provided me with new ways to approach my analytical skills
and how to review my papers.

A fair number of students also mentioned that their freshman writing classes
taught the value of organization and the importance of constructing logical
arguments:

[The course] has helped me organize my essay, have a concrete thesis, and have
backup information.

In freshman composition, I learned, specifically, how to reapproach essay organization, from the typical five-paragraph essay format to unlimited-quantity
essays where the thesis could be the first line of the paper and still come out
very strong. Learning different organization styles helped strengthen my writing
skills through organizational variety as well as helping in the skill of being clear
and concise in conveying the information of an essay.

The course that was by far the most helpful in strengthening my writing skills was . . . 155. I rely on the concepts, such as being able to back up every idea, knowing what to look for in an argument, and how to relate to your reader on a daily basis.

155 honors worked to improve my ability to formulate and express ideas. I was taught the fundamentals of argumentative essay writing and debating.

When it comes to instructor behavior, respondents most frequently mentioned the importance of faculty becoming involved in students' writing processes, as the following examples illustrate:

Unfortunately, the first essay I submitted I received a D+ grade. Although I worked hard and had my essay revised by a college graduate, I did not meet the requirements of the professor. The professor captured grammatical errors that I myself could not have caught, and he wrote advice on how to improve my writing. Every week my professor taught me something new that will help strengthen my paper, and it did. On the following essay, I took advantage of the advice the professor gave to me, and I placed those skills onto my paper. My professor was very proud to see my improvement in writing because I received a grade higher on my second test, which was a C+. . . . 155 was a very challenging class, but challenges only make you a stronger person.

My . . . 115 class, was one of my favorite classes at CSUN thus far. My professor always made sure she was available and always gave feedback on essays. She even would sit down with us and explain exactly how we could do better and how to revise the essays to help us get a better grade. This individual . . . definitely helped me to become a better writer in almost all of my other classes.

I think the most helpful aspect of this class was the one-on-one attention I received. The professor made it a requirement to meet up with her outside of class to work on the paper. Even though it felt like a drag to meet up with her, it proved to be the reason why I got a good grade in that class.

Finally, the importance of having to do so much writing in college was highlighted by a number of students:

My freshman year I took university writing, and I believe that was the most beneficial class I have taken while at CSUN. We had to do a lot of essays and writing exercises that not only helped the way my writing flows but also how I approach my assignments and handle my heavy course load.

This class just had a lot of writing assignments, and as much as I hated it, it helped because I had to write so much my writing would improve on each assignment.

A year ago I took . . . 115 with professor X, and it was very difficult but extremely rewarding. We always had homework which included writing at least a
page or two on a topic that was discussed in class. But by the end of the semester, I was able to write essays and reports for other classes with ease because I
had so much practice in English.

As the preceding discussion indicates, the LH writing study is notable
for its use of both empirical evidence that students' writing improved
between their freshman and junior years and reports by the students themselves, affirming that the first-year writing course helped them improve
as writers. These self-reports are in accord with Urie Bronfenbrenner's
concept of learning development, which challenges "the notion of development as simply getting better at the same task" (quoted in Carroll 2002,
22). Rather, statements by LH students indicate they learned strategies for
approaching a writing task more effectively and, in terms of their insight
into academic writing, "learned to accommodate the often unarticulated
expectations of their professor readers, to imitate disciplinary discourse"
(Carroll 2002, 23).

These are the learning goals that are most likely to facilitate "transfer,"
which in the field of writing studies refers to students' ability to apply what
they have learned about writing in one context to another context that involves writing. To some extent, the LH writing study findings constitute a
significant contribution to the ongoing "transfer debate," in particular, the
question of what should be taught in the first-year writing course. Students'
focus on process-oriented composing strategies and genre awareness is in
accord with the research of Anne Beaufort (2007), Irene Clark and Andrea
Hernandez (2012), Nowacek (2011), and Amy Devitt (2004). As Elizabeth
Wardle (2007) maintains, "Meta-awareness about writing, language and
rhetorical strategies in FYC may be the most important ability our course
can cultivate" (Wardle 2007, 82). Similarly, as Michael Donnelly (2006) has
argued, "There is no 'must' content; the only thing(s) that really matters is
what students are doing—i.e., reading, thinking, responding, writing, receiving (feedback), and re-writing. When these things are primary, and whatever
other content remains secondary, we have a writing course."

However, as is necessary in any assessment of student writing, we acknowledge the role of other factors, particularly the maturation that occurs
naturally during the college time period and the prior knowledge students
have upon entering a university. In fact, students' participation in the Learning Habits Project itself may have played a role in their development of self-
confidence, self-efficacy, and motivation.

Revised versus Unrevised Writing

Another factor that needs to be considered in interpreting the degree to which student writing improved between the first and third years is the extent to which submitted essays received feedback and were revised. In fact, because the first-year essays received considerable feedback from both peers and instructors and were revised significantly whereas the later essays may not have been, it is likely there was actually a higher degree of writing improvement than was indicated in the assessment scores. Based on curricular requirements, all essays written in students' freshman year were written in multiple drafts, repeatedly received both peer and instructor feedback, and were additionally revised for a department-mandated portfolio assessment that occurred at the end of the semester. The essays that the first-year students submitted to the LH assessment project were *revised* essays. Of course, juniors *may* have also revised their essays extensively, or brought them to the writing center for help, but it is likely that at least some of the junior-level essays had not been revised at all. It is possible that if the junior-level essays had received as much feedback as the freshman essays and had been equivalently revised, they would have received higher scores and the degree of improvement found in the assessment study would have been higher.

THE WRITING ASSIGNMENTS

An additional factor that is likely to have influenced the degree of improvement between the freshman and junior essays is the extent to which students understood what type of text they were expected to write, as presented in the writing prompt. Presumably, all faculty members provide detailed instruction about the requirements of the writing tasks they assign, instruction that often occurs in the classroom. However, the quality of the prompt itself, in terms of clarity and specificity, is likely to influence how successfully students are able to complete the assigned task, because they may not take adequate notes in class or forget at least some of what an instructor said. Thus, the type of assignment as it is presented in the prompt is a significant factor, as noted by John Bean in his widely used book *Engaging Ideas* (2011), in which he contrasts what he refers to as the "traditional," more general method of assigning writing to those that specify "thesis-governed argumentation" (Bean 2011, 90). According to Bean, the traditional writing prompt is often presented as follows:

> There will be a term paper due at the end of the semester. The term paper can be on any aspect of the course that interests you, but I have to approve your topic in advance. (90)

The student then submits a proposal that is often stated as a topic area or perhaps a tentative thesis, and the professor either approves the topic or refines and narrows it. The student may then be asked to submit an outline, but often there is no further contact between teacher and student.

Bean maintains that this type of writing prompt is quite suitable "for skilled upper-division students who have already learned the conventions of inquiry and argumentation in a discipline . . . but for many college writers, the freedom of an open-topic research paper is debilitating" (Bean 2011, 91). These students are not yet comfortable with "academic writing or with the discourse conventions of a new discipline," so the essays they submit are likely to be immature, "all-about papers" (papers that present information chronologically but have no main point), or "quasi plagiarized data dumps with long quotations and thinly disguised paraphrases" (Bean 2011, 91). For students in the Learning Habits Project, although all were admitted to the university with higher than average GPAs, the more traditional type of research assignment would most likely have posed a challenge. (In fact, many graduate students encounter difficulties with this type of assignment.)

In contrast to the traditional assignment prompt, Bean cites the work of Dean Drenk, who assigns thesis-support topics intended to help students understand that disciplinary knowledge is not "an assemblage of inert concepts and data but rather an arena for inquiry and argument" (quoted in Bean 2011, 91). In his chapter concerned with writing assignments, Bean emphasizes that assignments that specify "rhetorical context—purpose, audience, genre—can create significant differences in students' writing and thinking processes as well as in their final products" (93), a perspective that was supported in a recent large-scale study of writing improvement by Paul Anderson and colleagues (2015). That study emphasizes the importance of "*Clear Writing Expectations* [italics in original] which involve instructors providing students with an accurate understanding of what they are asking their students to show they can do in an assignment and the criteria by which the instructors will evaluate the students' submissions" (207). Assignment design as a factor in student success also is supported by Irene Clark's perspective on how to develop effective writing prompts, which focuses on the importance of defining the goals and exigencies of a writing assignment and of scaffolding the task—segmenting it "into various components that build upon one another" as a means of fostering students' understanding" (2012, 443). Clark notes several problems students at various levels have in completing a writing task successfully; in particular, they often

- are unaware of the necessity of having a thesis;
- do not understand the role of definition in academic writing;
- are confused by an assignment that asks a lot of questions; and
- do not know how to narrow an unfocused or vague assignment prompt (446).

Many of these problems, Clark maintains, can be avoided if students are given a clear, focused writing prompt that explains the nature of the writing task, thereby enabling students to understand its generic, rhetorical, and content expectations. In the LH writing project, most of the first-year writing prompts did fulfill these criteria because instructors were trained in assignment development. However, many of the junior-level essay prompts did not.

To illustrate the possible effect of a writing prompt that does not adhere to the criteria just outlined, we cite the example of a student whose scores declined by 15 percent between the freshman and junior years, as table 7.5 indicates. Although there are always factors that can contribute to a student's inability to complete a writing assignment successfully, an analysis of the writing prompts from both the freshman and the junior years suggests that this decrease was due, at least in part, to the clarity of the freshman prompt and the lack of clarity in the junior prompt.

Analysis of Freshman Prompt

The freshman prompt (page 167) specifies clearly that the student is expected to address a controversy and develop an argumentative thesis concerned with that controversy. The title of the prompt itself ("Techno Love or Hate") indicates that the topic is controversial; two readings concerned with the topic had been assigned and discussed in class. In addition, the requirement that the essay was expected to consider both sides of the controversy was indicated in the reminder to "include a counterargument." The need to write multiple drafts and revise them was foregrounded by the three due dates.

The essay the student wrote in response to this prompt demonstrates that he or she understood the expectations. The title of the essay, "Even Educational Games Can Have Negative Consequences," indicates that the student understood the requirement to address a controversy, and the first paragraph, which leads to the thesis sentence, further exhibits that understanding. The paragraph begins by referring to the prevalence of games for children, with one, the Webkinz brand, becoming very popular. The thesis statement, appearing at the end of the first paragraph as expected, is as follows:

> Although Webkinz provides a safe environment with educational games for children, if played too much, children will become socially awkward and lose the sense of having an imagination, if all rules and regulations are set up for them, as well as increase their health problems in the future.

Table 7.5. Student whose scores declined between the freshman and junior years

	Context and Purpose	Organization and Cohesion	Content Development and Coherence	Genre and Disciplinary Conventions	Sources and Evidence	Syntax and Mechanics	Total
Freshman Essay							
Assessor A	3.0	3.2	3.0	3.2	3.0	2.0	17.4
Assessor B	2.2	2.2	2.0	2.2	2.2	2.2	13.0
Resolved score	5.2	5.4	5.0	5.4	5.2	4.2	30.4
Junior Essay							
Assessor A	2.0	1.8	2.2	2.2	2.0	2.8	13.0
Assessor B	2.0	1.8	2.0	2.2	2.8	2.2	13.0
Resolved score	4.0	3.6	4.2	4.4	4.8	5.0	26.0
Difference between Freshman and Junior Resolved Scores							
(JR–FR score)	−1.2	−1.8	−0.8	−1.0	−0.4	0.8	−4.4 (**14.5%** **decrease**)

The Freshman Prompt

Stuff your eyes with wonder . . . live as if you'd drop dead in ten seconds. . . .
It's more fantastic than any dream made or paid for in factories.

—Ray Bradbury

Whether it is a blessing or curse, technology has influenced our lives as a generation. In this paper, you will choose a specific form of technology and make an argument regarding its effects on society. The following questions are concerned with readings we will discuss in class. Keep them in mind, but do not feel that you must answer them when dealing with your own topics.

[The instructor has listed four possibilities, but only the first, which is the one to which the student responded in the submitted essay, is listed here.]

Question 1. "What's the Matter with Kids Today" and "Can You Hear Me Now?" are arguing about technology, albeit a different form of it. These two authors discuss the influence of the Internet on children. What are your thoughts on the Internet? Is it hindering or helping our ability to read, write, and communicate?

Requirements

1. 4–6 pages, typed, double-spaced, 12-point font in Times New Roman and 1" margins
2. Thesis: A sentence outlining your argument must be in your introduction.
3. Follow MLA format.
4. 3–4 sources woven throughout the essay. Include a works cited page.
5. As always, you must include a counterargument in your essay. Keep in mind the lessons we have learned from "They Say, I Say." Feel free to try out the templates in your essay.

Due Dates

First Draft: 10/11
Second Draft: 10/18
Final Draft: 10/27

Of course, one might find this thesis a bit exaggerated in terms of how it assumes a direct causal relationship between playing video games and future
health problems, and it is hoped that as the student matures, he or she will become aware that a credible academic essay tends to be more nuanced. However, the essay does indicate that the student understood the exigence for the
writing and was able to develop an idea that could be supported with relevant
evidence from outside sources, which the student does. As a freshman essay,
it is not superior, but as the scores indicate, it is competent.

Analysis of the Junior Prompt

The specifications written in the following junior-level prompt suggest that
the instructor wants the student to do research on a specific person or topic
and develop a thesis that shows how this person or topic relates to a theme
discussed in the course (a standard academic writing trope, as discussed
in Wolfe, Olson, and Wilder 2014). However, that goal is not explicitly
stated in the prompt, requiring students not already familiar with the trope
to probe the prompt to figure out what is expected. Moreover, rather than
specifying what the student *should* do to fulfill the expectations of the assignment, the prompt contains injunctions about what the student should
not do (i.e., don't simply list what each author has said). The main instructions about what the student should do focus on the paragraph level (topic
sentence, one point, supporting point, and conclusion) and general admoni-
tions about craft, organization, and thoughtfulness.

   One can imagine that students receiving this prompt, which appears on
the next page, might have a number of questions—perhaps about how many
sources should be included, how many pages the essay should have, and
most importantly, about the purpose and genre of the assignment. Perhaps
this information had been provided during class. However, from the scores
this student received on the essay, either no explanation was given or the student hadn't understood it, because the only area in which the score increased
was in the rubric dimension for syntax and mechanics. An increase in this
dimension of the rubric suggests that the student's writing ability probably
improved at the sentence level between the freshman and junior years but that
the student did not understand the expectations as presented in the prompt.
In terms of context and purpose, the student's resolved score decreased by
1.2, and in terms of organization and cohesion, it decreased by almost two
full points. Reading through the essay, no thesis is discernible. Rather, the
essay consists of a great deal of information about Native American religious
beliefs and what happened to those beliefs when the Europeans came to
America, including a description of the diseases brought by Europeans (an

"all about" paper, as Bean would say). There is a lot of summary but no clear thesis or argument, even though the prompt (albeit obliquely) indicated that the instructor wanted a thesis. In terms of how outside sources were used, the essay does adhere to the injunction not to merely summarize what others have written, but few references to outside sources are used at all, and the ones that are included merely document facts, such as that Columbus came to the coast of Cuba in 1492. The fact that the student's scores declined, then, is not surprising; it is unlikely that the student understood what he or she was expected to write. Actually, the fact that the student was able to write in response to this prompt at all is impressive.

The Junior-Level Prompt

Note: Specific references to the course and discipline have been omitted to maintain privacy.

Instructions for Research Paper

I want you to choose a specific topic or issue that reflects one or more themes. Make sure the theme is specific and not general. For example, if you want to discuss X (topic omitted here to retain privacy), which encompasses the themes of identity, definitions of faith, assimilation, and pluralism, do not discuss the theme in general. Rather you should choose something specific, such as Y and his role in the development of the tradition in the US. So, your issue would be: what role did Y play in the developing of X in the US? Why did he think that Y would be appropriate for the group in the United States? In answering these questions, you should address the themes as well.

Second, I want you to carefully research your chosen topic or issue and carefully integrate the themes with your research in your mind before you write your paper. I do not want you to "list" what one author says and then list what the other author says without any thought to your overall thesis and its relevance to the themes.

Third, I urge you to carefully craft your paper. I do not want a laundry list of whatever facts, points, or sentences presented in each source, but rather I want you to present your research and conclusions in a thoughtful, well-organized way. You must do this in well-constructed paragraphs.

Each paragraph should contain *one* idea presented in three parts: the topic sentence that introduces the point you are making, supporting sentences, and a conclusion.

A Junior-Level Prompt for a Student Whose Scores Increased

The junior-level writing prompt discussed above may be contrasted with a more clearly written junior-level prompt assigned to a student whose scores increased significantly. Unlike the previous assignment, which required the student to figure out the exigence, purpose, and expected academic trope for the essay, this assignment makes these elements clear, focusing attention on particular parameters of the problem (what factor was most significant in causing the housing boom and bust?). Although one might wonder if adequate exploration of the problem could be achieved in a three- to five-page essay, given the scope of the topic, the student who wrote in response to this prompt received high scores in all dimensions of the rubric, increasing the total resolved score from 28.0 to 44.4.

A Second Junior-Level Prompt

- Buy and read Thomas Sowell's *The Housing Boom and Bust*.
- Familiarize yourself with the housing crisis using the *New York Times* website (website included).
- Write a 3–5 page essay on the following:

Consider the following explanations for the housing boom and bust:

1. Government regulation that increases housing prices
2. Government promotion of "affordable housing"
3. Choice by individuals to gamble on increasing housing prices
4. Failure of government regulators to monitor the lending activities of banks and other financial intermediaries
5. Other

Assign percentages to each possible explanation according to how important it was to causing the housing boom and bust. Justify your answer and explain if and why it differs from Sowell and the *New York Times*.

Table 7.6 displays the full set of scores of this student on both the freshman- and junior-level essays. The scores of the student who responded to

Table 7.6. Student whose scores increased between the freshman and junior years

	Context and Purpose	Organization and Cohesion	Content Development and Coherence	Genre and Disciplinary Conventions	Sources and Evidence	Syntax and Mechanics	Total
Freshman Essay							
Assessor A	2.8	1.0	3.0	2.2	3.0	2.2	14.2
Assessor B	1.2	1.8	1.8	3.0	3.0	3.0	13.8
Resolved score	4.0	2.8	4.8	5.2	6.0	5.2	28.0
Junior Essay							
Assessor A	4.0	3.8	4.0	3.2	4.0	3.8	22.8
Assessor B	4.0	3.8	4.0	3.8	3.0	3.0	21.6
Resolved score	8.0	7.6	8.0	7.0	7.0	6.8	44.4
Difference between Freshman and Junior Resolved Scores							
(JR–FR score)	4.0	4.8	3.2	1.8	1.0	1.6	16.4 (58.6% gain)

this junior-level prompt increased in all dimensions of the rubric, a result that could have been due to a number of factors. Nevertheless, the clarity and explicitness of the prompt is likely to have been a contributing factor.

Junior-Level Prompts for Students Who Improved Significantly

Moreover, what is particularly significant about all the junior-level prompts for students whose resolved total scores improved by more than four points (38 out of 76) is that each prompt had clear expectations—all of them, in fact, specifying patterns that Joanna Wolfe, Barrie Olson, and Laura Wilder (2014) maintain are typical disciplinary tropes, such as the necessity to address an issue of stasis (a central issue involving definition, causality, or evaluation), developing a proposal, or using a conceptual lens (apply a concept, term, theory, or hypothesis to a particular idea, situation, or text). Moreover, all specified the importance of developing a thesis or main idea. Several required multiple drafts, specified page length and other formatting requirements, explained the type and number of readings that were acceptable, and outlined the process that students were required to complete. A mathematics assignment, summarized below, was particularly well constructed—and notable because writing has not traditionally been assigned in mathematics classes. Some of its features included the following requirement:

> The assignment for the final paper asks you to research and report on connections between mathematics and a particular field or area that interests you. The key component of this paper is teaching your reader some specific mathematics topic. The paper should establish a clear thesis concerning the topic and goal for the paper in the opening paragraph.

The assignment prompt also outlines the "Process for Completing the Final Project":

The final project will be completed in a series of steps (please see course calendar for due dates):

1. Selection of the topic and proposed resources
2. Acquisition of resources
3. Detailed outline: Homework I (100 points)
4. Final paper: Homework II (200 points)
5. Revised final paper: Homework III (200 points)

Moreover, in addition to calling attention to the exigence of the assignment (to teach the reader some specific mathematics topic) the prompt also specifies the number and type of sources required, the necessity of having a well-developed thesis supported by evidence, and the requirements for formatting. This assignment prompt admirably fulfills the requirements discussed above by Anderson and colleagues, Bean, and Clark, and it is not surprising that this student's total resolved score improved remarkably, from 12.0 to 20.4—a 70 percent increase.

CONCLUSION

The LH writing assessment project yielded several important insights concerning improvement in student writing between the end of the first-year composition course and the junior year, as well as provided insight into the issue of transfer from one writing context to another:

- Students do make modest gains in writing between the end of their first-year composition course and the coursework attempted in their junior year.
- Improvement is most significant for students who arrive at college with less than adequate writing skills.
- Improvement is most notable in the use of sources and evidence.
- The curriculum emphasized in a first-year writing class can affect students' ability to engage with writing assigned in other academic and professional contexts, particularly if it emphasizes process and genre awareness.
- The specificity and clarity of the writing prompt in an upper-division class can affect a student's ability to complete assignments successfully.

The fact that writing improvement did occur, albeit modestly, and that the greatest improvement was made by students whose entry-level writing ability was less than adequate is particularly encouraging, given the fact that this study was conducted at a large, public, urban university enrolling many traditionally underserved and first-generation students. Although it is important to acknowledge that all writing assessments are situated in particular institutional contexts and must address additional factors, such as students' linguistic and cultural backgrounds, prior knowledge, and motivation, the results of this study are promising, suggesting potentially useful curricular directions for enabling writing improvement.

Table 7.7. Learning habits assessment rubric

Assessment	Superior	Competent	Satisfactory	Less than Adequate
Scores	**4.2, 4.0, 3.8**	**3.2, 3.0, 2.8**	**2.2, 2.0, 1.8**	**1.2, 1.0., 0.8**
Context and Purpose for Writing and Critical Thinking Includes considerations of audience, purpose, and the circumstances surrounding the writing task.	Skillfully demonstrates a strong understanding of context, audience, and purpose that is relevant to the assigned task(s) and offers a superior level of critical thinking to support the main claim.	Demonstrates competent consideration of context, audience, and purpose, and a clear focus on the assigned task(s). The task aligns with audience, purpose, and context. Offers a proficient level of critical thinking to support the main claim.	Demonstrates awareness of context, audience, purpose, and to the assigned task(s). Offers a sufficient level of critical thinking to support the main claim.	Demonstrates minimal attention to context, audience, purpose, and to the assigned task(s). Offers a less than adequate level of critical thinking that does not support the main claim.
Organization and Cohesion	Skillfully demonstrates ability to structure and organize material and ideas as a means of supporting the main claim.	Demonstrates competent organization and structure to support the main claim.	Adequately organizes and structures material to support main claim.	Attempts to organize and structure material but is often unsuccessful.
Content Development and Coherence	Skillfully uses appropriate, relevant, and compelling content that conveys the writer's understanding of the discipline and contributes to the coherence of the work.	Uses appropriate and relevant content to explore ideas within the context of the discipline and contributes to the coherence of the work.	Uses adequately relevant content to explore ideas within the context of the discipline through most of the work.	Occasionally uses appropriate and relevant content to explore simple ideas in some part of the work.

Genre and Disciplinary Conventions Formal and informal rules inherent in the expectations for writing in particular forms and/or academic fields.	Skillfully demonstrates successful execution of a wide range of conventions particular to a specific genre and/or writing task(s), including organization, content, presentation, formatting, and stylistic choices.	Demonstrates competent use of important conventions particular to a specific genre and/or writing task(s), including organization, content, presentation, formatting, and stylistic choices.	Follows expectations appropriate to a specific genre and/or writing task(s) for basic organization, content, presentation, and stylistic choices.	Attempts to use a consistent system for basic organization, content, presentation, and stylistic choices.
Sources and Evidence (as appropriate)	Skillfully demonstrates effective use of high-quality, credible, relevant sources to support ideas that are appropriate for the discipline and genre of the writing.	Demonstrates competent use of credible, relevant sources to support ideas that are appropriate for the discipline and genre of the writing.	Demonstrates adequate use of credible, relevant sources to support ideas that are appropriate for the discipline and genre of the writing.	Demonstrates an attempt to use sources to support ideas in the writing.
Control of Syntax and Mechanics	Uses fluent language that clearly and skillfully communicates meaning to readers and is virtually error free.	Uses language that clearly conveys meaning to readers. Language has few errors.	Uses language that conveys meaning to readers. Language may have some errors.	Attempts to use language to convey meaning to readers but is often unsuccessful because of errors in usage.

NOTES

1. It should be noted that the essay writers are somewhat less likely than other LH participants to be native English speakers (70 vs. 81 percent). The difference is modest, however.

2. During the years that the Learning Habits Project was underway, most incoming freshmen were able to choose a composition course from those offered by several departments. All had similar course numbers, however: 155 during the first years of the project and 113, 114, or 115 during the last years.

3. The runner-up was a related course: speech communication, which was mentioned by 6 percent of the students. This course is also offered by multiple departments and required of all freshmen.

REFERENCES

Anderson, Paul, Chris M. Anson, Robert M. Gonyea, and Charles Paine. 2015. "The Contributions of Writing to Learning and Development: Results from a Large-Scale Multi-Institutional Study." *Research in the Teaching of English* 50 (2): 199–235.

Bean, John C. 2011. *Engaging Ideas: The Professor's Guide to Integrating Writing, Critical Thinking, and Active Learning in the Classroom.* 2nd ed. San Francisco: Jossey-Bass.

Beaufort, Anne. 2007. *College Writing and Beyond: A New Framework for College Writing Instruction.* Logan: Utah State University Press.

Carroll, Lee. 2002. *Rehearsing New Roles: How College Students Develop as Writers.* Carbondale: Southern Illinois University Press.

Clark, Irene L. 2012. *Concepts in Composition: Theory and Practice in the Teaching of Writing.* New York: Routledge.

Clark, Irene L., and Andrea Hernandez. 2012. "Genre Awareness, Academic Argument and Transferability." *WAC Journal* 22: 65–78.

Devitt, Amy. 2004. *Writing Genres.* Carbondale: Southern Illinois University Press.

Donnelly, Michael. 2006. "What's the Content of Composition?" CompFAQs from ComPile. http://compfaqs.org/ContentofComposition/HomePage.

Drenk, Dean. 1982. "Teaching Finance through Writing." In *Teaching Writing in All Disciplines*, edited by C. W. Griffin, 53–58. New Directions in Teaching and Learning 12. San Francisco: Jossey-Bass.

Elliot, Norbert, and Les Perelman, eds. 2012. *Writing Assessment in the 21st Century: Essays in Honor of Edward M. White.* New York: Hampton.

Graff, Gerald. 2003. *Clueless in Academe: How Schooling Obscures the Life of the Mind.* New Haven, CT: Yale University Press.

Hamp-Lyons, Liz. 2007. "Farewell to Holistic Scoring?" *Assessment Writing* 27: A1–A2.

———. 2016. "Farewell to Holistic Scoring Part Two: Why Build a House with Only One Brick?" *Assessment Writing* 29: A1–A5.

Huot, Brian. 2002. *(Re)articulating Writing Assessment for Teaching and Learning*. Logan: Utah State University Press.

MacDonald, Susan Peck. 1987. "Problem Definition in Academic Writing." *College English* 49 (3): 315–31.

Nowacek, Rebecca S. 2011. *Agents of Integration: Understanding Transfer as a Rhetorical Act*. Carbondale: Southern Illinois University Press.

O'Neill, Peggy, Cindy Moore, and Brian Huot, eds. 2009. *A Guide to College Writing Assignment*. Logan: Utah State University Press.

Petraglia, Joseph, ed. 1995. *Reconceiving Writing, Rethinking Writing Instruction*. Mahwah, NJ: Erlbaum.

Russell, David. 1995. "Activity Theory and Its Implications for Writing Instruction." In *Reconceiving Writing, Rethinking Writing Instruction*, edited by Joseph Petraglia, 51–79. Mahwah, NJ: Erlbaum.

Soliday, Mary. 2011. *Everyday Genres: Writing Assignments across the Disciplines*. Carbondale: Southern Illinois University Press.

Thaiss, Chris, and Terry Myers Zawacki. 2006. *Engaged Writers and Dynamic Disciplines: Research on the Academic Writing Life*. Portsmouth, NH: Boynton/Cook.

Thompson, Celia, Janne Morton, and Naomy Storch. 2013. "Where From, Who, Why, and How? A Study of the Use of Sources by First Year L2 University Students." *Journal of English for Academic Purposes* 12 (2): 99–109.

Wardle, Elizabeth. 2007. "Understanding Transfer from FYC: Preliminary Results of a Longitudinal Study." *WPA: Writing Program Administration* 31 (1–2): 65–85.

Wolfe, Joanna, Barrie Olson, and Laura Wilder. 2014. "Knowing What We Know About Writing in the Disciplines: A New Approach to Teaching for Transfer in FYC." *WAC Journal* 25: 42–77.

Yancey, Kathleen Blake, Liane Robertson, and Kara Tacsak. 2014. *Writing across Contexts: Transfer, Composition, and Sites of Writing*. Logan: Utah State University Press.

8

Students and Technology

PowerPoint Fatigue and the Rabbit Hole of Internet Stuff

Donal O'Sullivan

Over the course of the Learning Habits Project at California State University, Northridge (CSUN), few areas have seen such rapid change as technology. When the project began, *some* instructors *sometimes* used technological tools to enhance classroom teaching. But far more commonly, the faculty used physical books to spread knowledge and blackboards/whiteboards and overheads in the classroom itself. The most frequent teaching tool involving technology was PowerPoint, seen in the classrooms of some early adopters. It was also by far the most referenced technology mentioned by learning habits (LH) students in the early years of the project. Even in 2007, there were no fully online classes at CSUN. Not a single classroom had been "flipped." There were no personal response systems ("clickers"). Not all students had cell phones, and none of these were smartphones. Social media was still in the MySpace era, and the learning management system (LMS) was WebCT.

By the end of the research period in 2014 the use of LMSs such as Moodle was widespread, instructors routinely assigned online texts, e-learning tools were making inroads into large classes, and the university library began offering e-books. PowerPoint was used almost universally. Many students accessed materials via their tablet or smartphone. Entire classes were fully or partly online, involving blended or hybrid learning models. And students had strong opinions about academic technology, as we can see in the LH student interviews.

It is clear that these dramatic changes in both technological advancement and widespread use of academic learning technology would create interesting questions. How has the use of technology changed over time? For example, at the start of the research period, instructors were reluctant to require students to use expensive technology, especially traditionally underserved students. As a result, implementation of tablet-based courses was slow across the university. Now that smartphones have increased capabilities, and nearly every student has a smartphone, how will that affect the future?

How are students exposed to technology during their academic careers? How do students perceive instructors' use of tech tools to facilitate learning? The inroads of social media into the lives of students have impacted the way they obtain information, organize their time, and collaborate on projects. How do successful students navigate their use of social media? Are they aware of the potential distraction from their academic studies? If they are aware, how do they handle the issue? How do they reflect on their peers' use of social media? Can we learn from the learners how they self-regulate and how we can teach a better use of social media?

From the instructor's side, we can ask how effective technology has been in classroom pedagogy. For example, how do students think about the "tech policy" prohibiting or allowing the use of laptops, cell phones, and tablets during class? How can instructors learn from the negative examples shared with us by students? How about the learners' assessment of the most ubiquitous of tech tools, PowerPoint? What are the pitfalls for instructors using technology?

Because of space constraints, this discussion only touches on some re-search results on the manifold issues of technology and learning. Recent studies suggest that students adapt to the use of technology in their own way. For example, a 2014 study among education majors by SuHua Huang and colleagues (2014) found that once the instructor uploaded the PowerPoint lectures on a specific textbook chapter to the course website, students did not read the chapter at all, preferring to simply review the slides (450).

The same study confirmed anecdotal evidence of inattentive students con-stantly looking at their cell phones. As the researchers observed in the class-room, "The use of hand-held technologies has reached the point of obsession, creating a distraction in academic engagement" (Huang et al. 2014, 451). But is looking at phones so different from daydreaming, a strategy previous generations of students were familiar with? How do instructors and students handle the challenges of technological addiction?

Recent findings from neuroscience also give us food for thought regarding the way the brain changes during learning. In the early period of the project, instructors often banned electronic devices in order to "force" students to concentrate. Another reason may have been that in a world where informa-tion is suddenly only a click away, anything the instructor said could be fact-checked instantly by curious or suspicious students, with potentially embar-rassing results for the instructor. As teaching faculties know, the accessibility of online information dramatically transforms the classroom environment today. It challenges the way educators need to think about conveying information, and it underscores the need for transformational teaching, enabling students to judge and connect evidence.

Commonly, scholars have attempted to distinguish "digital natives" from "digital immigrants," usually considering young adults in the former category and their older instructors in the latter. "Natives" would be comfortable with ever-changing technology and eager to adopt new tools, whereas "immigrants" would hesitate and display reluctance to adopt new software, generally requiring more assistance. Always eager to experiment and open to change, the "natives" were believed to be able to multitask, were demanding interactive learning platforms, and were quick to consider traditional teaching styles to be old-fashioned and boring. According to popular media, millennials growing up with game consoles and chat rooms would be clamoring for sophisticated teaching tools that capture their notoriously short attention span. However, serious studies found the divide to be more complex than anticipated, including the native equals young and immigrant equals old paradigm. "Like most things in life, the use of technology . . . differs with personal preference and according to individual differences" (Mellanby and Theobald 2014, 391). The digital divide cuts across age and involves socioeconomic factors as well.

Note-taking is another area where the use of laptops, tablets, and smartphones has had a noticeable effect. Studies do suggest that handwriting notes is a more effective way to enhance memorization of material than is typing classroom notes into a laptop or tablet (Mellanby and Theobald 2014).

LH students often reflected on strategies—their own and their instructors—discussing how they related to the use of technology both in the classroom and in their study habits. All use of technology needs to be well integrated into the course. Our sample students embrace teaching technology when they believe it is helpful for them. Many appreciate the university offering computer labs and often prefer studying there than working at home, in order to avoid family distractions. Many use social media to access information, including for academic purposes. They do, however, fear that social media can become a vortex threatening student success.

But they also voiced criticism of instructors who—in their view—did not use technology adequately. Here, successful students identified several methodological flaws of using PowerPoint. While they appreciated having visual aids, with some students explicitly identifying as visual learners, many felt a certain "PowerPoint fatigue." Among practices that met with the strongest criticisms were instructors reading verbatim from slide after slide; posting slides in advance and therefore inadvertently enabling students to cut class; or simply overrelying on this one tool to provide information to students.

DRAMATIC CHANGE

Excerpts from the full array of LH interviews illustrate the dramatic change of technological tools. In 2007, students entering CSUN as freshmen were discovering the electronic resources of the library. As one young woman remarked about electronic resources,

> I just recently started using them. In my English class, we went to the library, and a librarian was telling us about the library website. I didn't know about that, that you can get information from there that's reliable and stuff.

A junior, who entered in fall 2007, reflected back on the changes in her sociology classes:

> My first teacher writes on the blackboard whereas my last teacher—they're both sociology teachers—but my last teacher uses PowerPoint and a microphone and all this good stuff. So just totally different teaching styles, but I've learned from both.

Students tend to embrace change, as this woman who went from one LMS to another during her academic trajectory:

> So I used to use WebCT and I really liked WebCT. I thought it was simple and easy to follow, and I felt when Moodle came into the picture I was like, "What is going on? What is Moodle?" It was a little bit more difficult to learn Moodle, but once you had the hang of it, it's like, okay, just press this button.

A fall 2008 entrant recognized the transition as well:

> I know when I first came here PowerPoints were maybe one class a semester, and now everything is on there. Chemistry, biology, physics, all that's on PowerPoint. It's crazy, it's incredible. Is it good or bad? In some ways it's good, because the teachers say, "All my notes are online."

Another student had similar feelings:

> Last year I had no Moodle. This semester, they all just popped up and all of them were like, "Here's everything, everything's on Moodle," and I didn't know what to do because I'd never used Moodle.

The transition also affected study habits: "I got a tablet a couple semesters back, and I think that's really made things a lot easier. I get to load all my books as PDFs onto the thing, and then it can access files like syllabus, or lecture handouts. So, it makes it a lot easier, and you don't have to carry around all this paper." Students also noted some instructors enthusiastically embracing technological change:

> I had a class last semester where my professor encouraged us to bring computers or notebooks or tablets to class because that way—we had about 60 pages of reading a week, and he didn't want us to print all that out, so we were able to work with that. He was pretty strict about going off-topic online and he could tell if you weren't paying attention to the reading.

Some were also excited about being able to quickly view material previously difficult to access. A junior recalled,

> Use of technology I think was helpful. Teachers who were able to pull up what was on their laptop on the big screen, and sort of lead us along on our laptops to show like, "This is how this is done," that was helpful.

Of course, some students were familiar with technology in the classroom prior to going to college, such as this freshman speaking in 2008:

> They had SMART Boards at my high school. So it was kind of like a familiar thing with me. [The professor] incorporated some YouTube videos—because we're doing political candidates and writing about their essays. She showed us a lot of stuff like that. The lectures that are incorporated with technology really focus a student on it more because we're already so involved with technology. And if you just remain with the chalkboard, it's hard to pay attention, you know? So I really like how she involved technology with that.

Another student attributed faculty use of technology to age, saying, "I've generally had really young professors, and they're all on board with technology." Another praised online books: "I would always prefer to have an online book than a hardcover. . . . Then with technology, I can just search for key words and things like that really quickly. So I much prefer online books to the hardcovers." A woman student developed an affinity for educational technology after being exposed to it:

> I never really used technology before in my course. Like I said, I'm more of a note-taker. I don't bring my laptop to class. But having those deadlines all in Moodle, it'll tell you, and exactly on Friday at 11 p.m., this is when that journal assignment is due. And if you don't turn it in, you know you'll get points docked off. . . . So it's really gotten me to time management skills; it's really helped.

Appreciation extends to other delivery methods: "[A] lot of the professors used lecture capture. So that really helped a lot because I was able to see the video and see the notes that they were writing or the slides that they had. That helped a lot."

One student commented, "I like almost all technology that professors bring in. I think that PowerPoints are great because they give you a clear outline. And I really like it when a teacher hands out PowerPoint notes before."

However, electronic delivery of course materials has its critics. Students tend to enjoy highlighting and marking their texts, and this was initially not possible online. One said, "Honestly, I'd rather have the physical [copy] in my hand because I can mark on it and make notes on it and whatever. . . . Technology can only be used so far." Then, of course, apps appeared, making highlighting and marking possible. "I use my iPad a lot when teachers or professors upload readings; I'm able to download it on my iPad and make notes on it, and highlight on it, and then it's still in that digital format."

POWERPOINT FATIGUE

The students' comments are indicative of a general openness toward new educational technology. However, students have mixed reviews of the most commonly used tool, PowerPoint. It's not the tool itself that students dislike; it's the way some instructors use it. They display a critical attitude toward faculty members who rely too much on PowerPoint. Here are two:

> One thing I didn't mention is the use of PowerPoint, and [I] generally find that's helpful, especially if they provide the slides. That does let them move a little faster sometimes, but I found differences with how they interact with it, and one thing that I found really helpful is when the teacher doesn't just read off the PowerPoint, or even just present them, but actually interacts with it.

> Well, [in] most of the GE classes all they have done is PowerPoint, and now one of my teachers is implementing YouTube to show us videos as well, which is kind of cool. I mean if she's just reading what's on the slides, then I feel like I'm not going to pay attention. It makes me lose interest. . . . I'm here to learn and you're just reading what I can read at home.

Clearly, students suffer from "PowerPoint fatigue." But they also acknowledge good practices, as this student remarked:

> My Biology teacher this semester uses PowerPoint for notes. He provides the notes through Moodle. But he leaves blanks so that we have to fill them out during class. So I feel like that's very effective because you have the notes in front of you, but you're also paying attention to what he's saying.[1]

HYBRID AND ONLINE CLASSES

Another major change over the course of the project saw the introduction of hybrid and online classes at CSUN, with our sample being the first generation of students experiencing this new teaching model. Some students prefer hybrid to fully online classes: "The hybrid class, I found that to be better because there was time in the classroom and you actually met the professor face to face so it was easier to come to office hours."

In fully online courses, students say they often miss both personal interaction and qualitative feedback from the instructor. One woman student commented on her class experience:

> I like that I don't have to go sit in a class for an hour and fifteen minutes and I can kind of do it on my own time. I'm in one right now where it just seems like I have no idea where I stand in that class. The instructor doesn't use Moodle. I mean [the course is] on Moodle, but he doesn't really communicate through Moodle. He communicates through e-mail so we just have reading every week and then we write a reflection and submit it. And his responses are, like, two words, like, "Okay."

Another student explained simply, "The only reason I took online classes is because I didn't have time." A third said, "I don't feel online classes benefit me in any kind of way, especially on a subject that I have no interest in, or I don't understand very well." But others do just fine, such as this young man: "Some online courses are actually a lot of fun. One of my geology courses, not the lab, I took the lecture online. Just looking at the videos and having a visual to go along with it, is quite helpful. Sometimes it's not."

Students also reported birthing pains after enrolling in hybrid or online classes as soon as they were offered at the university. One student said about her hybrid biology course,

> I'm good at technology. I know how things function. I know how to get it to work and stuff. That's not my problem. It's just that I would like—I like the atmosphere of having people around and talking to them personally, and I think that's very important, especially when doing résumés and actually when they give you recommendations and stuff.

Another student, studying to be a teacher herself, felt dismayed when she found out that she had enrolled in a hybrid class. "Technology just takes over now, and my religion class is supposed to be two days a week, and he made it one day, just because the Internet can take care of the other half. And I don't see the point of that. You can't really substitute." Few topics elicited such an emotional response as the issue of online classes: "I took one online course my freshman year. I hated it, so I swore I would never take one again." Another said, "Online courses are horrible, I've never had a good experience with them."

DOWN THE RABBIT HOLE OF INTERNET STUFF

Our LH students, while excited about new pedagogical tools in general, were at the same time conscious of the distraction potential of technical gizmos. One junior said she would never use a computer or a phone in class because she wanted to focus. She said she even noticed an adverse effect on student learning when an instructor posted the PowerPoint slides before the lecture: "I just sometimes find that having PowerPoints students don't concentrate as much in class because they already know they have it." Two others offered similar remarks:

> I really like when teachers just use the whiteboard or the chalkboard, because I can't learn from PowerPoint presentation. I can see the words they're showing me, I can see the step by step, but until they show me how to do it step by step and what I should be thinking, how I should be going about it, I don't feel I can learn anything.

> I like interactive. Because most professors just use PowerPoint, and I find that to be a little boring. I'm taking Spanish this semester, and he doesn't use any technology at all. He does just conversation, interacting, student between student. I find that to be a pretty good way to learn.

Not only are students divided about the level of technology in their classroom, they use the whole spectrum of tools available to them—and this may include old-fashioned pencil and paper. It turns out students pick and choose different note-taking methods for different classes: "I can take notes in class on a laptop in certain courses, but if it gets to another course I just have to just like write it down, like notes in class, and just, you know, take in information that way."

To avoid distractions, some students choose physical strategies: they like to sit in front of the class to avoid getting distracted by fellow students. They say they hate it when students look at other websites unrelated to the course material. Yet, most of them admit doing it themselves. In the words of one student, "Because on the cell phones they're texting and you can hear the click, click, click. Or the computers—technically, they're taking notes, but they're not really taking notes. So it's like, what are you looking at?" A junior explained how it impacted him:

I notice a lot of students now, nowadays, during the middle of lectures or such, they'll bring out their laptops, their iPads, their phones, and they'll just be distracted by technology. So last semester that was what I did. I'd played on—play on my iPad, go on the Internet, do stuff like that, and I found out that my grades weren't the best. I came back this semester, turned it off. . . . If I felt like it was going to be a distraction, I'd put it in my backpack or somewhere where I can't reach it that easily.

Other students called the practice of surfing the Web during class downright rude. But they also confess to falling into "the rabbit hole of different Internet stuff." Some students said they benefited from professors banning devices altogether:

My one professor for film, he's a big stickler on no technology, no computer, no phone. So at first that was frustrating for the note-taking process because he does lecture quickly, but it's slowly turned into—I felt more—I felt like I actually was taking in everything that he was saying.

Another physical strategy some students choose involves a change in their environment. They report that during study time, they try to forestall distractions by cleaning their desk of clutter and switching off their phones to focus on the reading. They are grateful for the university environment and often prefer it to studying at home with its manifold distractions. One student stated,

I think it's great. I am like living in the computer room and the library a lot, doing homework and stuff because it's so much easier and then being in an academic environment, it's easier to focus on that instead of being at home and having video games and food and all that.

In general, LH students appreciated the use of course websites that allow them to check on assignments and revisit content. One student said, "I liked that my grade is on there and I can keep track of what I'm doing and if I'm missing anything because it keeps me focused." But a small group reported that using websites such as Moodle was challenging at first, especially having to invest time to learn how to upload their assignments. They also reported that while some instructors spent a lot of time on the technical aspects of the specific learning management system, others simply assumed students knew how to handle the course website.

A significant takeaway from our study is that instructors are often too quick to assume all students are "digital natives." "I absolutely hate PowerPoint assignments," said one student. "I'm not very good with technology, and having to put it on a PowerPoint, for me, is harder because I'm just focused on what needs to be on the PowerPoint rather than what I should be learning from the PowerPoint. So I don't like that." Another confessed to being uncomfortable with the newfangled ways:

> I am more of a paper book [person], I guess. So all of [the instructor's assigned readings] are like e-books, and you have to learn your concepts and you have to take hundred-question tests on that e-book. So it's really hard, whereas [professor X] is traditional; you write notes, and you do all this while the e-book is just ewww.

One junior reflected on her own relationship with technology and came to the following conclusion: "I use the computer all the time and I see the advantages, but I don't like resorting to a computer. I am very much the type of person who likes doing an assignment and write it in hand, and turn it in in hand. Technology for me, I feel like it then puts me out of control." Others echo this discomfort. A senior said,

> I've tried to . . . like e-books and kind of bringing technology into the classroom, but it's never really worked for me. I guess I'm just so used to reading by the book and writing notes that when I'm trying to use a tablet or a laptop to take notes I find it very difficult because I can't do the kind of note-taking and coding that I do in my real notes.

Student learners were also quick to point out inadequate methodology and bad teaching practices. One student said,

> When I come to school I prefer the teacher to teach me so since like today we showed up in class, and he is like, "Oh, I put my lecture notes on Moodle. Did you guys get them?" And we were like, "No." He answered, "Well I put them at 11 o'clock last night," but what he did was he just opened a PowerPoint and read right off it.

By 2011, students were experiencing a lot more technology in their classes. "Most of my classes have online components. I do homework online. I do—get all the study guides and the PowerPoints from the lectures, so I'm on my computer a lot."

Project students were also aware of their own weaknesses when it comes to the use of technology. One junior said,

> The only thing I honestly should improve in is time management because it's very—I can get off track very easily, like, with studying. So the whole Internet and technology oftentimes, I have social networks on there . . . so I just need to, like, be sometimes more focused and be able to balance my time and manage it better.

Students also have had painful experiences with failing technology, as this young man recalls: "I usually don't trust iCalendar or anything like that because I've had so many times where my phone gets broken, my phone gets lost, my computer crashes. I would really love to trust my technology, but at this stage of my life, I don't have enough money to buy trustworthy equipment." He says he now uses a paper planner.

Students agree on one point, however: the better organized the instructor is, the more they get out of the class—with or without technology.

> What I've noticed is if the teacher is organized, then the class flows better. I've had teachers where they'll bring up a 50-slide PowerPoint and they'll jump around and they'll bring things from different websites, and it's so hard to concentrate on what the main idea is. So when the teacher's really organized I find that really helpful.

CONCLUSION

As seen repeatedly in the LH participant responses, successful students welcome technology and are comfortable using it for academic purposes, both inside and outside the classroom. They have become accustomed to accessing educational materials online and have few issues with electronic submissions, chats, and e-mail communication—even though the learning curve was steep for many, especially in the earlier years of the study. Some students demonstrate a critical awareness of technology, critiquing inadequate teaching practices, in particular, those connected with PowerPoint. Many are aware of the distractions of social media, but even good students experience difficulties "switching off." Many report getting sidetracked while studying. Many of the successful students display excellent time management skills, also assisting them in their effective use of technology. Fully online classes still have to win over students. However, students overwhelmingly embrace technology if they are convinced it will help them succeed.

In reaching these conclusions about the introduction of educational technology, several points stand out after listening to the learners:

- Successful students welcome technology if it assists their learning goals.
- Learning management systems such as Moodle have made a positive impact.
- PowerPoint continues to be a useful tool, especially for visual learners. However, feedback also suggests the need for updating faculty skills, involving the best use of tools such as PowerPoint, perhaps through the auspices of faculty development offices.

- Overall, the faculty would do well to remember that students at large urban institutions do not necessarily merit the label "digital native" and may require step-by-step guidance through any electronic tools connected to a course.
- Many of these students appear to possess the self-discipline and time management skills to avoid getting sidetracked by their use of social media. However, this is hardly true of most students.

As Michelle D. Miller (2014, xii) writes, the mere presence of technology does not promote learning. Rather, "what technology allows us to do is amplify and expand the repertoire of techniques that effective teachers use to elicit the attention, effort, and engagement that are the basis for learning." Key for the future seems to be facilitating a dynamic process of adopting and adapting technology according to its usefulness, shaped by evidence-based research. Students and instructors need "to develop the ability to use technology effectively to enhance our own cognitive processes and capacities" (Mellanby and Theobald 2014, 391).

NOTE

1. For a fuller discussion of this approach, see chapter 9 in this book, "Sliding into Learning."

REFERENCES

Huang, SuHua, Matthew Capps, Jeff Blacklock, and Mary Garza. 2014. "Reading Habits of College Students in the United States." *Reading Psychology* 35 (5): 437–67.
Mellanby, Jane, and Katy Theobald. 2014. *Education and Learning: An Evidence-Based Approach*. New York: Wiley Blackwell.
Miller, Michelle D. 2014. *Minds Online: Teaching Effectively with Technology*. Cambridge, MA: Harvard University Press.

9

Sliding into Learning

The Power of Webnotes

Carrie Rothstein-Fisch and Sharon M. Klein

INTERVIEWER: Can you tell me a little something about how you approach your studies these days in terms of the strategies you're using inside the classroom and outside the classroom to study for tests and do assignments?

JUNIOR STUDENT: Okay, so number one, I recommend that all professors try and record their lectures and post them on Moodle (electronic learning platform). I mean, it does help students out, I believe, and it's not just from my perspective. I've heard it from other friends as well.

How do faculty members help students learn? Specifically what do students find most helpful to their learning? Through longitudinal data collected at California State University, Northridge (CSUN) by the Learning Habits Project, this chapter explores students' perceptions of instructor practices that have been beneficial to their college success. The nine years of project data provided the opportunity to learn from students whose records of success before and throughout their undergraduate experiences reflect an awareness of how to navigate the territory of college—as different as their individual experiences can sometimes be. We look to what the students said—individually and collectively—in order to uncover some of the strategies used for successful engagement as undergraduates. We were curious about what students perceived as helpful to their learning and why, but we also wanted to know how those perceptions have changed with time and maturity. Ultimately, we wanted to contextualize students' ideas about the roles faculty members play in promoting student success in college.

As noted in chapter 1, interview transcripts were coded thematically. General themes emerged, revealing subtopics under the more general categories. For example, under the general theme "Effective Teaching Practices Encountered," four core subthemes emerged: (1) the instructor's approach, including his or her focus on student learning, enthusiasm for the subject, approachability, and style of presentation; (2) course structure and organization; (3) instructor attention to guiding students toward successfully completing tasks, such as discussing procedures for writing papers and preparing for exams; and (4) other teaching practices that facilitate learning, including low-stakes in-class quizzes and making lecture notes available.

The overall findings from interviews with learning habits (LH) students are captured in tables 9.1 and 9.2, indicating the number of responses related to each theme found throughout. In other words, if a student was discussing her study habits, she might describe what her professor did that was helpful, but another student might have mentioned it in a different context. Thus, students' descriptions of instructors' practices were interspersed throughout the interviews, even when the prompt signaled a different topic. Ultimately, teaching

Table 9.1.   Freshman interview data: effective teaching practices encountered at CSUN (N = 1,134)

General Themes: Level 1	Theme Elements: Level 2	Nuanced Elements from Level 2
Instructor approach 52.5%		
	Style of presentation 19%	
		Humor 8.6%
		Making the class interesting 5.5%
		Drawing the students into the discussion 4.1%
Course structure 27%		
	Small-group work 12.1%	
	Appealing organization 5%	
	Utility of assignments and tests 3.8%	
	Integration of readings into class 2.2%	
Other teaching practices 23.3%		
	Making lecture notes available 12.5%	
	In-class quizzes 8.0%	
Instructor's attention to successfully completing tasks 13.1%		
	Preparation for exams 7.3%	
	Procedures for written assignments 3.8%	

Table 9.2. Junior interview data: effective teaching practices encountered at CSUN (N = 271)

General Themes: Level 1	Theme Elements: Level 2	Nuanced Elements from Level 2
Instructor approach 43.5%		
	Style of presentation 10%	
		Making the class interesting 4.4%
		Humor 3.3%
		Drawing students into discussion 3.0%
Other teaching practices 26.9%		
	Making lecture notes available 19.6%	
	In-class quizzes 8.5%	
Instructor's attention to successfully completing tasks 23.6%		
	Procedures for written exams 8.9%	
Course structure 22.5%		
	Small-group work 11.1%	
	Appealing organization 0.9%	
	Utility of assignments and tests 3.8%	
	Integration of reading into class 2.2%	

practices that benefited student learning were captured along the four general categories described above.

This chapter begins with general findings across freshmen and juniors. Thereafter, the focus changes to an in-depth examination of one unexpected related finding because students had many insights on a relatively new teaching and learning practice: webnotes. Webnotes, defined as "lecture notes that are made available 'in parallel' with the delivery of lectures in electronic form, typically through a virtual learning environment (VLE) such as Blackboard" (Sambrook and Rowley 2010, 119), seemed to make a significant difference in how students engaged with their learning.

FRESHMAN RESPONSES TO EFFECTIVE TEACHING PRACTICES

In their freshman interviews, first-year students were asked, "In the classes you have taken at CSUN thus far, can you think of approaches or techniques used by some of your instructors that were particularly helpful in enhancing your learning?" Student responses (N = 1,134) emphasized instructors' overall approach to the course (52.5 percent). Within that, style of presentation (19 percent) was frequently mentioned, including instructors' use of humor (8.6 percent), making the class interesting (5.5 percent), and drawing students into the discussion (4.1 percent).

After overall approach to the course, the next most frequently cited cluster of effective teaching practices centered on course structure (27 percent). Within that category, small-group work (12.1 percent) was the most frequently cited. Students referred to the frequent hands-on activities instructors develop within a class setting so that students work collaboratively—in a low-stakes environment—to respond to prompts, solve problems together, come to conclusions, and then compare the groups' work in the context of a classroom exercise. As one male freshman explained,

> We do group study in class, some classes, and that helps when we stay on topic because it's good to get insight from other people . . . and if you didn't understand something and they might have understood it better than you did, then it's good to ask them.

Students often spoke about learning from others in a group—having someone else enhance their own understanding of a topic or problem. But importantly, students also spoke about the value of having to explain something to others—to be put in the position of an instructor; in a sense, acknowledging that teaching something is one of the best ways to understand it:

> [My high school teacher told us that] you memorize 30 percent of what you write, 20 percent of what you hear, 90 percent of what you teach. So when you're in class discussion, you're teaching, you memorize a lot more effectively. . . . The chem professor . . . made us split off into groups of approximately four students every day. This was a Monday, Wednesday, Friday class, 50 minutes a day. And what we'd do is we'd cover a particular topic, discuss it, do problems on it. For example, if we had to convert moles to grams, or grams to atoms, we'd do the problems, check with our neighbors, and [see] if we got it.

To a lesser degree, other comments (all ≤ 5 percent) included content organized in an appealing manner (5 percent), utility of tests, papers, assignments (3.8 percent), and integration of reading material into class sessions (2.2 percent). In the context of tests, we found students reporting that they preferred more frequent quizzes and exams to just a midterm and final. According to one freshman,

> I like the material spread out more and the testing spread out more. I prefer, actually, more tests than less because it gives you a chance to catch up. And for

me, at least, if it's a whole three months or two months of work combined all into one test, it becomes a lot more difficult to organize that information and to retain a lot of information. . . . Even if you can retain it, you confuse it at some point during the test and it doesn't give you much of a chance to make that up. So personally, I don't like the two-test-in-one-semester [approach]. I prefer to have, like, maybe four tests or two tests and four quizzes or some other work on the side, like, papers and all that.

We turn to a set of responses that surprised us enough to make it a focus of this chapter. Nestled in a category dubbed "other teaching practices that facilitated learning," we found that "making lecture notes available to students" scored frequently (12.5 percent), contributing more than 10 percent of all the overall comments. Table 9.1 summarizes the data from LH freshmen.

JUNIORS' PERCEPTIONS OF EFFECTIVE TEACHING PRACTICES

While the question for freshmen that was targeted to elicit approaches or techniques used by instructors that were particularly helpful in enhancing learning, the third-year prompts were more generalized and related to "interactions with faculty" or "skills learned over the past two years." Despite the slightly different set of prompts, the same themes about effective teaching practices emerged for juniors (N = 271 responses) as for freshmen: the ways in which instructors approached the course was most important (43.5 percent). Within this theme, the most frequently cited elements of teaching practices were "conveyed the desire to foster student learning" (11.1 percent) and "style of presentation" (10 percent), which included making class time interesting (4.4 percent) and using humor (3.3 percent). "Other teaching practices that facilitated learning" accounted for 26.9 percent of the responses, of which the largest component was "making lecture notes available to students" (19.6 percent). In other words, juniors classified lecture notes as "teaching practices that facilitated learning" about 20 percent of the time. Recall that table 9.2 summarized the general themes and subthemes for juniors.

Why might lecture notes (we assume including presentation slides) be so important to student learning?

LECTURE NOTES AND WEB-BASED
PRESENTATION SLIDES FOR LEARNING

As noted earlier, we adopted Sally Sambrook and Jennifer Rowley's definition of webnotes as "lecture notes that are made available 'in parallel' with the delivery of lectures in electronic form, typically through a virtual learning environment (VLE) such as Blackboard" (2010, 119). At CSUN, the platform used during this study was Moodle, which, like most course management systems, provided a variety of options, including posting syllabi, assignments, readings, and lecture or webnotes. We note that there are no data to indicate the extent to which lecture notes or presentation slides are provided across our campus. Also, in the interviews, it is unclear if students are referring to copies of faculty-authored presentation slides, textbook publishers' slides, lecture notes/outlines, or other media, unless explicitly stated in the students' comments. However, what comes through clearly is that the availability of these kinds of resources is deemed important by students.

We delve into the topic of webnotes mindful that another chapter in this volume is devoted to the use of technology in student learning. That chapter (chapter 8, "Students and Technology") is a perfect complement to this chapter. Donal O'Sullivan takes a broad perspective and explores the use of smartphones, tablets, laptops, and the changes in technology used from 2007 (when LH began) until the project's conclusion in 2016. Taken together, these two chapters provide a wider view of how technology has impacted student learning.

Because the role of webnotes was a surprise to us, we explored the literature to find other studies targeting that learning resource. The next section begins with a brief overview of studies on the topic of webnotes and student learning. Following that brief review, we present an array of students' voices from many different majors and from a variety of cultural and ethnic communities. In this examination of individual students' use of webnotes, we discovered some interesting convergences around topics such as note-taking, class participation, and the visual aspects of learning. Finally, we consider the emerging themes, many of which have implications for future research and professional development.

LITERATURE ON THE USE OF WEBNOTES

Webnotes are a relatively new phenomenon, existing for only the past 10 years or so (Sambrook and Rowley 2010). As with any new technology, some instructors were quick to test and implement webnote use while others may not be inclined to use them. Reviewing the related literature, we explored attitudes and use of presentation slides as a study guide (Kozub 2010), ambivalence toward presentation slides (Hill et al. 2012), student preference for printing out slides before class (Apperson, Laws, and Scepansky 2008), and student attitudes and use of webnotes (Sambrook and Rowley 2010).

Robert Kozub (2010) studied student attitudes toward and use of presentation slides as a study guide in undergraduate accounting classes. The group of students (N = 480) were equally male and female, and over 90 percent were either sophomores (48 percent) or juniors (44 percent). All were offered supplemental lecture notes from the course website. The majority of students did not see the webnotes as substitutes for class attendance and participation, and there was no significant difference in this regard across gender, year of study, or major. The influence on student performance was not measured, and the author concluded that this topic remains a subject for exploration.

In their article "I'm Ambivalent About It: The Dilemmas of PowerPoint," Andrea Hill and colleagues (2012), surveyed undergraduate students (N = 384) across eight courses, along with 33 sociology instructors. Students reported that PowerPoint slides were "almost always" or "always" effective for aiding exam preparation (56 percent), enhancing comprehension of course material (52 percent), and improving attention in class (38 percent). Not surprisingly, slides were deemed less useful for writing papers and for engaging in discussions. The authors did not indicate whether the slides were also available as webnotes (although it seemed implied), but they noticed that "some students and most instructors also acknowledged that it [the use of such slides] may often result in passivity and disengaged entertainment" (249). This finding is consistent with O'Sullivan's chapter in this volume, as well as with Sambrook and Rowley's work (2010). Ultimately, Hill and colleagues identified a tension inherent in providing these slides—a tension between the clarification of key ideas on the one hand and the potential to oversimplify them on the other.

Jennifer Apperson, Eric Laws, and James Scepansky (2008) assessed student preferences for presentation slide structure in undergraduate courses. Psychology students (N = 275) at two different universities (one large public and one small liberal arts college) completed a 36-item, 7-point Likert scale on a "Student PowerPoint Preferences" survey. The students reported their preferences for having slides available before class. However, there were no data collected to demonstrate how this insight might be translated into learning strategies, study habits, or academic success.

> Students preferred that faculty make slides available from PowerPoint presentations electronically for printing before class, with no significant difference in their preference for a password-protected system like Blackboard or by the Internet. . . . Furthermore, students indicated a preference for copies of actual presentation slides, including pictures, graphs or charts, significantly more than text alone, $t(270) = 8.74$, $p < 0.001$, $d = 0.68$. They also reported that access to copies of presentations prior to class would not decrease their attendance, nor

would they find it easier for their minds to wander during class. (Apperson, Laws, and Scepansky 2008, 151–52)

Finally Sambrook and Rowley surveyed 162 business students at Bangor Business School in the United Kingdom regarding their attitudes and use of webnotes. The students indicated they were averse to making their own notes and much preferred "adding their notes to the lecture notes/slides" (2009, 35). Students preferred to have webnotes before class to better prepare for the discussion and did not report attending class less frequently as a result of webnote availability. Also discussed was the concept of "gapped webnotes" (38), described as purposely incomplete webnotes requiring students to attend class and pay attention.

Themes found in the literature were supported by comments from CSUN's LH students. For example, the availability of lecture notes for printing before class was deemed very helpful, as was the inclusion of visual elements, such as pictures or diagrams.

Some interesting comments by students identified the relationship of webnotes to increased class participation. Students mentioned how webnotes helped with comprehension of material and related these to studying for exams. They also described how webnotes helped to target their engagement with assigned readings. In the section below, we offer some representative voices from our students.[1] We specifically target the junior voices because they seemed best at articulating their learning needs, with more nuanced and interesting narratives. Note that throughout, the comments represent a variety of majors, indicated at the end of each quote.

The students' voices described below represent our campus diversity, making note to remember that these are students identified as successful. The voices include Latina/os (N = 7), European Americans (N = 6), Asians (N = 4), Armenians (N = 3), and African Americans (N = 1). In addition, the voices are mostly female (N = 15) compared to men (N = 6). However, these are only a small subset of the many students who reported the use of webnotes. We mindfully selected those who seem to represent others with similar comments. Therefore, no generalizations should be made with regard to gender or ethnicities other than that our students are very diverse with regard to cultural backgrounds.

STUDENT VOICES: JUNIORS DISCUSS WEBNOTES

Listening and Comprehension

Students observed that by posting webnotes, professors made learning easier. Knowing the notes were available not only allowed students to listen more but also liberated them from having to frantically try to "transcribe" lectures.

I love PowerPoints because I'm visual, so I like that we can print it out and we can follow along. I love when things are bulleted as opposed to paragraphs, or the book, yeah. I love the bullets. I love it. (preaccounting)

I'm a public health education student . . . a lot of the professors in that major like to use PowerPoints. So I find it kind of convenient to take a laptop because they usually will post the slides up online or something. So it's easier for me to follow while they're on their slides. I could type some notes in, different things like that.

I have had one professor where you print out the lecture. You have this option to go on his website, print out the lecture and it's an outline . . . everything that's on the PowerPoint . . . so then you can just take notes instead of worrying what's on the PowerPoint. You already have it which is great because then you're not writing everything on the PowerPoint. (deaf studies)

Most of my classes offer outlines or notes available online, so I usually, if I can, I print them out ahead of time, and instead of writing down what's on the screen I write down what they say or write down what they're embellishing that's not just on the outline, and then that's what I really look at when I'm studying for tests and highlighters are my best friend. (organizational systems management)

My biostatistics teacher . . . on his website he posts up notes like outline notes ahead of time so that we can print them out and read them and have them ready during class, and his lecture corresponds to the notes that he has given us so it's not all, you know, brand new stuff. . . . That's what I love about professors when they do that—there's a lot of professors that actually, you know, want to make it easier for you—so it's better for you to understand. When professors do that when they have, you know—I'm not saying it's like lazy for us—but it's more of a helpful tool for them to have notes for us ahead of time or to let us know actually what we should be learning . . . but actually tells us what part in the book to pay attention to or what to look out for and what's going to be on the homework. (kinesiology)

The things that I don't understand I try to look at, for example, PowerPoints. When a teacher gives PowerPoints, those are really helpful because it is the summary and the main points of what they are teaching. . . . This semester, with three of my classes I have all PowerPoints, and I was very happy with that. I remember my first semester my chemistry teacher would just write stuff on the board. I didn't really understand her handwriting. (biology)

I look at the PowerPoints before class, and then I just make note of, did they follow their PowerPoint specifically, or did they deviate. . . . And if they deviated, what section did they deviate from? And that section I will read in the book. So it's more just getting to know your professor. That's what I found most helpful in bio classes. (biology)

It appears from many of these responses that familiarity with the content of a class session ahead of time might facilitate learning. In many cases, students were given the notes before class and could preview the concepts, creating a mental schema for the content of the upcoming class meeting. Such engagement might function either to reduce confusion or anxiety or to excite the student about the next class. In either case (or in both), by the time students were juniors, they seem to have figured out strategies for using webnotes (such as the preview function) to facilitate their comprehension and learning.

Visually Oriented Courses

Being able to print out webnotes before class seemed especially helpful where there were a lot of visual images associated with the course.

> I know like some professors, they'll post their PowerPoints online before a class. And that's helpful. For my physiology class, she posts the slides, and mostly they're pictures or diagrams that she talks about in class. And then we also have to write notes on it, so it's helpful to look at the PowerPoints. (kinesiology)

> I like when teachers use PowerPoints, because . . . they can put whatever they want on there . . . they can have it like an image, and then they can expand the image. Because if you were to tell your students to go to page 50 in your book . . . some people won't have the book. So I know, one of my professors, they say, "I know you guys aren't going to have the book, so I'm going to use parts of the book on the PowerPoint," which was very useful, because, say, if we didn't bring a book today, he would have part of the book on the PowerPoint, like, just like figures. (sociology)

Not Having to Take Notes in Class

As we observed above, and as research has revealed, note-taking in class can be very challenging for students; this may be especially true for male students ($p < .001$), who seemed to have more difficulty with handwriting speed, working memory, language comprehension, conscientiousness, and note quality (Reddington, Peverly, and Block 2015). Our interview transcripts, however, uncovered some interesting factors with regard to note-taking, particularly around the issue of increased listening and class participation.

> Well, just this year, I've found it helpful to print out the lectures. So that way, I could really focus on what the professor is saying and take side notes, because I would find it a little harder to try to copy down notes and put side notes around. So now, I think that's a good way—when it comes to taking notes, it's like, I have it there, I'm listening. (psychology)

In some classes, teachers that use PowerPoint and then post the PowerPoints for you to use, I usually find that I do better by not taking notes because some classes, when you're so busy trying to take notes, I'm not actually learning it. I'm just trying to write it all down. So, if I have the opportunity to not take notes and just focus on class and, you know, participate in the discussion and really understand it, I do. . . . And so, yeah, and then I usually try to participate as much as I can in class because I found that, I don't know, it just works in your favor, like if your grades are borderline, a teacher knows you and knows you're trying. I've seen that help me a lot usually. . . . And I always go to classes. I don't miss class unless it's like, you know, some classes, there's a class you can get away with not going. But I try not to do that because even if they don't take attendance, they know who was there and stuff, so, like, if they get to know your name and it comes up and you didn't do that well, I know that'll help [with the instructor's perceived impression of the student as a participant in class]. (journalism)

In this quote, the student reveals a fascinating integration: the webnotes contributed to more opportunities to listen, thus opening up the possibility for increased class participation. In turn, the greater participation in class was related to becoming better known to the professor. In courses where participation is included as part of the grade, having the webnotes ahead of time may actually contribute to improved grades.

I have my psychology class for child development with [professor X, who] would post her PowerPoints on Moodle and then we would print the PowerPoints out in class. And next to the PowerPoint, there was the image of the PowerPoint. . . . Once she put that PowerPoint on there and she was lecturing, I would write notes right next to . . . the PowerPoint, you know, so it was really helpful. . . . It's almost like notes that she's already done for us, you know, and we add onto it and she said, . . . "It's helpful if you add your notes to that." So instead of taking a notebook to class for example, I would just have those PowerPoints. (English)

In this example, the professor was very explicit about two important learning strategies, suggesting to students that they (1) print out the webnotes and (2) add notes to the printouts during class. While this may already have been part of some students' approach to using webnotes, to others, it will be novel but highly useful—with the potential to generalize to other courses.

Lecture Notes: Fill in the Blank

One idea that we found unique was the "fill in the blank" element, although we later found that Sambrook and Rowley (2010) mention "gapped webnotes" in their study. With this method, faculty provide *some* of the information they want students to acquire but incentivize attendance and attention in class by making the notes incomplete until the lecture/discussion occurs in class. In some ways, this is a hybrid of providing all lecture notes versus not providing them at all. These kinds of incomplete notes encourage more interaction and engagement by students, compared to passive consumption of complete notes.

> Then recently I had a professor who [provided] slideshows on the website. But they had missing words . . . missing paragraphs and stuff, so you had to come to class and write . . . to fill it in. I think that was one of the things that—one of the great things. I was, like, oh, wow, that's really smart. . . . I can add to it. I like that. (psychology)

> Yeah, but my biology class . . . she left blanks in the [slides] so we had to pay attention and kind of fill in the blanks. Because we didn't know what the words [were going to be]. I liked it because I was paying attention . . . I had to focus. (sociology)

> For one of my psychology classes this semester she puts [slides] up [online], but she puts blank spaces . . . we'll fill it in while she's lecturing. Other classes they show PowerPoints in class, but they won't post it on the Moodle site or they won't send it to us. Other classes they'll give us the PowerPoint ahead of time and then it's the same PowerPoint that they use in class. . . . It's different from all of my teachers. I prefer when they put it online in class—because I feel like, you know, when you're trying to listen to what the professor is saying but you feel like what is on the PowerPoint, it's vital. That method where you have to come to class to find out the missing answer, it gives people, I guess, a reason to go to class . . . and also we're able to refer back to it if we don't get to copy everything down. (undecided)

> He has the PowerPoints given to us. We can get access to it online. But there's blank spots, so then you have to attend class and fill it in. But then he also has the lecture online. So . . . you should still attend the class, but if for some reason you can't, the lectures are all available online and you can do it at home. [*interviewer question:* Are they videotaped lectures? What's the format?] There's some that are just mp3, but the other ones are just the PowerPoint with audio over it. So it helps me when I—'cause then we should listen to it before going to the lecture, so it's nice to have them—to hear it on a lecture, and then in class I can ask him a question about, "Oh, I didn't understand this about the lecture, can you go into more detail about it?" It's like a hybrid, but more. (liberal studies)

Students Who Did *Not* Prefer Lecture Notes

Another surprise was the perspective of students who did not like having the lecture notes/presentation slides available. This response was most frequent if the online notes were identical to the class presentation and the students cited redundancy as the issue.

> I don't like it when they put notes online and then go over it in class. I find that really redundant. . . . It's fine when they put the slides online and they elaborate in class, that's fine. I have one of my teachers who does that and I like that. (biochemistry)

> I really enjoy my classes where the professors try to engage with the students. I have my history class, the professor doesn't have a PowerPoint or anything, he just talks the entire time, and we're taking notes on that. And he doesn't give us any notes or anything, it's all knowledge that we take from the book and from his lectures. So that's really helped me out, to do things on my own. [*interviewer question:* So maybe in some ways, having a sort of structured PowerPoint kind of lays everything out for you and makes it too easy. And so having to kind of work for it a little bit is really sort of more enjoyable?] Yeah. Because I have other classes that do have PowerPoints, and while you're trying to take the notes, then you're not focusing on what the professor's saying. So it's easier to read the book on your own and get the basic idea, and then during the lecture the professor sort of goes deeper into the subject. (physics)

In some cases, students prepared by reading the book first and awaited the instructor's deeper exploration of the subject in class. This observation takes us back to more generally traditional college teaching and learning, where the text, read prior to class, served as the platform from which discussion developed. Interestingly, this seemed unrelated to the student's major. In the quote above, the physics major's comment about her history instructor's approach was valued despite its seeming distance from her major.

> I don't like PowerPoints because I find it hard to keep up with, but a lot of teachers have an extra copy on Moodle, which is fine. But I really like it when a teacher just talks and just whips out the board marker and as they go, kind of write it because I don't bring an iPad to school. So everything that I do is by hand, so I like that better. (business law)

Thus, it appears there are some students who prefer organic kinds of teaching and discussion. A more traditional approach does not have to be eliminated from college pedagogy, but it should not be a surprise if students prefer a pacing that is more class driven ("in the moment" and engaging) and discussion based, as opposed to a class meeting that is organized solely around and even somewhat scripted through a PowerPoint presentation.[2]

SUMMARY AND IMPLICATIONS

Why did webnotes seem so valuable for many students' learning? LH
juniors at CSUN revealed that having notes available beforehand helped
them use class time more efficiently, allowing them to focus on pertinent
information. They mentioned that being able to pay closer attention to
discussion without having to write constantly was helpful. Students found
webnotes to be particularly valuable when visuals were involved, especially
having a copy of the selected pictures or graphics to go along with content.
Webnotes were also associated with students' ability to engage more in
class discussion—freeing them from frantically trying to capture new ideas:
even as they were rendering them into notes, students reported they could
more fully engage in class discussions. Nevertheless, we recognize that not
all students appreciate webnotes. But is there more to webnotes than just
the value of note-taking and studying?

Making webnotes available before class also seems related to other major themes in "effective teaching practices"—such as course structure and
instructor's style of presentation. The identification of lecture notes being
available (19.6 percent) was nearly equal to the overall comments regarding
the instructor's focus on student learning (20.7 percent). Do webnotes convey
that faculty members care about their students and their learning? Would this
be particularly true for students who downloaded "fill-in-the-blank" webnotes because they felt their learning really mattered? Perhaps the webnotes
signify a genuine interest in helping and caring about students, making the
effort to post notes prior to class. The webnotes may also indicate a well-
organized class that could translate into students' engagement, with the idea
that "this professor really cares about my learning, so I do too."

Another critical and intriguing theme points to the possibility that webnotes
liberate students from the perceived need to try to "transcribe" lectures, allowing them to have additional opportunities for interaction and engagement.
This could be especially true where instructors designed the "fill-in-the-
blank" format to entice students into attending class while providing a learning challenge that could be solved like a puzzle. Liberated from the anxiety
of missing something they couldn't transcribe, students could instead listen
more intently for clues to the identity of information that would complete the
notes. Looking forward to completing notes in class, either individually or in
a group, could support students' class attendance or increase their participation. On the other hand, verbatim in-class use of the same slides that had been
posted online may prompt feelings of disengagement and alienation, perhaps
conveying the feeling that the instructor didn't care enough to prepare novel
learning experiences in class.

The extent to which students perceive that their learning matters to their instructors is important. And it may not be just the students' overall feeling that is affected: as a result of feeling valued, perhaps students are more motivated. LH students' responses suggest they don't value or seek being fed information. Rather it's the guided challenge of having the chance to interact with the material. This disposition is clearly consistent with current findings in the contexts of encouraging transparency (Winkelmes 2013), developing students' growth mind-sets, and teaching them about their own metacognition. "Transparency," in Mary-Ann Winkelmes's terms, refers to the explicit discussion with students of any assignment's purpose: what it actually requires students to do, that is its tasks, and the criteria by which students' work on the assignment will be evaluated. Such knowledge, along with the development of a growth mind-set (Dweck 2015), involves students recognizing (and ultimately appreciating) that the difficulty of a challenge is not a measure of its being insurmountable and that working toward meeting such challenges leads both to achievement and to the confidence that is a corollary to such achievement. Through understanding the interrelatedness of transparency and the growth mind-set, and applying these to their learning, students develop a sort of metacognitive disposition toward their own educations, making it more likely that they'll be prepared to navigate challenging learning. These "learning habits" are at the heart of what we hoped we would find at the onset of the project.

IMPLICATIONS FOR PROFESSORS' PROFESSIONAL DEVELOPMENT

This chapter suggests a number of possibilities for faculty members to pursue as they develop their own approaches to a more extensive use of online resources for their students:

- Overall, students appreciate webnotes posted *before* class. This reflects a combination of their perceptions of the benefit of previewing concepts, of having a source of accuracy, and of freeing them from writing constantly. In addition, webnotes provide a way to portray visuals with precision and may foster greater class participation because students are liberated from intensive note-taking. In addition, supplying webnotes may convey the sense that instructors really care enough to provide useful resources ahead of time.
- Instructor motivation for students' use of webnotes should be explained explicitly. This theme came up in the study by Sambrook and Rowley (2010) as well. Instructors' explanations should include the value of

printing out webnotes, previewing them before class, and then bringing them to class for additional annotation. It is important to tell students that the webnotes were designed to enrich their engagement with the material, free them to participate more fully in class, and deepen their learning. Such discussions should also help students integrate webnotes with other learning resources, such as texts, lectures, fieldwork, or library use. Letting students know that there is an infrastructure for them to make use of in navigating the course's conceptual territory is important. Explicit discussion of goals, uses, and benefits of webnotes enables students to maximize their learning.

- Posted webnotes should not mirror class sessions but should be suggestive of key ideas or terms. Heavy narrative in the webnotes should be avoided. Class sessions should not be used merely to read each slide. This coincides with the study by Apperson and colleagues (2008).

- When novelty is included (such as blank spaces and "gapped," or what one CSUN student dubbed "vague," slides), students may be more likely to engage in their own learning. The use of fill-in-the-blank webnotes may be a good idea for some courses, some of the time. A variety of strategies for different ways to create gapped notes could be developed to keep novelty and interest alive. Students reported that incomplete notes seemed to draw their attention and provided a worthy incentive for class attendance.

- Experimenting with webnotes may allow faculty members to meet the needs of diverse learners. For example, vocabulary and other comprehension supports may be helpful for multilingual or international students. Students with special needs should also have our attention. For example, CSUN is home to the second-largest population of deaf and hard of hearing students in the United States. (Gallaudet University has the largest.) Webnotes could add positively to their other learning supports, such as interpreters, note-takers, and captioning. Students with either identified or suspected learning challenges might find webnotes extremely helpful in remembering key ideas. Webnotes can be especially valuable for male students who have a more difficult time taking notes (Reddington, Peverly, and Block 2015), with implications related to gender topics examined in chapter 4. While this did not come up in our data and discussion per se, gender does seem to have a role in predicting graduation rates. (See chapter 10, "Factors Influencing Academic Help Seeking by College Students.") And we did find that the majority of juniors' quotes regarding webnotes came from women, so perhaps the men have not figured this out yet.

- Graphics and pictures play a special role for students in webnotes, especially important for visually driven courses, including the arts, biology, and engineering. Not only can visuals make webnotes livelier and more engaging for many learners, but also they are able to capture images far too complex for students to re-create accurately in their notes.

Faculty members should be explicit about the goals they have for using webnotes. Faculty development programs should include instruction in the use of webnotes, with a variety of styles, formats, and content, through both workshops and online posting, especially for faculty members wanting to ramp up their use of technology. This might be especially important for new faculty members (Uz, Orhan, and Bilgiç 2010). While individual instructors may find webnotes too simplistic in some cases or core and essential in others, access to information is critical. Just as we would wish students to be curious learners, we hope that faculty members will explore the promising practices identified in this chapter and continue their journey to promote the successful learning habits of all students.

NOTES

1. These are direct quotes, but comments such as "like" are often omitted. Ellipses are used to consolidate the student's comment around the same topic.

2. However, as we note in some detail, and as chapter 8 (O'Sullivan) aptly observes, "[technology] challenges the way educators need to think about conveying information, and it underscores the need for transformational teaching, enabling students to judge and connect evidence." Instruction has always needed to be "transformational," that is, a core, if unspoken, goal of education. New technologies have never failed to present new challenges for making it so.

REFERENCES

Apperson, Jennifer M., Eric L. Laws, and James A. Scepansky. 2008. "An Assessment of Student Preferences for PowerPoint Presentation Structure in Undergraduate Courses." *Computers and Education* 50: 148–53.

Dweck, Carol. 2015. "Carol Dweck Revisits the 'Growth Mindset.'" *Education Week*, September 22. Accessed September 22, 2015. http://www.edweek.org/.

Hill, Andrea, Tammy Arford, Amy Lubitow, and Leandra M. Smollin. 2012. "I'm Ambivalent About It: The Dilemmas of PowerPoint." *Teaching Sociology* 40 (3): 242–56. doi:10.1177/0092055X12444071.

Kozub, Robert M. 2010. "Student Attitude towards and Use of PowerPoint® Slides as Study Guides in Undergraduate Introductory Financial Accounting." *Journal of College Teaching and Learning* 7 (3): 40–47.

Reddington, Lindsay A., Stephen T. Peverly, and Caryn J. Block. 2015. "An Examination of Some of the Cognitive and Motivation Variables Related to Gender Differences in Lecture Note-Taking." *Reading Writing* 28: 1155–85. doi:10.107/s1145-015-9566-z.

Sambrook, Sally, and Jennifer Rowley. 2009. "Student Attitudes toward and Use of Webnotes." *International Journal of Management Education* 8 (2): 31–42. doi:10.3794/ijme.82.252.

———. 2010. "What's the Use of Webnotes? Student and Staff Perceptions." *Journal of Further and Higher Education* 34 (1): 119–34.

Uz, Çiğdem, Feza Orhan, and Gülşah Bilgiç. 2010. "Prospective Teachers' Opinions on the Value of PowerPoint Presentations in Lecturing." *Procedia: Social and Behavioral Sciences* 2: 2051–59.

Winkelmes, Mary-Ann. 2013. "Transparency in Teaching: Faculty Share Data and Improve Students' Learning." *Liberal Education* 99 (2). https://www.aacu.org/.

Part Four

FOSTERING STUDENT INITIATIVE

Both the face-to-face interviews and end-of-term survey responses provided learning habits (LH) students with the opportunity to comment on their evolving ability to take control of their own learning, the focus of this section. The topics they discussed, as is evident from the three chapters included, often focused on seeking help with their academic work, as required; finding means of successfully regulating and mastering academic demands; and becoming more thoughtful about their learning.

This introduction sets the stage for these more focused discussions by providing a brief overview of the beneficial co-curricular activities that the LH participants enumerated. Although much of the discussion during the interviews focused on coursework and study habits, students commented on the value of their cocurricular campus activities with some frequency, when given the opportunity through targeted questions.

In both first- and third-year interviews, students most frequently mentioned one or more of the following activities when identifying those that were helpful: campus services, such as the library and the learning resource center (LRC); on-campus student clubs; and study groups. The proportion mentioning any one of these activities ranged from approximately one-fifth to one-half. More importantly, some noteworthy shifts in emphasis emerged between the first and the third years: fully half of the first-year students singled out campus services as beneficial. Said one student, "Last semester I had a stats class, which was a pretty tough class, but I went to the LRC and I got help, and it really helped." Others noted the following:

> And for English, I . . . went to LRC appointments where they helped me brainstorm before I write my essays. And then that really helps me a lot. . . . Sometimes

I have an idea kind of thing and they tell me if it's clear or not. [They] help me clarify my thoughts and my ideas and stuff, and they tell me what to elaborate on more because it's not understandable. . . . So I like going—I like bringing my essays to LRC appointments.

The [academic] advisement center, I use that a lot because, I don't know. I just want to know that I'm on track, keeping [up] with all my stuff, and making sure I'm taking the right courses at the right time.

I use the library resources because I had a couple of research papers I had to write. . . . If I can't always go [to] the library, I really like the fact that I can chat to someone, like online, to ask about the library resources. So, I was really glad I could do that because sometimes I'm so busy that I really can't go to a library.

Ever since the rec center opened, I have been trying my very hardest to be there every single day. Basically, if I'm at CSUN, I will go there for at least, at minimum, half an hour of workout. I've been playing soccer since I was four. And I'm used to that being my form of exercise. And since I don't have that, I've been trying to use the gym.

The third-year students, in contrast, were most likely to mention the benefits of participating in campus clubs and organizations, with two in five doing so. The following are illustrative of their comments:

The Blues Project—basically, we're a program that's dedicated to help you understand depression and suicide and why it happens and how we can help prevent it or work on it. So I like—I do that. It's really fulfilling to be able to help people because there's a lot of people who are not knowledgeable, you know.

The camaraderie, it really did help me out. Like I was never shy in high school—I was completely the opposite of shy. Then once I hit college, I'm, like, I wasn't really out there much. But once I got into the fraternity, then it completely switched, like it made me more active in everything. Not only did it get me active in the fraternity, but now I'm in all sorts of programs, you know. I wouldn't even be able to list how many things I'm in.

So coming from being a cheerleader and like being very social in high school, it was weird not having that around. So I kind of didn't want to come to school because it's like I don't know anyone. But then I joined the sorority and then I got to know a bunch of people. . . . Like, it just kind of makes your experience better. And then you're more motivated to come to class.

I am in Project Date this semester. . . . Well, we're a sexual assault and rape peer education program here on campus and we do presentations on and off campus to kind of, you know, to spread awareness and. . . . And I'm also doing the CSUN Help Line, which I'm enjoying.

The third category of response focused on study groups and was mentioned with approximately equal frequency, regardless of interview time. The flavor of the responses emerges from the following examples:

> Usually when I do study groups with friends, I'm usually kind of the one that leads it and sets it up and has it organized. And like for my math final last semester, we got one of the study rooms [in the library], and I would go up there and I was doing problems and kind of leading them through it, which really helps me a lot. You know, it helps me because when you teach someone I feel like you learn the material more. And I feel like study groups, also, when we do those kind of things, they're more effective.

> I found a good group of people that wanted to do well in class, and they wanted that A. And I found that that made me want the A. So, I did better when I was working with them. So I still do that. I still find the people that I work well with, and especially in my major, we're taking all the same classes. So we try to coordinate which classes we're taking each semester so that we take them together.

In terms of the benefits of participating in various campus activities, one reason stood out for everyone: strengthening academic skills, as a number of the comments above illustrate. However, the virtue of strengthening academic skills was a less dominant theme in third-year interviews, with the benefits of career guidance—hardly mentioned by freshmen—assuming considerably more importance. Such comments were often linked to descriptions of students' internships, which were almost exclusively discussed by the third-year students:

> It's kind of hard to pinpoint, but I guess, over summer was kind of an "aha" moment just because I was working and interning, and it's kind of like I saw the direction that I wanted to go in.

> I recently got an internship over this past summer for the transit coalition. And it mainly deals with public transportation. And I was, a long time I was on the fence, because for urban planning, they have you choose a specialization, like housing, transportation, the environment, or whatever. . . . And I still had no idea, up until this past summer, I realized I really do enjoy public transportation.

A fair number of students also mentioned the importance of the friendships that participation in campus activities give rise to. Said a freshman about participating in one of the student musicals in the theater department, "But that's been another great experience, like, making friends, and it's very much like a family bond."

As expected, the clubs chosen vary wildly by student, from the math club to the photo club, from performance to the Greek system.

> And so I started going [to the math club] and, you know, interacting with people there and I was like, "Oh, this is really great." And I'm actually part of starting a student chapter for the Association for Women in Mathematics. So that's just starting at CSUN right now. And I'm part of that as well.

> I think that my social skills [have grown the most]. Meeting my friends now through photo club. I think without photo club I wouldn't have met these people that are so close to me now.

With one exception, the emphasis on academic benefits prevailed in all cocurricular activity clusters identified. The exception is the activity grouping encompassing student clubs and organizations, where the beneficial effect on friendships is on a par with the academic benefit.

Factors Influencing Academic
Help Seeking by College Students

Mark Stevens and Peter Mora

In this chapter, we explore a key factor contributing to the retention and graduation of college students: the willingness of students to seek academic help in a timely and effective manner. Analysis of interview data from California State University, Northridge's (CSUN) Learning Habits Project helped shape the content of the chapter. Participants were selected based on their academic record in high school, SATs, and college readiness (i.e., placement in freshman-level math and English classes, without remediation). They represented students who were most likely to succeed academically and graduate from CSUN.

To provide a context for the reader, the chapter begins with a "big picture" view of help-seeking behaviors and attitudes, and the influential factors that shape them. Next, the authors provide a brief literature review of factors influencing academic help-seeking, setting a frame to discuss the learning habits (LH) student interviews. Lastly, based on findings, we provide specific suggestions for students, faculty members, staff members, and administrators to increase the likelihood that students will seek academic help with increased frequency, timeliness, and self-empowerment.

Students were interviewed across time, from the year they entered as freshmen to their graduation semester. Subsequently, self-reflection about developmental changes regarding their academic help-seeking behaviors is presented.

BIG-PICTURE VIEW OF HELP-SEEKING BEHAVIORS

Seeking help is a necessary part of life. In order to survive most of us must rely, at times, on someone else or something for information, guidance, and emotional and physical support. As infants, help is provided without our asking. The same can usually be said in times of grave circumstances. The renowned developmental theorist Erik Erikson (1950) discusses that as children grow older they are tasked with the developmental challenge of independence (self-reliance) versus dependence (reliance on others). While observing toddlers you can hear some say quite proudly, "Let me do it myself" while others proclaim, "I can't do it; I need your help." Much later in life you can observe the struggle of the elderly, resisting attempts by family members to agree to give up their car keys.

Throughout life this developmental challenge emerges and plays itself out differently, depending on an assortment of contributing factors including environment, socioeconomic status, health, self-confidence, gender socialization, context, age, availability, and knowledge of resources. Why, when, where, and how a person seeks help are essential questions to ask when understanding help-seeking behaviors. Help-seeking decisions are learned behaviors, often related to the individual's perception of the usefulness of past help seeking and their interpersonal experiences with helpers. Help seeking is often contextual in nature. One might be comfortable asking for help dealing with being lost yet reluctant or avoidant in asking for help in connection with having difficulty in a class.

ACADEMIC HELP-SEEKING BEHAVIORS AND ATTITUDES

Asking for academic help is a necessary and key component of student success. But what do college students do when they encounter a roadblock that interferes with their understanding of academic material? Such roadblocks include everything from not understanding how to complete an assignment to not comprehending a conceptual aspect of the material.

Ironically, students who are more confident in their academic capabilities ask for help more often and in a more timely fashion than those who feel ashamed of their abilities. The anticipated "shaming" or "reshaming" factor associated with academic help seeking is shaped by mini-traumas (Stevens 2016) experienced by students, as well as gender-role socialization. Males are generally socialized to view seeking help of any sort as being weak; they want to hide their sense of vulnerability from others. Students tend to avoid or delay learning behaviors, such as academic help seeking, if there is anticipated anxiety associated with the task, so for those students who have felt humiliated and ashamed about their academic abilities, seeking help can be quite difficult. Faculty members who are perceived by their students as too busy or who seem annoyed by the quality of students' questions can unintentionally inhibit students from seeking their guidance. Especially for first-generation students who may not have the academic capital (Stevens 2016) of confidence and entitlement, these types of interactions with faculty members (authority figures) can become an even greater obstacle to them asking for academic help.

LITERATURE REVIEW: HELP-SEEKING BEHAVIORS IN HIGHER EDUCATION

Academic help seeking can be the difference between a student entering higher education destined to face challenges that may lead to dropping out or one successfully identifying a challenge, building self-efficacy, finding support, and overcoming the challenge presented within their journey. Margaret Taplin and Olugbemiro Jegede (2001) found that "effective help-seeking is an important strategy that is fundamental to successful learning whenever the student's knowledge or comprehension is insufficient to enable independent resolution of a problem" (136).

The playing field may be uneven when it comes to academic help-seeking behaviors. Greta Winograd and Jonathan Rust (2014) found when students seek help early on their higher educational journey, they appear to benefit in terms of having a greater grade point average and having an improved persistence throughout their educational journey. The authors also found that first-generation students, who often experience an uncertainty of belonging, do not seek support in a timely manner and often feel intimidated to seek help from their professors. In his research on stereotype threat, Claude Steele (1997) found that ethnic minority students avoid running the risk of appearing less capable than their peers, and subsequently are more reluctant to seek academic help.

Gender also creates an interesting lens to understand academic help-seeking behaviors. Tracy Morgan, David Ness, and Maureen Robinson (2003) found that women indicated a higher likelihood of seeking help than men. Previous research has concentrated on the challenges presented in male students seeking academic assistance as they confront challenges in attaining their goals.

David Wimer and Ronald Levant (2011) found that "having a high degree of conformity to masculine norms was associated with men being even less likely to seek academic help" (266). According to the authors, men are more likely than women to drop out of school and not to seek help from teachers when struggling academically. Self-reliance and dominance were two masculinity measures that Wimer and Levant found hinder men from seeking academic help. The authors state, "It makes sense that males who adhere to the cultural myth that men should be self-reliant would be reluctant to seek any form of help, including academic help" (2011, 268).

Students' perceived academic self-efficacy impacts their academic help-seeking behaviors. When students reported being unsure of their abilities, they were more likely to feel threatened and reported a greater likelihood of avoiding help when needing it (Ryan and Pintrich 1997). The authors found that lower-achieving students and students who believe they are not able to achieve believe their need for help is evidence that they are incapable of completing the tasks required in a scholastic setting.

Some students prefer a less interpersonal context for academic help seeking. Anastasia Kitsantas and Anthony Chow (2007) examined how college students' help-seeking behavior varied across different instructional learning environments. They found that students enrolled in courses with an online computer component reported feeling less threatened and had higher instances of help-seeking behaviors, particularly from instructors. Participants stated that seeking help through e-mail allowed them to engage in "private dialog, and gives [the students] ample time to construct a question" (392).

WHAT LEARNING HABITS STUDENTS TAUGHT US

Several themes emerge from the narratives of the students we interviewed over time, from their entry as freshmen to the semester in which they graduated. This section of the chapter allows the authors to summarize these themes and provide the reader with relevant quotes.

How the Faculty Encourages Help-Seeking Behavior

Dozens of LH students spoke about how the faculty encouraged them to seek help. Sixty-five percent of the first-year students in the study reported how useful it was when instructors made help seeking a class requirement (or extra credit). Here are accounts from two first-year students:

> So we had to go to LRC [the learning resource center, the university's tutoring office] for each essay and then having other people help you with it besides the teacher and . . . they always had me read aloud which I never do but then I would catch all my little mistakes. I continued to go even when it was not a requirement.

> Our university 100 [freshmen seminar] professor insisted on [us] visiting our professors just so we have a connection with them, and they said to make yourself known.

Because of time challenges associated with outside work and family demands, faculty members having flexible office hours was viewed as important. One freshman said, "Most office hours are during class or when I work, and some professors won't move around their office hours or make a time for you. So I've had to miss class in order to go on office hours." Students were also encouraged when professors spoke enthusiastically in class about the variety of campus resources available to them. "They talked about all of the different programs and things that we have here at CSUN that help outside of just academics . . . that I had no idea were here."

By far the most influential "variable" that encouraged and reinforced the help-seeking behavior of our students was the "vibe" felt from the individual instructor. Traditionally underserved and first-generation students particularly noted this.[1]

> You get that vibe that they're very helpful and they're very willing to see you in their office hours, like they're a mentor. They've been through it. They can help you.

> For example, my professor for psychology—Yeah, she likes that we go to her office and ask for help.

A third student described her instructor talking to the class, saying, "'Listen, like, you need to feel comfortable. Like, we're all here for you,' and stuff like that, kind of made me feel better."

Many students—especially first year and first generation—are too intimidated to seek help from the faculty, not knowing if they will be shamed or understood. LH students said the approachability and empathy of the faculty played a significant role in the interaction.

> And understanding that if we come to the office hours for help, we're not just saying, "I'm getting poor grades . . . because I'm not studying." But I'm coming, you know, to your office hours for help.

The Challenges of Seeking Help

By far the greatest obstacle and challenge related to seeking help is the emotional difficulty of asking, according to student comments. "I really should have asked for more help with math, and I'm disappointed in myself with that. I'm retaking the class this semester," one freshman told an interviewer. Said another, "I find it kind of weird. I don't know. . . . Sometimes I do go up to a professor, but most of the time I get scared. I won't go to office hours." And a third said, "I've never liked talking to teachers or professors. This stems all the way back to kindergarten. I just get it in the class. I sit there. I sit in the back, and then I leave."

Of course, many students do seek help, but some report not knowing what to do when they receive advice that contradicts what was taught in class. "Well, when I went to tutoring . . . I found out that my professor is teaching us a completely different way." Too many students reported feeling shamed when they asked for help.

> I will ask her for help, but the way that she answers me, it's as if I should know this and I should have known this for two years before. It's a very . . . almost sarcastic.

> And he was very rude. Like incredibly rude. Like, just like I'd ask a question I didn't understand. He would say—literally, he said this to other students in my class too, like he'd say, like, "Are you stupid?"

Other students reported feeling rushed and not knowing how to be assertive to get what they needed. "I attended tutoring a lot, and sometimes some of the tutors were kind of fast, like they kind of expected you to already know what you're supposed to be doing."

Student Attitudes that Encourage Them to Seek Academic Help

LH students reported developing a variety of strategies and attitudes to overcome their reluctance to seek help. Understanding that you are not the only one who feels lost or does not understand the material is one strategy: "So what I learned was, I wasn't the only [one]; other people didn't know what was going on." They also shared how to reduce their fear and have an attitude of empowerment, most often expressed by students at the junior level:

> I've met students who say that they feel dumb asking for help. Really, it shouldn't be that kind of mentality. If you need help and you know it, then you should get it. You shouldn't just say you'll figure it out or refuse just because you don't like asking for help. That's not a good way to go about things in college or in life, I think.

> Like I said, I'm not afraid to ask for help because it's on me, and I'm not just going to sit there and let something else determine my grade without me having a say.

Of course, some first-year students learn this earlier. "If you're sitting at home, and you're pulling your hair out over a certain thing that you just don't understand, just put it down and go see a tutor. There's no shame in seeing a tutor. Like, it sucks that you have to go see a tutor, but they'll help you." Others acknowledged that it happened over time:

> It's probably different now. I don't think I'm—I'm not as hesitant to ask questions because now I figure that if I don't know something, then I'm better to ask it than not to ask it. Whereas before I would probably have tried to figure it out by myself rather than ask the question.

While a useful attitude to increase help-seeking behavior, only a few students mentioned feeling "entitled" to the services. "I actually use a lot of resources. I try to take advantage of the resources because I am paying for them."

Learning over Time How to Ask for Help

One of the project's interview questions—and a favorite among both interviewers and students at the junior level—asked what the student would "tell your freshman self" if you ran into him or her on campus. It revealed rich answers and insights about how help-seeking attitudes and behaviors changed and, more importantly, improved over time. More self-reflection was reported.

> Because what I've learned is, like, when you're having academic difficulty I think stepping back and just looking at the bigger picture and then just slowly going, "This is what's wrong, this is what's wrong," and just have . . . mapped out what's the problem and then slowly tackle each one.

A higher priority on asking for help also was reported.

> Never stop asking questions. If you need help, there's going to be someone who's willing to help you. Sort of like not to be afraid to seek out that help. I guess . . . because it's similar to my story, but you have to prioritize and you have to take into account what's most important.

> My freshman year I would hardly really talk to any of my professors. Now I do. [*interviewer question:* What made you change?] When I failed that course—it goes back a lot to that course. I never really asked for help, and I didn't search for it at all. I thought I had it under control. Now, a lot, what I do is take advantage of those office hours.

Get to know and seek guidance from your classmates was a frequent response. One first-generation student noted that she would tell her freshman self to

> start talking to people she was sitting around in class. [*Laughs*] 'Cause all those people I had in my freshman class and all those people—I mean, if I would

have gotten to know them quicker, or opened myself up faster I wouldn't have struggled so much in that one semester where I almost changed my major, just because it was so hard. So trying to be an island doesn't work. [*interviewer question:* Asking help from friends, is that something that's shifted?] Yeah. I didn't want to as much because I was just thinking, oh, well—I didn't want them to know, oh, I don't understand it or something because if they understand it then I thought oh, I'd look dumb. But then I'm just thinking, no. It should not be that way.

Wishing they had used office hours more often was a common theme for the juniors. "Talk to your professor. Go to their office hours. They're there to help you and not there to make you fail." Something they wished they had done more of—and do now that they are older—is getting other points of view and ideas from a different person.

I would definitely say try to get a tutor. Even if you think that you don't need one, trust me you need one. Get a tutor, get—at least find a study buddy that you can sit down with and review the courses because hearing the same ideas from a different individual will help you so much.

A more mature perspective on help seeking also developed. Said one junior, "If a class gets hard, if there's a hard topic, don't stress over it. Just find a way to work over it. Find a tutor, or just study more or something like that, instead of just getting frustrated and worrying yourself."

The Benefits of Virtual Help Seeking

Students reported using online resources to answer questions when they were not comfortable asking for help in person. "[The professor] wasn't very friendly or open about answering questions. I had to, number one, reteach myself the material through either going online [or] watching videos." In contrast to this student, who was forced by unfriendly faculty to go online, other students were encouraged by their instructors to seek help online to do better in the course. "That's what my professor recommended us to do; she was like, 'Yeah, go on Google and look up test-taking strategies,' and—which I [did]—that's why I liked that professor so much."

Students reported seeking help online was convenient and fit their schedules. "Because if I can't always go in the library, I really like the fact that I can chat to someone like online." Said two other students,

And the Cramster site basically is like an online tutor for you and shows you step by step how to go through the problems, you know. And last year I was looking at these calc-2 problems, and I'm just like, I have no idea where to even start. . . .What I can do on Cramster in 30 minutes would take me two hours at the tutoring center.

I've been e-mailing professors if I couldn't make it to office hours, 'cause I'd have class like all day. So it wouldn't like—it wouldn't mesh well with my schedule.

Students also reported online help fit their learning style:

I went on YouTube, and I found a whole bunch of things about astronomy so they like talked—it would talk about it, then show the picture and everything, you know, more like a visual learning instead of just looking at it flat in the book.

Effective Ways to Ask for Help

When students shared some of the assertive strategies they used, being clear about what help they wanted from the instructor was a common response.

So, what I do is that I go to my professor's office hours when I can when I don't have a class that day or I just go in there. "Excuse me, can you help with this? I didn't understand." Or if I didn't get something from an exam or a quiz, I'll just go ahead because I don't want to repeat the same mistake on my final.

The other common student response was asking the faculty member how they could raise their grade, which typically led to an academic help referral or other good advice. "Um, well for the last semester in my English class I got a C on my first paper, and I was like shocked that I got a C. And then I asked my professor how I can, like, raise it for my next essay and then she said I can go to LRC (learning resource center)."

Students also reported on the advantages of asking to review their work with the professor and preparing beforehand for the meeting. Said one junior, "Then I have had essays reviewed before I went in and turned it in and it helps in leaps and bounds to do that." Another junior had a similar point of view but stressed the need to be prepared: "So being able to get that feedback but studying before I go to see the professor."

Help Seeking and Male Students

Generally speaking, male students in the Learning Habits Project paralleled many of the attitudinal and behavior obstacles discussed briefly in the literature review and more extensively in numerous studies. One hindrance was being the "lone ranger." "I don't have that much time, but—I don't know. I kind of like to do things on my own," a first-generation junior said. Another admitted,

I have been trying to get more help with work 'cause before I was able to do things on my own, but somehow classes seem to be getting a little harder so I kind of. . . . I search online for help. I try to get some tutoring. And it helps me out, but then I go back to kind of falling behind so I have to go back to getting tutored.

Pride (expressed in a variety of ways) was often reported as an inhibiting factor. "I was just, like, no, I don't, like, no. I just feel stupid if I need a tutor," and "you know it's really bad to say, but I had to go to the math tutoring. It was the only way I could pass that class."

Men also reported disproportionately not knowing or remembering where to go for help. "I mean, I never really, like I knew there was some kind of math tutoring on campus, but I never really went out to search for them." Overconfidence also appeared to be a hindering factor.

I think I should have asked for more help, and I just wasn't that committed back then, like it wasn't my primary focus, and I guess I never thought that I could actually do poorly in a class until it really happened.

On a more encouraging note, men in the fraternity system reported the benefits and increased level of comfort in asking their fraternity brothers for academic help.

So the house will do anything they can to get your GPA up. I mean, like, it's not just like, "Okay, you're not smart. You're out." Like, they'll actually try and help you with it. Those 60 guys, they know something about a subject that I don't, that I might need help with.

Parents as a Source of Help

The option of asking parents for academic help is not available to all students, particularly our first-generation students, whose parents may not have knowledge of the subject matter and of navigating higher education, as discussed in chapter 3. However, some students—especially first year—sought relief and guidance from their parents rather than go to campus resources and some said it was more comfortable to rely on a family member:

I called my mom and I was like, "I'm stressed, please help me," and she talked me through it and she was like, "Don't worry about it. It's just a test," you know.

And my dad would just be helping me, tutoring again. We would spend hours. I mean I would spend hours and hours.

My mom's dad was a mathematician but she has been a great help with my math as well.

Some Positive Consequences of Academic Help Seeking

In addition to improved academic performance, LH students reported a variety of positive consequences associated with their help-seeking experiences, including building academic confidence.

> So I thought about quitting the class, but then I stuck to it because he had really good tips. Like, there are a lot of new techniques that I didn't learn before. So that's why I was frustrated because I didn't know how to do them. But then once I finally figured it out, it was really helpful and my essays got a lot better. And then getting it checked at the LRC helped me even more.

Other students reported feeling comfortable and a sense of belonging at the LRC: "I've gone there and not needed any help. Check my answers there, cool, but it's just a quiet place to just do it." Students also reported receiving useful guidance, not just academic help. "It is really great, because like if we have questions, then we can ask her (the tutor), and it is not just about classes, it is about the entire school in general."

A significant number of students reported positive relationship building while visiting faculty members during office hours. Here are two juniors speaking:

> So I kind of feel [that] going to the office hours kind of built up a personal rapport with him, which kind of helped me out. And also educationally helped me.

> It's weird, because they seem a little bit strict in class, but when you see them individually, it's different. They're kind of more open and friendly. They're not as intimidating when [there's] just you and the professor, so it's pretty cool.

The Useful Role of Peers

Students reported that going with peers to ask for outside help reduced the intimidation factor. Others said it was easier to ask peers for help, instead of seeking it elsewhere.

> And, you know, it's hard to go alone, so I went with friends too sometimes. And we just kind of had like a group study session with a tutor who had already taken the class . . . because it might be intimidating at first to go just alone, kind of, for me at least. So what I did was . . . I had friends in the class, and we just said, two of us or three of us, "Let's go together to tutoring."

> So I always ask a classmate first, and if they don't know then I always go to the professor, his office hours or her office hours.

> I also depend a lot on, like, my peers. . . . If someone's around to me, I'm not afraid to say, "Hey, do you think you would mind helping me out with this?"

> These people are cool just like me. They are having a hard time, why not just
> hang out with them but study with them.

Some students found it was easier to ask their peers to be direct and honest,
without being embarrassed about the outcome. "I usually have my friends
look over my papers and I tell them, I say, 'Be brutally honest with me.'"
Approximately 55 percent of the first-year and first-generation students found
a "collectivist environment" to be helpful to studying.

> The students help each other find all kinds of ways to do good in the class. It's
> everybody wants to do good, and if you find out you can do better by helping
> somebody else and they help you there is no reason why you wouldn't want to
> do that.

> [We feel] more free 'cause we're not worried about what we're saying, what
> we're speaking, you know. So I think that was really helpful.

Finally, a number of LH students reported the usefulness of being tutored
by their peer-like supplemental instructors, older students who have previously taken the class and work with current students in special sections or
individually.

CONCLUSIONS

Academic help seeking is a skill set that is developed and usually improves
over time. In the academic environment seeking help is both encouraged and
discouraged by a variety of environmental, interpersonal, and intrapersonal
factors, intentional or not. Students seek academic help in a variety of effective ways and from a variety of resources because one size does not fit all,
particularly in a large, diverse urban institution like CSUN.

Students, many of whom were first generation, often enjoyed and found
comfort working in a collectivist-type learning environment, that is, formal
and informal study groups. First-generation college students often do not
have the option of going to their parents for academic help, and they experience more reluctance to go to office hours to ask their instructors for help.
First-generation students, who do not have as much academic capital as their
peers, are more sensitive to authority-type issues.

For many of our students, seeking help is an act of courage, as they are concerned with being shamed or viewed as not being smart. Students in this study
overwhelming reported how intimidating it is to ask questions in class and see
their professors during office hour. How students perceive faculty members'

availability, willingness to take time, patience, and friendliness when approached significantly impacts their academic help-seeking behaviors.

Students report being surprised at how beneficial the help-seeking experience was to them, not only academically but also in increasing academic confidence. Peers were often viewed as a great resource of support. Study groups, while not for all, were experienced as a great way to meet students' academic and social needs. Male students tended to try to figure out academic challenges on their own and delayed, sometimes for too long, seeking help. Virtual help seeking seems to be a barely tapped resource, yet a useful one for students tight on time and reluctant to have face-to-face help.

Lastly, students benefited from class assignments and reminders throughout their time at CSUN about when, where, and how to seek academic help on campus.

RECOMMENDATIONS

The Learning Habits Project at CSUN provides us a glimpse into the challenges, rewards, reinforcers, strategies, and mind-sets of our students in the context of academic help seeking. Universities could benefit from developing an academic help-seeking "strategic plan," one that corresponds to the needs of their particular students. Below is a list of recommendations to consider in developing such a plan.

1. Provide ongoing professional development and training (virtually and in person) to faculty members, tutors, supplemental instructors, and academic advisers on best practices for encouraging and providing academic help.
2. Develop an informed, culturally responsive approach and strategy for providing academic help to first-generation students and other groups less inclined to seek help, such as male students.
3. Develop a student-oriented website that includes videos and other materials on campus resources, online and virtual academic help resources, tips on how and when to ask for academic help, and psychosocial educational materials on the challenges and rewards of academic help seeking.
4. Evaluate academic help providers regularly with the goal of improving the experience for students.
5. Develop an academic help-seeking campaign on campus. Let students know what help is out there.
6. Even small and specific changes can prove helpful, such as providing

- signage around campus that encourages academic help seeking;
- more flexible faculty office hours;
- ideas for the faculty around class assignments/extra credit for help seeking, syllabi that include academic resources, restructured classes to encourage students to network for peer-to-peer help seeking, and opportunities for students to reflect on help-seeking obstacles, specific to the course;
- academic help providers with the ability and opportunity to teach how to ask questions in a way that would be most effective to the goals of the student, and with the knowledge and skills to have strong empathy for the courage it takes for many students to ask a question in class and seek academic help; and
- ongoing encouraging and empowering messages to students that they are entitled to take advantages of the academic help resources on campus.

NOTE

1. Five subgroups make up the larger set of students stemming from traditionally underserved backgrounds: American Indians, Pacific Islanders, African Americans, Latina/o, and multirace. Others are referred to as stemming from better-served backgrounds. Further, within the context of this book, first-generation students are defined as those whose parents have no more than a high school education. This definition is narrower than the one relied on by the federal government, which considers first-generation students those whose parents lack a four-year college degree.

REFERENCES

Erikson, Erik H. 1950. *Childhood and Society*. New York: Norton.

Kitsantas, Anastasia, and Anthony Chow. 2007. "College Students' Perceived Threat and Preference for Seeking Help in Traditional, Distributed, and Distance Learning Environments." *Computers and Education* 48 (3): 383–95.

Morgan, Tracy, David Ness, and Maureen Robinson. 2003. "Students' Help-Seeking Behaviours by Gender, Racial Background, and Student Status." *Canadian Journal of Counselling* 37 (2): 151–66.

Ryan, Allison M., Lynley Hicks, and Carol Midgley. 1997. "Social Goals, Academic Goals, and Avoiding Seeking Help in the Classroom." *Journal of Early Adolescence* 17 (2): 152–71. doi:10.1177/0272431697017002003.

Ryan, A. M., and P. R. Pintrich. 1997. "Should I Ask for Help? The Role of Motivation and Attitudes in Adolescents' Help Seeking in Math Class." *Journal of Education Psychology* 89, 329–341.

Steele, Claude M. 1997. "A Threat in the Air: How Stereotypes Shape Intellectual Identity and Performance." *American Psychologist* 52:613–29.

Stevens, Mark. 2016. "Utilizing the Experiencing Confidence and Enjoyment of Learning (ExCEL) Program as a Culturally Responsible Teaching Tool with Underrepresented Students." Paper presented at the conference at California State University, Fullerton.

Taplin, Margaret, and Olugbemiro Jegede. 2001. "Gender Differences in Factors Influencing Achievement of Distance Education Students." *Open Learning* 16 (2): 133–54. doi:10.1080/02680510120050307.

Wimer, David J., and Ronald F. Levant. 2011. "The Relation of Masculinity and Help-Seeking Style with the Academic Help-Seeking Behavior of College Men." *Journal of Men's Studies* 19 (3): 256–74.

Winograd, Greta, and Jonathan P. Rust. 2014. "Stigma, Awareness of Support Services, and Academic Help-Seeking among Historically Underrepresented First-Year College Students." *Learning Assistance Review* (TLAR) 19 (2): 17–41.

11

Self-Regulated Learning Habits

Daisy Lemus and Mary-Pat Stein

There is something to be said about learning difficult things. Heart surgery. A foreign language. Singing opera. We all know of people who have succeeded at learning and mastering impressive skills and knowledge. They must have started somewhere. But where did they learn to learn and not get discouraged by challenges? What enabled them to be "good" students and master the information? How is this kind of learning different from how college students learn? Would this type of learning help students attain academic achievement?

The questions about what makes college students academically successful are not new. Some may argue that what is new is the rapidly changing demographic of today's college population—students who are accompanied by a variety of experiences and cultural influences that shape how, when, and what they learn. And yet, our focus in this chapter is on the processes of learning, irrespective of all of the differences. Ultimately, we argue, learning is about a relationship with the mind that needs to be understood, cultivated, and monitored. The question we should be asking is how do students teach themselves how to learn? We advance the notion that students who are self-regulated in their learning process better understand what they know and do not know, find motivation in their learning experiences, and take control of learning to yield desired results.

In describing self-regulation in learning, Barry Zimmerman and Dale Schunk (2011) assert that key to student achievement is self-awareness before, during, and after the learning process. Engaging in self-reflectivity and feedback loops allows students to choose one approach to studying, see the results of that practice with respect to their performance in a course or assignment, and then alter the approach based on their findings. Sabra Brock (2010) establishes that critical reflection has been shown to drive "transformative learning" or the changing of worldview; the self-regulated learning approach centrally positions the sorting of information in a conscious decision-making process as catalytic to active learning, as opposed to simply relying on routines students were taught to follow and not question. Linda Nilson (2013) notes, "Learning is about one's relationship with oneself and one's ability to exert the effort, self-control, and critical self-assessment necessary to achieve the best possible results—and about overcoming risk aversion, failure, distractions, and sheer laziness in pursuit of real achievement" (xxvii).

In sum, the type of learning that scholars define as self-regulated involves proactive activities, processes, and beliefs that drive an awareness of the learning process and an unfolding of developmental markers that allow students to better understand their academic achievement.

In this chapter, we examine the strategies, activities, and practices identified by selected students at California State University, Northridge (CSUN) that they believe made them successful academically. We posit that there is something unique about these Learning Habits Project students: they demonstrate the key elements of self-regulation while representing a diversity of profiles that span across gender, racial, socioeconomic, and academic preparedness differences. The process of interviewing these students and exploring their self-reflection has provided an insight into self-regulation and specifically into their metacognition.

We examine what students indicate contributed to their success and how they express themselves to reveal self-regulation as a core component to their learning habits. We arrive at a better understanding of how their motivation and positive feelings in the learning process significantly contributed to their academic success. Without realizing it or knowing how to label it, our students exhibited the qualities of self-regulated learners: they have a desire to learn, demonstrate initiative, are intrinsically motivated, and take responsibility for their own learning.

THE PSYCHOLOGY OF LEARNING

The literature is replete with terms that describe student learning and the understanding of that learning by students, both young and adults. In fact, researchers have explored learning dimensions with respect to both processes and individual traits associated with adulthood. For example, "self-directed learning" is a term originally associated with adult learners who learned outside a classroom environment, on their own, by trying different strategies and assessing the outcomes of those strategies (Saks and Leijin 2014).

Malcolm Knowles (1975) advanced the foundational definition of "self-directed learning" as a process in which individuals take the initiative to diagnose their learning needs and create goals and the necessary resources to achieve those goals, while choosing and implementing appropriate strategies, and consequently evaluating outcomes. More recently, "self-direction in learning" has combined the external process of self-directed learning (planning, implementing, and analyzing outcomes) with the internal desire to learn and acknowledge the responsibility of learning as a personality trait of the learner (Brockett and Hiemstra 1991). Conversely, "'self-regulated learning' is an active, constructive process whereby learners set goals for their learning and attempt to monitor, regulate and control their cognition, motivation, and behaviour, guided and constrained by their goals and contextual features on the environment" (Saks and Leijin 2014). That is, whereas self-directed learning focuses on the external forces that influence learning, self-regulated learning emphasizes the internal motivation and acceptance of responsibility for the process.

Students' self-regulation with respect to learning involves the ability to identify and pinpoint which activities and behaviors lead to being academically successful. The literature defines self-regulation of learning as a mind-set and behaviors that are activated and lead to following processes that enable achievement (Zimmerman 1990). Self-regulation requires goal setting, implementing strategies, assessing progress, and adjusting along the way to persist. Self-regulation entails developing self-efficacy, learning from feedback loops, and help seeking. Most importantly, in addition to high motivation to learn and the ability to recognize behaviors that contribute to goal achievement, self-regulation involves metacognition.

Metacognition is the identification and awareness of one's own thinking (Schoenfeld 1987). It is a critical aspect of self-regulated learning because it is not an implicit state but rather requires learners to exert effort in understanding themselves. In the broadest meaning of the term, all students are aware that if they do not study, the results they can expect on a given exam or assignment will not be as good as if they had studied. This awareness allows students to engage in various activities, including studying to learn the materials to excel in a given exam or assignment. All students use metacognition at varying degrees of complexity with regard to their study habits. What makes self-regulation assist in improving student achievement is the activation of metacognition *where the student is aware and reflects upon the learning process as it is happening.* Irrespective of the motivation behind the learning, or the behavior in regard to self-discipline or choice of learning activity, without the self-knowledge of their cognitive processing capabilities, students will not maximize the effort and investment in active learning.

THE LEARNING HABITS PROJECT

This study does not endeavor to determine if students are demonstrating self-direction or self-regulation. The purpose of this chapter is to better understand learning habits from the perspective of the students themselves, which happen to involve both self-direction and self-regulation. Nor do we suggest that we can establish that students have, indeed, used self-directed learning to identify the processes they believe have made them successful. Instead, we identify and discuss the importance of our need to understand what students think makes them "good" learners and academically success-ful. The focus is on students and, more specifically, what this population thinks is important for them to succeed. By understanding what our students believe to be their strengths, we may be able to identify the gaps and provide additional tools they can use on their paths to success. Furthermore, identify-ing and understanding what students believe may help us—as educators and facilitators of student learning—to understand misconceptions that poten-tially cause problems for them.

As a Hispanic-serving institution (HSI) and as one of the largest public undergraduate institutions in California, CSUN is a culturally and ethnically diverse environment where many students are first generation or come from traditionally underserved populations in Los Angeles.[1] The discussion here, therefore, represents specific strategies, activities, and practices that a subset of this population has identified as helping them succeed. This subset repre-sents students with experiences that may not be found in traditional students. In some cases, our students come from low-income homes where they hold full-time jobs to financially support themselves and their families. In other cases, our students come from cultural groups that are inexperienced in how to best support and encourage students in a college environment.

Nevertheless, we found that our students were what Mark Kroll and Mi-chael Ford (1992) regard as "task-oriented students" who are motivated to work hard to master tasks and tend to feel less concerned with demonstrat-ing their abilities for the sake of showcasing a positive image to others. This motivational orientation to focus on securing the achievement rather than emphasizing self-image explains why these students tend to be more self-reflective and make internal attributions for unsuccessful academic outcomes (Dinsmore and Parkinson 2013). In sum, our students' personal experiences and diverse backgrounds, as well as their task orientation, establish a solid foundation for developing self-regulated learning habits and strategies that lead to academic success.

COMMON SELF-REGULATION LEARNING STRATEGIES

In both face-to-face interviews and questionnaires, learning habits (LH) students described strategies that allowed them to figure out what was best for their own success; these strategies developed over time through trial and error, demonstrating metacognition of the process and practices that help them learn to learn. Several common themes were evident. Overarching concepts identified by students as critically important to their academic success included time management, organization and planning, and their polar opposite, procrastination. Strategies around social support, including group work and studying with others, were also identified as playing a role in their success. As Philip Winne (2004) suggests, during self-regulation, these strategies encourage learners to engage in self-regulated learning rather than assuming the use of these strategies will cause a particular desired effect.

Time Management

Time management is a recurring theme, especially in regard to self-discipline. Many LH students identified issues with both procrastination and allowing other distractions to prevent them from succeeding. They were keenly aware of which time management strategies worked for them and identified common obstacles to successfully managing time. Awareness of such problems and a variety of time management tools allowed many students to "set themselves up for success." Reflecting on the maxim "If you want something done, give it to a busy person," many students reported that having a busy schedule helps them focus on what needs to be done. One student said, "I think when you're busier you just get more stuff done, which is kind of counterintuitive, but you do," and continued, "because you're on a schedule and you have to do it." Other students reported that scheduling their time helps them to focus on what they need to do and use their time more efficiently. A student noted, "When you only have a certain amount of time, it's like your brain almost clicks into a different mode."

Moreover, many students discussed taking advantage of their "breaks" (time between classes and before or after work) as a way to optimize time in their busy schedules. A number actively try to schedule their time so they are not wasting it. One student noted,

> So it's like, the more other things I have going on, the more focused I am on getting my assignments done and my work done, because I know that I don't have any other time to do it other than . . . between my breaks, and stuff like that.

The strategic arrangement of their schedules was the key that kept students busy and allowed them to monitor and regulate procrastination, which was the expected tendency. One student noted, "If you stay busy, then you won't have a lot of time, so you'll have to, like, designate time when you have to study or when you have to do that."

Interestingly one student went so far as to frame time as a commodity that needed to be managed and even preserved. This reflection is indicative of metacognitive judgments that are integral to the success of the learning process. Patricia Alexander (2013) points out that making self-regulatory judgments about understanding, readiness to learn new tasks, or how much effort to expend are difficult but important to strategic behaviors in the learning process. For example, one student said, "And for me, personally, I feel like keeping myself busy is what helps the most, because if I have too much free time I will squander it."

Overall, students realized that managing their time required them to be reflective and adjust their schedules to force themselves to be more productive. Students clearly realized the tendencies to waste time, even referring to "squandering" it if they have too much free time. The solution for many is to make sure they are busy.

Organization and Planning

Successful students also identified planning, goal setting, and organization as strategies leading to academic success. These help to shape learning behaviors and, consequently, learning habits. Predominant in the research on self-regulation is the notion of forethought, or a type of awareness necessary to complete a task and achieve learning goals (Zimmerman 2000). Forethought with respect to what one needs to do during an entire semester, a week, or even just a day demonstrates the capacity to organize both time and materials, and plan how best to proceed in order to achieve the desired outcome (goal). The ability to organize and plan, regardless of whether the student later analyzes the outcomes and changes or modifies strategies, was clearly perceived as a tool required for student success.

Successful students organize not only their time but also information, and they anticipate the need to recall what they learn. A common strategy was the physical organizing of their work to better understand what they were learning. One student explained,

> I make sure I have different notebooks for different subjects and mark them clearly so I don't have to search in the morning and get lost. I have folders for everything, you know, [and] make sure I have my syllabus.

This example demonstrates that students recognize the importance of organization, even at the level of organizing their papers and notes. Additionally, the student signals the importance of the course syllabus, a document that is inherently designed to organize the course content to help students visually and conceptually map out what they will learn.

LH students also reflected on their planning activities, more specifically noting that planning meant the need to retrieve information in an efficient and organized manner for future use. Planning, for example, in reviewing course materials prior to class, helps students to organize information for later recall. One student noted,

> So I don't necessarily study the textbook in depth, but by reading the chapters, I get a sense of where the lecture's probably going to be going. So I'm prepared and I have some exposure to the topics.

Prior preparation enables students to organize information in the larger context. Furthermore, when students know that future assignments have specific associated tasks, they are better able to prepare themselves for those tasks (i.e., plan ahead). For example, one student explained that she characterized her successful learning habit as having multiple types of preparation for different courses. She explained,

> Definitely each class or course has a different type of preparation you have to do for it. I don't like taking laptops for bio courses only because the professor likes drawing a lot of diagrams and different charts and stuff. And it takes up a lot of time when you're trying to insert a diagram and do different things like that on the laptop. Rather [you should be] writing it down and trying to listen to what he's saying. Otherwise, you're losing a lot of information. And then I have my courses for . . . a public health education student. So a lot of that stuff, a lot of the professors in that major like to [use] PowerPoints. So I find it kind of convenient to take a laptop because they usually will post the slides up online or something. So it's easier for me to follow while they're on their slides. I could type some notes in, different things like that.

The use of exams as a form of assessment allows students to evaluate their state of knowledge and anticipate tasks required for academic success. Students' awareness that they will be required to recall information on a particular day allows them to plan and organize their studying around those particular days (also another form of time management). One student tried to cover all possibilities:

> So what I do is, for my tests, I'll study at home in the quiet and then I'll study in the cafeteria where it's loud—and I'll study with music so that way, I have

all the different kinds of environments so that if my class is quiet or it's loud or there's noise, like, I'm ready to take the test in every way.

This example also demonstrates that some successful students recognize their environment as an important factor in their ability to succeed. Different environments differentially prepare students. A prime example of how students assess the practices that help them learn is their intentional preparation in multiple types of environments to prepare for all contingencies on exam day.

Additional Learning Strategies

A variety of other behaviors and techniques—in addition to time management, planning, and organizing—are noted as contributing to academic success. Our LH students were asked to discuss strategies they were using inside or outside classrooms to complete assignments/projects and study for exams, and then to compare these strategies with those they used in high school (for freshmen) or when they first entered CSUN (for juniors). They identified many simple study techniques, such as taking and rewriting notes, using flash cards, and reading textbooks. However, as we examined the responses more closely, it was apparent that some students displayed metacognition with respect to *why* one technique produced better outcomes than another did. Thematic examples of metacognitive behaviors students identified for success are discussed below.

Students overwhelmingly reported that taking notes in class on lecture materials and outside of class on assigned readings was critical to their success. One student said, "I take a lot of notes in class . . . because I can remember better when I'm actually writing things down." Another elaborated,

> That is when I really began to understand the whole concept of not reading passively, but actively. And that really helped me internalize everything . . . because I would write it down in my own words.

These students were describing active learning, in which they not only listen or read information but also actively think, summarize, evaluate, and transcribe that information as it is received. The conversion of information into "their own words" further demonstrates comprehension, even if students do not specifically recognize this metacognitive aspect. One student described an important self-regulation learning habit: "I find that if I write something down, I remember it really well. I write it by hand—'cause if I write on the computer, it doesn't sink in as well [as] when you're writing by hand." And another said,

Note-taking does a lot of help because you go over the notes, and it's not [what] somebody else has wrote, it's something you have wrote. . . . So when you're going over it and you're reviewing it, things are clicking in your memory.

Many students "know" that writing information down helps when retrieval of that information is required later. However, whether students are aware that this behavior uses the kinesthetic process of writing to stimulate activity in cerebellar cells, making brain connections that allow for easier retrieval at a later date (Sweller 1994), is doubtful. But one student semi-articulated it as "because when you write things by hand, it connects somehow, you know, with your mind."

Successful students also reported using what they considered their "optimal times" of the day for learning. Some reported being better able to study/ learn in the morning (or evening) and scheduled their classes accordingly. Most CSUN students juggle full academic schedules with heavy workloads to afford college and fulfill family obligations, so optimal "time to study" may not be easily arranged. However, the ability to identify optimal learning times and schedule accordingly increases the likelihood those students will achieve their academic goals. One student reported, "I'm not a night person at all. After 8:00 p.m., my mind shuts off, and nothing sticks anymore." Another reported scheduling 8:00 a.m. classes as a freshman and then determining over time that going to work first and then attending school was ideal for his learning process. A third strategy was to switch from early classes to classes later in the day to allow time in the morning to do homework. One student explained, "Come here early, and I have like two hours to do my homework in the morning. . . . And it helps me focus better. And then I start classes."

These students not only engage in time management but also reflect on what works for them and adjust their strategies accordingly. A key lesson for them is to become aware that planning their optimal study/work schedules is an important aspect of the learning process.

Students indicated the importance to success of practicing what they learn, through either repetition or working practice problems, depending on the discipline. In order to improve writing skills, one student said that getting ideas down on paper with "free writing" was the best way to start a written exercise. The student described "free writing" as, "I go onto the computer and I just start typing and it's random and then I can take my thoughts and rearrange them into paragraphs."

One key explanation for why students believe that strategies such as brainstorming and free writing improve their achievement has to do with self-efficacy. According to Barry Zimmerman and Albert Bandura (1994), students develop their writing skills because as they practice and adopt learning strategies, they are simultaneously building self-efficacy perceptions of their writing skills. Furthermore, the authors assert that such self-efficacy, coupled with motivation, yields greater academic achievement. Another student exemplified the interaction effects of self-efficacy and learning strategies:

> It's a lot of practice. It's a little bit of terms and a little bit of the concepts. Like, for essays, preparing for in-class essays—if you just get your own style, if you understand your style of how you like to write, it'll save you from being nervous in class.

Another student noted that doing practice problems allowed for engagement with the material and warming up to the cognitive effort required for the task. A third described his process as follows: "They have a lot of problems online with solutions. So just go and practice those so I can get the concept." Meanwhile, a fourth found her professor's online resources useful to developing mastery. She explained, "He has previous tests from previous semesters online, so I go back and I do all of those."

The deeper understanding of how these practices improve performance on exams and assignments was not discussed, but students clearly state that practice was an important component of their success. As Schunk and Zimmerman (1998) explain, self-regulation takes learning about the practices and their benefits and then wanting to implement these practices and reaping the positive outcomes of the successful strategies.

And, finally, a clear example of how metacognition interacts with motivation to learn is exhibited in one student's response:

> I think it all does begin with how you were in school previous to college because if you just were never set up in a situation where you enjoyed doing your schoolwork or wanted to try to get through it with the best of your ability, it's hard to change that and flip to the other side of the coin. Mostly I try and would, say, find a subject you really enjoy. That way, obviously, I prefer one film book over another, but it all comes back to something I'm really passionate about. I constantly have to remind myself on days when I'm like, oh, "I don't want to read this," or "I don't want to watch this thing for this class." Like, no, this is what you want to do. This is what you care about. Why did you choose this major in the first place?

Social Support to Promote Self-Regulation

Asked to reflect upon their learning and to attribute a locus of their success, students sometimes mentioned their instructors. Faculty can be instrumental in promoting or hindering self-regulation in learning. When analyzing interview excerpts that discussed self-direction in learning and faculty, several themes emerged. One common theme centered on the simple realization that seeking faculty support is dramatically helpful. Following reflection on what they learned from their freshman to junior years, students noted that learning could be augmented and improved if they sought help from their professors: "I realized it was just so much easier to go to the professor and talk about problems, or see what I missed, or what I could do better for studying habits or to study better." Another student reported improvement in seeking help from the faculty over time:

And I just felt like okay, I can relax and be honest [and say] I really don't understand this and that. [And if] I have an extra maybe five minutes or ten minutes after class where I have to go into office hours, I'll go in and do it real quick, run over there. So I think I've come a long way as far as being able to communicate with the professor when I need help.

While extra instructor contact can help learning, students also revealed the ease with which the opposite dynamic can quickly squelch those seeking out support. One student recalled a highly negative experience visiting an instructor during office hours, despite her clarity that she needed help. She noted, "I mean, at least for this professor she wasn't very helpful, just not very pleasant. So I kind of felt dumb, although I knew that I needed help. So that was very difficult." While this might exemplify a personality or demeanor that hinders students from seeking contact, other faculty members use pedagogical strategies to encourage habits of self-regulation. Several students mentioned they had been in classes where the instructor mandated attending office hours. One shared how this faculty strategy had a lasting impact on self-discipline to use social support, even when students don't think they need it. She said,

She made sure we were on the subject and studying by requiring that we go in for office hours and then we also had homework to do. So that's what started what I do now. The fact [is] that I do have to study, and I get in the habit of going to tutoring as well, even if I feel like I don't need it.

Carol Dweck and Allison Master (2009) examined the environmental factors, such as social support, on persistence and achievement. They assert that providing feedback about performance and guidance on metacognitive processes positively influences student effort and persistence with difficult tasks. Monique Boekaerts (2009) explores social support as a mechanism to explain the different values student ascribe to academic achievement goals. She indicates that social relationships and personal goals of interaction with others motivate students and provide an additional source of energy for students to strive to learn. A common example of a learning activity that serves as a driver for students' learning habits is group work. A student describes how group associations in class serve as an additional mechanism:

> The first thing to do is find someone in your class to make—at least two people to be friends with, and then have a study partner where you could trade notes and trade information. And then if you miss the class, you can ask what you missed. Always talk to the professor.

CONCLUSIONS AND RECOMMENDATIONS

It is clear from our analysis of interviews that LH students engage in self-regulating behaviors and that they are aware of what works for them. They adjust their behaviors based on context and experience. They reveal a "desire to learn, intrinsic motivation and responsibility for their learning."

In the course of this project, we gained a better understanding of what LH students think makes them good learners. We noted that although they come from diverse backgrounds, they shared similar stories of their metacognitive process, even when they did not label it as such. They recognized the importance of time management, a particularly significant issue for students who often work full-time in addition to attending school. Students explained how they planned on completing assignments, studying for tests, and even preparing for class. They knew what they needed to do and were motivated to do what was necessary for their own success.

LH students recognize the value of note-taking and commented that by taking notes and rephrasing readings in their own words, they were better able to remember information. Without analyzing why this works, they "know" it helps. Many students commented on how practice promoted their learning. Practicing problems, for example, before a test aided students' ability to do well. Finally, students become aware of how social support enhances their learning at the university. Visiting faculty members during office hours becomes more comfortable as students realize the many advantages in talking to instructors outside of class.

How can the faculty capitalize on students' ability to use self-regulated behaviors? These successful students can suggest strategies for both the faculty and other students. Students appreciate an organized course with specific assignments and dates for completion. Faculty can motivate students to think about their time management. Visiting during office hours can be enthusiastically encouraged and even mandated. By inviting students to office hours, instructors encourage those too intimidated or reluctant to seek help. Once they have a positive experience, they may reflect and visit other faculty.

Table 11.1. The strategies of "good learners" in the eyes of the LH students

	Specific Strategies Identified by Students
Time Management	• Maintaining a "busy" schedule • Avoiding procrastination • Optimal scheduling
Planning and Organizing	• Different color notebooks and folders • Planning how to collect information based on the course (handwriting versus typing) • Understanding in different environments in order to be prepared for all situations
Skills/Strategies	• Note-taking, particularly by hand • Identifying optimal times for studying (overlaps with time management) • Practice and repetition
Faculty Support	

If, as we have come to believe, one of the most significant results of the Learning Habits Project is the value of students' thinking about their learning, then that should be an important focus of how to proceed with what we have learned. All students should be encouraged to engage in self-reflection as part of their learning experience.

NOTE

1. Five subgroups make up the larger set of students stemming from traditionally underserved backgrounds: American Indians, Pacific Islanders, African Americans, Latina/o, and multirace. Others are referred to as stemming from better-served backgrounds.

REFERENCES

Alexander, Patricia A. 2013. "Calibration: What Is It and Why It Matters? An Introduction to the Special Issue on Calibrating Calibration." *Learning and Instruction* 24: 1–3. doi:10.1016/j.learninstruc.2012.10.003.

Boekaerts, Monique. 2009. "Goal-Directed Behavior in the Classroom." In *Handbook of Motivation at School*, edited by Kathryn R. Wentzel and Allan Wigfield, 105–22. New York: Routledge.

Brock, Sabra, Ionut Florescu, and Leizer Teran. 1992. "Tools for Change: An Examination of Transformative Learning and Its Precursor Steps in Undergraduate Students." *ISRN Education* 2012: 1–5.

Brockett, Ralph G., and Roger Hiemstra. 1991. "A Conceptual Framework for Understanding Self-Direction in Adult Learning." In *Self-Direction in Adult Learning: Perspectives on Theory, Research, and Practice*. London: Routledge.

Dinsmore, Daniel L., and Meghan M. Parkinson. 2013. "What Are Confidence Judgments Made Of? Students' Explanations for Their Confidence Ratings and What That Means for Calibration." *Learning and Instruction* 24: 4–14. doi: 10.1016/j .learninstruc.2012.06.001.

Dweck, Carol S., and Allison Master. 2009. "Self-Theories and Motivation: Students' Beliefs about Intelligence." In *Handbook of Motivation at School*, edited by Kathryn R. Wentzel and Allan Wigfield, 123–41. New York: Routledge.

Knowles, Malcolm S. 1975. *Self-Directed Learning: A Guide for Learners and Teachers*. New York: Associate Press.

Kroll, Mark D., and Michael L. Ford. 1992. "The Illusion of Knowing, Error Detection, and Motivational Orientations." *Contemporary Educational Psychology* 17: 371–78. doi: 10.1016/0361-r76X(92)90075-A.

Nilson, Linda B. 2013. *Creating Self-Regulated Learners: Strategies to Strengthen Students? Self-Awareness and Learning Skills*. Sterling, VA: Stylus.

Saks, Katrin, and Ali Leijin. 2014. "Distinguishing Self-Directed and Self-Regulated Learning and Measuring Them in the E-Learning Context." *Procedia—Social and Behavioral Sciences* 112: 190–98.

Schoenfeld, Alan H., ed. 1987. *What's All the Fuss about Metacognition?* Hillsdale, NJ: Erlbaum.

Schunk, Dale H., and Barry J. Zimmerman, eds. 1998. *Self-Regulated Learning: From Teaching to Self-Reflective Practice*. New York: Guilford.

Sweller, John. 1994. "Cognitive Load Theory, Learning Difficulty, and Instructional Design." *Learning and Instruction* 4: 295–312.

Winne, Philip H. 2004. "Students' Calibration of Knowledge and Learning Processes: Implications for Designing Powerful Software Learning Environments." *International Journal of Educational Research* 41 (6): 466–88. doi: 10.1016/j .ijer.2005.08.012.

Zimmerman, Barry J. 1990. "Self-Regulated Learning and Academic Achievement: An Overview. *Educational Psychologist* 25: 3–17.

———. 2000. "Self-Efficacy: An Essential Motive to Learn." *Contemporary Educational Psychology* 25: 82–91. doi: 10.1006/ceps.1999.1016.

Zimmerman, Barry J., and Albert Bandura. 1994. "Impact of Self-Regulatory Influences on Writing Course Attainment." *American Educational Research Journal* 31: 845–62.

Zimmerman, Barry J., and Dale H. Schunk. 2011. "Self-Regulated Learning and Performance: An Introduction and an Overview." In *Handbook of Self-Regulation of Learning and Performance*, edited by Barry J. Zimmerman and Dale H. Schunk, 1–12. New York: Taylor & Francis.

12

Encouraging Students to Be Thoughtful about Their Learning

Bettina J. Huber

Examination in the second chapter of the persistence and graduation rates of learning habits (LH) students indicates they were disproportionately likely to complete college. This was evident in two regards. First, LH students are more likely than similarly qualified freshman entrants to persist to graduation. Second, typical differences in the persistence of students from traditionally underserved and better-served backgrounds are attenuated among the LH students.[1]

To a large degree, LH students performed so exceptionally well in college because overall they entered better prepared than students who could have joined the project but, for various reasons, did not. However, the data also suggested that aspects of the LH experience facilitated participants' persistence to graduation. The aim of this chapter is to highlight key project features likely to have played a role in fostering such success by locating students' reports of how they benefited from participation within the context of recent advances in the neuroscience of the brain. Although many said that the early registration provided by the project was helpful, even more pointed to the thoughtfulness about learning that project participation fostered. This last is likely a result of the repeated need to respond to end-of-term questions requiring students to describe key features of those just-completed courses that made them particularly good learning experiences.

RECENT ADVANCES IN NEUROSCIENCE

Neuroscientific research undertaken during the past 30 years has revolutionized our understanding of how the brain functions. The new research suggests that the brain "learns" by constructing increasingly complex neural pathways and webs that connect its specialized areas (cf. Zull 2002, 91ff). Since neurons repeatedly fire for different purposes, developing stable links between them takes time, so lasting learning requires experimentation and repeated practice with the knowledge or skills being mastered. By the same token, once established, people tend to be resistant to altering modes of learning encoded in neural pathways, whose creation required significant effort and persistence.

How effectively neural pathways function depends, in part, on the chemicals surrounding the neurons in question. Bodily functions and reactions play a key role in determining chemical levels in the brain. These bodily functions and reactions, in turn, are set in motion by perceived signals from the surrounding environment (cf. Zull 2002; Zeki 1993). For example, abnormal amounts of a chemical (cortisol) produced by moderate levels of stress will, if present for extended periods, adversely affect the neural circuits involved in learning and memory. Such a situation is particularly destructive for young children (National Scientific Council on the Developing Child 2005). In short, the prevailing atmosphere in diverse social settings, including the college classroom, is key to students' willingness and ability to acquire new knowledge and skills.

One of the most striking things revealed by recent neuroscientific research concerns the plasticity of the brain. Contrary to long-standing belief, the brain does not attain its final form during childhood but continues to mature until well into our thirties, when our abstract capacities are fully formed. More than that, the brain is endlessly mutable: regardless of age, it remains capable of forming new neural connections of great complexity, provided we continue to attempt to master new skills or knowledge. And if the environment becomes more supportive, the brain is often able to overcome early childhood deficits, such as exposure to chronic stress.

At the most basic level, neural pathways are formed to ensure human survival, our concern with which is centered in the area of the brain regulating emotion. Since our feelings are tied to fundamental notions of survival, the motivation to master new things rests on their perceived relationship to our immediate well-being (Zull 2002, 238ff). This is as true of newly enrolled college students facing a strange environment as it is of newborn babies trying to make sense of their nurseries. In the case of the former, the challenge for instructors is not to motivate students to learn in the abstract—our need to survive ensures that—but to find ways of drawing them into the subject at hand by making them feel they have a stake in it. This means relating the subject, no matter how distantly, to their survival.

As new insights about brain function began to be widely disseminated during the early 2000s, a lively debate began about their implications for both cognitive science and learning within educational institutions, be they pre-K or postgraduate. Scholarly conferences featured presentations about the implications of the discoveries, while scholarly journals of all stripes published articles (e.g., Halpern and Hakel 2003, 36). In 2007, a new journal titled *Mind, Brain, and Education* appeared to champion the intersection of neuroscientific insights and improved educational practice (Fischer 2009).

As research has flourished during recent years, along with articles about means of strengthening college-level teaching and learning, new "metacognitive" principles—or new ways of thinking about thinking—have emerged. These have generally been directed at providing instructors with better means of conveying new knowledge to their students (e.g., Fischer and Rose 2001; Immordino-Yang 2011). A more direct approach has also been in evidence, as courses designed to convey a sense of the new understandings of brain function have sprung up at colleges and universities. At California State University, Northridge (CSUN), for example, several upper-division courses in cognitive psychology and neuroscience have been offered for a number of years. Elsewhere, well over 100 institutions now offer neuroscience majors, according to a listing on the College Board's website.[2]

Although these courses are designed to convey an overview of rapidly evolving fields, students taking courses in neuroscience and related fields undoubtedly become aware of the implications for their own study habits. Still, students who benefit in this manner represent a small portion of those enrolled in any college or university. Thus, the experience of the Learning Habits Project in fostering what might be labeled a metacognitive perspective on learning among its participants is noteworthy, given the approach's potential for widespread replication. As the remainder of this chapter documents, participating students became more thoughtful about their learning through being required to respond to several questions repeatedly posed during the end-of-term surveys.

STUDENT VIEWS OF PROJECT BENEFITS

A two-part question posed to learning habits students just prior to graduation asked them how participation in the project affected their college experience:

1. Has your participation in the Learning Habits Project made any difference in your experience here at CSUN? For example, has it affected the time it has taken you to obtain your degree?
2. Which, if any, aspects of your periodic face-to-face interviews have been helpful to you?

Table 12.1 summarizes responses to these questions that dealt with students' perceptions of how project participation contributed to their college success. As is evident from the last row of the table, the number of responses to the above questions is considerably smaller than was the case for interview questions posed during the freshman and sophomore years. The primary reason for this drop in response is that one of the key incentives for project participation—early or priority registration in the next like term—fell by the wayside as students approached graduation.[3] According to the top row of table 12.1, just over half of the respondents said that the early registration provided by LH was a plus, frequently because it allowed timely graduation. As students commented,

> I think that one of the big things with the learning [habits] project is you get early registration. And every time I was registering for classes, I was so thankful that I had that, because without early registration, I don't know if I would have been able to graduate in four years, just because getting into classes is so challenging. . . . And so being able to get into those classes gave me even more motivation to do well, because I knew that I was in the select few that were able to get into that class.

> Oh, [the Learning Habits Project] has been so helpful. I mean, selfishly it was so helpful. I wouldn't have been able to graduate in four years if I didn't have priority registration. And that was a huge incentive.

> Well first of all, you guys gave me priority registration, so that was really beneficial. I don't know if people mention that, but that made a huge difference in my learning because I got to pick the classes that I wanted to take before my other classmates, so I didn't fall behind, so I was really lucky in that way. And I know because my sister didn't have priority registration, and she got the worst classes, and she's behind a year.

Unfortunately, early registration is a nonreplicable benefit, since if everyone has it, no one has it. Nonetheless, students' appreciation of this benefit points to the importance, for timely graduation in particular, of offering sufficient course sections to meet the needs of all students. And doing so probably requires not just offering the needed sections but also offering them at times that students find appealing.

In addition to early/priority registration, another benefit stood out in students' eyes: just over three-fifths noted that project participation fostered reflection and self-awareness, most particularly by providing insight into their own strengths, weaknesses, and study habits (see II.A. in table 12.1). The following provide a flavor of the responses:

Table 12.1. Student views of how participation in the Learning Habits Project affected their college experiences (senior interviews)

		Percent	(Number of Responses)
I.	Provided Early Registration	52.0	(191)
	I.A. *Allowed students to graduate on time*	23.2	(85)
	I.B. *Afforded more flexible schedule (with courses, employment, etc.)*	7.1	(26)
	I.C. *Other*	24.0	(88)
II.	Learning Habits fostered reflection and self-awareness	63.2	(232)
	II.A. *Afforded insight into personal strengths, weaknesses, habits*	56.4	(207)
	II.A.1. *Writing Skills*	5.4	(20)
	II.A.2. *Other*	48.2	(177)
	II.B. *Afforded insight into the effectiveness of professor's teaching style*	7.9	(29)
	II.C. *Generated expressions of gratitude, appreciation*	2.5	(9)
	II.D. *Other*	6.0	(22)
III.	Learning Habits created opportunities for involvement	20.2	(74)
	III.A. *Students felt they were part of the CSUN community*	3.3	(12)
	III.B. *Provided an opportunity to help others (e.g., students felt empowered)*	15.8	(58)
	III.B.1. *Current students (via tutoring, mentoring)*	2.7	(10)
	III.B.2. *Future students (via project publications, conferences, siblings)*	7.4	(27)
	III.B.3. *Other*	3.8	(14)
	III.C. *Other*	1.6	(6)
IV.	Learning Habits interviews allowed for personal connections	17.2	(63)
	IV.A. *Students felt appreciated, valued*	4.4	(16)
	IV.B. *Appreciated informality of interviews*	7.6	(28)
	IV.C. *Improved self-confidence*	3.8	(14)
	IV.D. *Other*	3.5	(13)
V.	Other	10.6	(39)
	Senior Excerpts Created (N for percent)		(367)
	Senior Interviewees		329
	Excerpts per Interview		1.12

I feel like after the first interview I started thinking about what I do more, and that maybe even helped me understand better what I should be doing. I guess it's helpful just to reflect on things, you know, to take the time to think, "Yeah, that did help me." Or, "I should do more of this or whatever."

I think for me, it makes you think more definitely about how you learn. Some of the questions make you think. . . . Like how much do the syllabi really matter to you? But it's not until someone poses those questions to you that you realize, okay, well this works for me, this doesn't work for me, and this is what I want. So I think ideally it's helped me in thinking what have I gotten, what haven't I gotten, and I think it would really help me in graduate school.

I think that, you know, throughout my classes I don't really think about the Learning Habits Project, but at the end of every semester, we have a survey that we have to fill out with some questions, and it helps to reflect on my classes and to really be able to think about what strategies I have used and what has been helpful for me. And to think about what I wished people had told me. So I do appreciate that time of reflection. It's kind of cathartic at the end of the semester. . . . It's just a way to kind of put everything into perspective and see how you're progressing.

[The project] does help me, kind of, question what I have learned in the classes before, with the surveys at the end where it's like well, what class do you feel you learned the most in. And, I think, without those questions . . . it would just, kind of, fly by where it's just like, oh yeah, those were just classes, instead of: I actually learned something in these classes, here's what I learned, and here's the professor I should be thanking, kind of thing. So it's helped me better appreciate what I've had here.

I liked taking the surveys because it made me reflect on the past semester. . . . I got to really talk about the professors that I really liked. And I could pinpoint exactly what they did and why I liked it. And so I figured out, like, things about myself. Like, oh, I love it when a professor, like, teaches this way, because I pick up things more easily.

I feel like it's been a good reflective journal that I should keep in my own room. . . . It would kind of help me think about, okay, who really made an impact on me in terms of the professors, and how did it kind of sculpt how I see things and how I can move forward. I mean, it was significant, even though it was like a small reminder or something, it pushed me to write that little summary.

In addition, two other project benefits were mentioned by close to one-fifth of the respondents. The first reflected on the opportunities for involvement that participation provided, with an emphasis on the opportunity to help others (see III.A. in table 12.1):

I mean in the back of my mind it was always nice to know that I was probably helping out the school or helping out somebody a lot.

So I know that . . . a lot of information I'm giving you, where it's maybe different studying strategies, might be used to help incoming freshmen or for, you know, maybe things that could be tips for other students so they could be successful. So I feel that's why I've always felt good about participating.

[The project] makes you feel good that people want to study how you work, and it kind of makes it worth it. Going through all the hard work that I put in trying so hard. And then people appreciate it. They want to know how I do it. And I think that's also been a huge part of it, knowing that I'm not only doing this for myself. I'm doing it for the school and this program and trying to help people that are coming in. So I think it's been a mutually beneficial experience, and I'm so glad I was a part of it.

The last benefit mentioned with some frequency involved the opportunity for interpersonal connections that project participation provided. Here, the informal interchange that characterized the LH interviews proved key (see IV.B. in table 12.1), as is evident from the following responses:

The face-to-face [interview], I think, was definitely something to look forward to, because you feel like you're getting some true feedback. You know? As in the happy expressions on your face when I say funny things or things that are important to you that you know, that you respond to. That's been really nice.

I mean, there is not much that I have done, other than come in for interviews. I mean it's nice to, you know, talk about these things. So I'd say it's like a stress reliever, like, kind of like a therapy session. . . . I think the best aspect of the program are these interviews, because you actually hear what the students have to say on a personal level, how they feel, you know, their education, . . . what their plans are for the future. . . . So I would say the interviews are the best benefit for the research.

You can get priority registration with other things, but you guys actually call us for interviews. . . . So it's cool that you guys want to like, you know, communicate and hear our feedback.

Table 12.2 shows differences in response for three key background characteristics: gender, racial and ethnic background, and first-generation status. The most striking thing about the table is the absence of subgroup variation. Across the board, the majority of respondents in each subgroup mention the two key benefits of LH participation: greater reflection and self-awareness about learning and the advantages provided by early registration. Further, a fifth in each subgroup consistently comment that the project provided opportunities for involvement.

Some modest variation is evident among participants commenting on how project participation fostered personal connections. Here, first-generation status is the differentiating factor, albeit in an unusual fashion. Participants whose parents have some college education, who usually fall in between the other two subgroups, are the distinct ones. They are less likely than other respondents to note that participation in LH had interpersonal benefits, largely because none said that participation made them feel valued or appreciated.[4]

Table 12.2. Student views of how participation in the Learning Habits Project affected their college experiences by selected background characteristics

	Gender		Racial Grouping		Parental Education		
	Women	Men	Traditionally Underserved	Better Served	High school or less: both parents	Some college: one or both	Four-year degree: one or both
I. Provided Early Registration	50.6	55.3	50.8	52.3	52.9	52.9	52.6
I.A. Allowed students to graduate on time	22.9	23.7	22.2	23.2	22.1	21.8	25.3
I.B. Afforded more flexible schedule (with courses, employment, etc.)	5.1	11.4	7.9	6.3	13.2	3.4	6.7
II. Learning Habits fostered reflection and self-awareness	62.8	64.0	65.1	62.0	61.8	59.8	66.0
II.A. Afforded insight into personal strengths, weaknesses, habits	55.7	57.9	57.1	55.7	50.0	54.0	59.3
II.B. Afforded insight into the effectiveness of professor's teaching style	7.1	9.6	10.3	6.8	11.8	8.0	7.2
III. Learning Habits created opportunities for involvement	20.6	19.3	20.6	20.3	22.1	21.8	18.0
III.A. Students felt they were part of the CSUN community	2.8	4.4	4.0	3.0	5.9	3.4	2.6
III.B. Provided an opportunity to help others (e.g., students felt empowered)	15.8	15.8	16.7	15.6	17.6	17.2	13.4
IV. Learning Habits interviews allowed for personal connections	16.2	19.3	19.8	16.0	22.1	12.6	16.5
IV.A. Students felt appreciated, valued	4.0	5.3	4.8	4.2	7.4	0.0	5.7
IV.B. Appreciated informality of interviews	7.5	7.9	6.3	8.4	7.4	6.9	7.7
IV.C. Improved self-confidence	4.0	3.5	5.6	3.0	7.4	2.3	2.6
V. Other	12.6	6.1	10.3	11.0	11.8	8.0	10.3
Senior Excerpts Created (N for percent)	(253)	(114)	(126)	(237)	(68)	(87)	(194)
Senior Interviewees	228	100	114	210	63	78	170
Excerpts per Interview	1.11	1.14	1.11	1.13	1.08	1.12	1.14

Among the small number of other respondents who did mention feeling appreciated, the following responses are typical.

> [The Learning Habits Project] makes you feel good that people want to study how you work, and it kind of makes it worth it. Going through all the hard work that I put in trying so hard. And then people appreciate it. They want to know how I do it.

> The interviews actually helped my self-esteem because like someone is willing to talk to me about how I study.

HOW THE LEARNING HABITS PROJECT FOSTERED THOUGHTFULNESS ABOUT LEARNING

A key benefit of LH participation—the opportunity to reflect upon both one's own and one's instructors' approaches to learning—was not purposefully built into the project, unlike priority registration, which was. Most likely, however, it was achieved through the small set of questions posed in every end-of-term survey:

1. Thinking back on the courses you took in [term], was there one in which you learned a great deal more than in the other courses you took? [If not, respondents were told to skip the next question.]
2. What was it about this course that made it such a good learning experience for you? Please be as specific as possible in responding, and mention all relevant aspects of the course in question (e.g., its structure and organization, your interest in its content, your fellow students, the instructor's style, the exercises required in class or as homework, etc.).
3. In the courses you attempted this past term (other than the one mentioned above), were there techniques, exercises, or approaches that your instructors used in one or more that made a significant contribution to your learning? [If not, respondents were told to skip the next question.]
4. If yes, please describe the techniques or exercises that were so helpful. (If you covered one or more of these in your response to question 2 above, confine your response here to helpful techniques in the other courses you took this past term.)

Through time, students became familiar with these questions and expected to have to answer them repeatedly. The questions served to focus their attention on the issues addressed. That is, they encouraged students to develop a metacognitive perspective on their learning. Or, as they put it, to become more reflective and self-aware.

The LH approach to encouraging thoughtfulness about student learning differs from that employed elsewhere. As preceding discussion has indicated, fostering a metacognitive perspective generally involves one extended discussion, often in an advanced course, of the implications for learning of recent decades' fundamentally new understanding of brain function. In contrast, our approach involved repeated short exercises designed to make students more thoughtful about their learning. Since data reviewed here suggest that these exercises had the desired effect, devising means of implementing them in more common university venues should prove fruitful.

Just how one might induce similar thoughtfulness in all undergraduates by means other than involving them in a multiyear research project is not self-evident. One possibility would be to require all students to respond to the questions prior to being able to access their end-of-term grades. Another possibility is to have the questions posed and discussed repeatedly in a set of classes or gatherings. Possible candidates include the first session of each semester's classes in a student's major, although this would require the participation of a wide range of faculty. Another possibility would be to mount repeated face-to-face discussions within the context of special university programs such as the Educational Opportunity Program (EOP), which sponsors regular meetings with the same set of students.

Another possibility, probably only feasible in small majors, is to invite students to participate in periodic face-to-face interviews focusing on the value of the recent courses they have completed in the major. Such an approach has the added advantage of corresponding nicely with the increased emphasis on assessment, especially as part of departmental accreditation and program review. Ideally, such face-to-face conversations would take place at the completion of a gateway course in the major and be repeated annually. In majors with many students, such an approach is not likely to be feasible. But the other options proposed above might be. As the following illustrate, such approaches are in keeping with the LH students' appreciation of the interview context.

It's also been really cool to, you know, to do these kind of interviews because, you know, hopefully what we're saying will be taken into consideration. Because we're not the minority. I'm sure a lot of people learn the way that we do.

Well, I can say that with the interviews, you guys always ask me about my study habits, and it's the only time I ever actually think about it. So, it's pretty much the only reflection time on studying habits and all that.

I think it's been the interaction. I know, at least in one previous interview, the interviewer recommended something she had done—making multiple tests for yourself and administering them as preparation. And I found that helpful. So I think it was fun both ways.

I think being able to tell someone, "This is what's going on, like this is the real deal" helps because you get to let someone know, someone who has the authority or the power to actually make a change to help other students, to help even the faculty improve their skills.

NOTES

1. Five subgroups make up the larger set of students stemming from traditionally underserved backgrounds: American Indians, Pacific Islanders, African Americans, Latina/o, and multirace. Others are referred to as stemming from better-served backgrounds.

2. Institutions offering such majors encompass a wide range, including American University, Baylor, Brown, Colgate, Duke, Earlham, Michigan State, Middlebury, Oberlin, Princeton, Texas Christian, Tulane, several University of California campuses, and Vassar (https://bigfuture.collegeboard.org/).

3. Some drop-off in response, of course, can be attributed to the fact that not all participating students graduated within six years. This is not the key factor, however, as is evident from the fact that the seniors interviewed constituted only 57 percent of the LH participants in the first three entry cohorts who graduated within six years (329 out of 580).

4. A similar pattern is evident for participants differing by Pell Grant status. Here the Pell Grant recipients are more likely than other respondents to note the interpersonal benefits of project participation (6 vs. 3 percent). This difference in response involves very few students, however, which is why the breakdown has not been included in table 12.2.

REFERENCES

Fischer, Kurt W. 2009. "Mind, Brain, and Education: Building a Scientific Groundwork for Learning and Teaching." *Mind, Brain, and Education* 3 (1): 3–16.

Fischer, Kurt W., and L. Todd Rose. 2001. "Webs of Skill: How Students Learn." *Educational Leadership* 59 (November): 6–12.

Halpern, Dianne E., and Milton D. Hakel. 2003. "Applying the Science of Learning to the University and Beyond." *Change* (July–August): 36–41.

Immordino-Yang, Mary Helen. 2011. "Implications of Affective and Social Neuroscience for Educational Theory." *Educational Philosophy and Theory* 43 (1): 98–103.

National Scientific Council on the Developing Child. 2005. "Excessive Stress Disrupts the Architecture of the Brain." Working Paper 3. http://www.developingchild.harvard.edu.

Zeki, Semir. 1993. *A Vision of the Brain*. Oxford, UK: Blackwell Scientific Publications.

Zull, James E. 2002. *The Art of Changing the Brain*. Sterling, VA: Stylus.

Part Five

CONCLUSIONS AND RECOMMENDATIONS

13

Conclusions and Recommendations

What Did You Learn? What Are You Going to Do About It?

As we were nearing the end of the Learning Habits Project and editing this book, one of the editors had lunch with an acquaintance, a generous donor to the university who has an abiding interest in higher education. Hearing a fairly detailed account of the project and the purpose of *Learning from the Learners*, she asked, "What did you learn? What are you gonna do about it?"

It made the editor stop and think. Sure, we know what the project was intended to do and we know what is discussed in each chapter. But we hadn't sat down to brainstorm about the edited volume's conclusions and recommendations. So, we did. Here is what we learned and what we're doing with the information.

WHAT WE LEARNED

To state the obvious, by listening to students we heard what they had to say. They had something valuable to tell us about how they learn, how they navigate higher education, and what techniques work best for them—whether the instructors' or their own, whether technological or traditional. Many studies of college students' learning are based on quantitative data, but their voices are not there. In this study, we not only look at quantitative data but also hear and evaluate the learners' reflections on their college experience.

We aren't the only ones who learned from conducting this study. What came as revelation to us was often revelation to them as well: the learning habits (LH) students repeatedly told us that thinking about their learning helped them to be successful, made them aware of what worked for them academically, and highlighted how to apply what they discovered about one class to others. We concluded that students can be reflective about their learning (metacognitive, if you will) if they are helped to do so. It may often be left to us as faculty members, support staff, and administrators to offer that help and do the guiding.

We learned that statistically, differences in persistence and attainment of degree are modest when we look at the demographics of gender, race, and ethnicity, as examined in part 2. Differences in familial background in higher education do make a difference, however not always in the way we expected to find. So, while students who have family members with some degree of higher education often have an edge in learning how to navigate the university setting, students whose parents had no higher education often had a different edge. As one of our authors noted in his chapter, "Parents with degrees may pass on critical knowledge sets or academic skills to their children. But other parents, perhaps with modest educational backgrounds, have given their children the gifts of grit, persistence, and determination, which often prove just as critical to succeeding in college."

Part 3 of this volume looks at issues around teaching and learning. One theme that comes through clearly is the impact on students of the atmosphere in the classroom and the climate for learning. For one, students thrive with faculty members who are passionate about their subject matter, who care about student success, and who demonstrate that caring. For example, one student spoke eloquently about an instructor who turned him onto a love for history, even though the student was an engineering major and remained so. Why? Because the instructor was passionate about history. Another student commented on his major professor's passion for business law and how it made him stick with the discipline even when it was a struggle.

A number of LH students noted that the instructor simply knowing their names made a difference in how they engaged with the class. "She was really relatable," said one young woman, seemingly a bit surprised. "She got to know her students. Like she actually learned most of our names." Students also reported especially liking faculty members with a sense of humor; who not only were available during office hours but also encouraged students to come in, even just to chat; who literally kept their office doors open; and who made such visits a course requirement.

Project students had lots to say about specific teaching and learning techniques, ranging from the use of technology to small-group work and from course organization to structure. Students love technology—if it's used correctly and thoughtfully. As a result, technology (discussed in chapters 8 and 9) came in for the most praise and criticism, not only for the type of technology used by faculty, but also for how well individual instructors integrate it. For example, students both loved and hated the use of PowerPoint, saving special criticism for faculty members who read the PowerPoints to them in class. Many students appreciated faculty members who e-mailed or posted the next day's PowerPoint or webnotes before class, but others thought it encouraged skipping class and led to boredom if you attended. Here is one student's experience:

> Well, I'd say that right now for my philosophy class I just love the class. And before he would just like [be] spontaneous, so he'd have an idea what he wants to talk about . . . and he'd make scenarios [and we would talk]. . . . And not so long ago he started using PowerPoints and I found myself—I don't learn well with PowerPoints. . . . And he even asked us to give feedback on that as well. And I'm like, "I can't focus with those PowerPoints," and he heard that from a lot of students because we all talked about how before he's made us interact with him and we'd argue back, have valid points and stuff. And he thought he might even go back to it because, like, more people prefer him talking than just going from a PowerPoint.

Among techniques and approaches particularly relevant to students were those used by the faculty to address students' inability to read discipline-specific texts. As cited in chapter 6, one professor reported student "amazement" when she told them that she often had to read an academic article—even one in her own discipline—more than once before she could understand it fully. Her modeling of her own behavior made students more willing to engage in this difficult reading rather than simply give up and skip the article. Other approaches cited by students as valuable include faculty members who create context by making the purpose and importance of the reading assignment clear, and faculty members who create reading guides for approaching difficult texts. Clearly articulated writing prompts also result in better writing (chapter 7).

For the most part, students were positive about group work, especially when it took place in the classroom. They valued the interaction with other students. Asked what skills would help him become a good dentist, one student replied,

> I have a speech class where there is a lot of interaction and group work and things like that, and some of my other classes have that too . . . like the lab work I have in the chemistry and biophysics labs; it is a group which is more hands on and group-working with someone.

Students generally praised faculty members who include small-group activities in class but also found some limitations. "And when everyone's involved and engaged, it's good, but then when you don't have everyone who's involved and people are kind of, you know, making it difficult, then that's when it's not so fun."

It appears that group work can contribute to classroom climate and enhance learning, especially when professors establish ground rules and all students buy into the process:

> So it really helps when we get in a circle. We get to critique their work. And it's really enlightening because we make sure we're polite and we make sure we respect the people. The teacher makes it very clear, like, we don't want to have anyone putting hate on someone's work.

Finally, students were appreciative of faculty members who were organized, whether or not the instructor used technology (PowerPoint and webnotes) or more traditional teaching tools. Students agreed on one point: the better organized the instructor is, the more the students get from the course—with or without technology. And from a practical viewpoint, their grades improve:

> I've found that I do a lot better in classes that are more structured and organized, such as the teachers are organized and are clear about what they want, versus teachers who are just all over the place and you never know what makes them happy, and you never know how to get a good grade in their class.

Most LH students used multiple success tool kits and valued different faculty strategies as they applied the experience of one class to others. As many noted, students need to evaluate what matters to the instructor and respond accordingly. Said one, "I don't read the book, I read the teacher."

In part 4 we learned interesting aspects of students' attitudes toward seeking academic help; it became clear from the interviews and questionnaire responses that help-seeking behavior improved over time. As freshmen, LH students were reluctant, and even too frightened, to ask for help. Some saw seeking academic help as a failure and weakened self-confidence. However, once students gained the courage to visit a professor during office hours and had a positive experience, they became more comfortable in visiting other faculty members. Instructor attitudes are extremely important; if they encourage and even require office hour visits, students respond well. Faculty willingness to work with students outside regular class hours communicates that they care about the student's success, our participants said.

Students used a number of resources to get help, such as the learning resource center at California State University, Northridge (CSUN), the tutoring and academic support operation that received positive reviews. A less used and potentially enormous support opportunity is "virtual help seeking." For those who are employed and have limited time on campus, this was a good resource. More importantly, it also seemed to be less intimidating to many than face-to-face encounters. Students also found that peers were a great source of support, and, for many, forming study groups was a way to meet their academic and social needs.

The Learning Habits Project raised awareness for both student and faculty participants of how metacognition—thinking about one's own thinking and learning—adds to students' ability to learn in various contexts. We heard repeatedly in the junior/senior interviews that the act of reflecting on how they approach their courses made students more adept at modifying their learning habits or adding new ones. In effect, the requirement that they speak with us about their learning habits semester after semester added to their success tool kits. Whether they know it or not, successful students repeatedly evaluate what works for them and strategically adjust to various learning environments.

WHAT WE CAN DO WITH WHAT WE'VE LEARNED

Each of the project's researchers ends his or her chapter with a list of recommendations for applying what our LH students taught us, and we recommend that you turn back to those for their insights. However, in this final chapter, we discuss some of the overarching ideas generated by the research, several of which have been instituted at CSUN and many of which still await application.

Faculty Development

In the second decade of the 21st century, most institutions of higher education have some formal faculty development, whether situated in an office; offered through meetings, seminars, and retreats; or provided through a campus website. This book can serve as a resource for such faculty development operations. The purpose is to help faculty members, whether brand-new or longtime members of the educational community, by offering them new techniques for teaching and learning, or by reminding them of how to use "rusty" ones better. We know that many graduate schools nationwide have added some emphasis on good teaching to the more traditional focus on discipline-based research. However, new faculty members may still need help in the classroom. One example shines some light: we all know how to make/design/create a PowerPoint by now. But how many of us know how to use one so that students get the most out of it? Is e-mailing/posting each PowerPoint before class the best idea? How do you encourage students to attend class—assuming that you want them to—if they have a complete and full set of notes? Overall, we need to learn to use technology better. As our students repeatedly told us, using technology badly is worse than not using it at all. Not all students like it, and no student likes it badly done.

How do you evaluate what you are using, make changes, and reevaluate? By now, we are all familiar with assessment of student learning, and most of us apply it. But do we regularly assess our teaching tools and techniques?

Faculty development has a 25-year history at CSUN. But the Learning Habits Project has prompted the CSUN community to respond in a number of additional ways. The faculty, the staff, and students benefit as the research is disseminated. Our Office of Faculty Development and the newly established Office of Student Success Initiatives created a website devoted specifically to the work of the Reading Matters Initiative (chapter 6), offering model assignments and suggestions for helping students with complex readings. Plans are in place to share what we have learned about the use of technology, especially PowerPoint.

The faculty will be invited to learn more about how to design effective assignments and reading prompts, based on the research summarized in chapter 7. One of the most useful methods for disseminating the information from the Learning Habits Project is the CSUN "Teaching Toolkit," an online resource for faculty.

Faculty/staff participants in the LH seminars—some for the life of the project and others taking part for only a year or two—agreed that the process was both interesting and extremely valuable to their own teaching and work. They enjoyed not only interviewing students but also listening to their colleagues' comments. Given time to spend in a nonpolitical, interdisciplinary discussion about teaching and learning is a rare treat in a university setting, although it should not be. Faculty members reflected on their own responses to interviews, and as they shared their research, they evaluated their own teaching. One professor said, "My experience in the Learning Habits Project has also taught me to be less concerned about covering every little piece of the content. Rather, I like my students to learn strategies how to learn. If they miss a bit of Russian history because of that shifting emphasis, so be it."

Student Development

As we have noted before, students who participated in the Learning Habits Project frequently credited their participation with becoming more thoughtful about their academic experience and teaching them "how to learn." In effect, many reported that having to answer annual questionnaires and respond in one-on-one interviews made them more aware of what worked and what didn't. Some said they spent time on their questionnaire answers and interview preparation because they wanted to "do well," even though they understood we weren't "grading" their answers. Responding to as basic a question as, "What was your favorite class this year and why?" made them think about their "academic" style.

Armed with this knowledge, it is important for us to create opportunities for students to reflect on their learning. While we do not suggest it is possible for every institution to engage in a process such as the Learning Habits Project, it is possible to use the framework on a smaller scale to help both students and the institution identify what works best—and what doesn't. A very short end-of-the-semester questionnaire could give insight to an instructor about his or her class, to a department about the techniques being used in its curriculum, or to general education.

We also learned from our students that seeking academic help is often one of the most difficult things to do and downright impossible for some. Encouraging the faculty and the support staff to reach out and constantly remind students of what is available to them is critical. As a result of the early years of the project's student interviews, we created a booklet—printed and electronic—that was distributed to all first-time freshmen at CSUN orientation. It was designed by graphic arts students and formatted in the shape and size of a CD cover, convenient and accessible. We included quotes from LH students on such subjects as where to study and where to find help, time management, and so forth. It has been used in the freshman seminar (University 100).

Not all needed help is about coursework and academics. As we learned in chapter 3, first-generation students often struggle because family members (parents and siblings) have not been to college and do not have the answers and advice that families with a history of college would have. That makes the first year for a new student much more difficult. To help alleviate the problem and accompanying anxiety, obvious sources of information—online, in person, in seminars, and so on—must be created and available to new students. The same is true, as we learned in chapters 4 and 10, for male students, many of whom see seeking help, working in groups, and other support as signs of weakness.

SIGNIFICANCE OF THIS STUDY

The Learning Habits Project was a massive undertaking in that it spanned ten academic years, involved more than 700 students in more than 1,400 interviews, and involved close to 50 faculty, staff, and administrators. As wide-ranging as this volume is, it doesn't begin to mine all of the data we assembled. So the data set is ripe for follow-up by other interested researchers.

That is what happened at CSUN, in fact. In 2015, under the auspices of the project and financial support from the provost's office, a competition was run for LH fellows, offering three units of reassigned time for faculty members interested in using the data for research in their own areas of interest. Eventually, six fellows were chosen, all using the LH database to examine a wide variety of projects, ranging from student interest in engineering disciplines to characteristics of high-achieving Latinas.

The Learning Habits Project focused on the success, not struggles, of self-selected groups of students who are a reflection of the many large, urban, diverse institutions of higher education in the United States. Asking these students to teach us about how they learn resulted in a constantly replenishing fountain of information, some expected and some not. The university came in for criticism and praise—but so did their fellow students and themselves. Listening to LH students supplied us with insights that no other method could provide—insights that can and are being applied to helping their peers succeed. It also confirmed our pride in our students as we saw them mature and gain confidence.

Appendix 1

Participants in the Learning Habits Seminar

First Name	Last Name	Position	Category	Department	Years of Participation
Coordinators					
Bettina J.	Huber	director	staff	Institutional Research	2008–2016
Elizabeth	Berry	emeritus professor	staff	IR/Undergraduate Studies	2008–2016
Administrators					
Elizabeth	Adams	senior director	staff	Undergraduate Studies	2012–2014
Judith	Hennessey	associate dean	staff	Dean's Office, B&E	2011–2013
Karen	Kearns	associate dean	staff	Dean's Office, AMC	2008–2011
David	Levin	director, academic technology	staff	Information Technology	2008–2012
Juana	Mora	special assistant to the dean	staff	Humanities	2010–2012
Janet	Oh	acting director	staff	Institutional Research	2015–2016
Thomas	Piernik	director	staff	Student Development and International Programs	2010–2014
Cynthia Z.	Rawitch	vice provost	staff	Provost's Office	2008–2016
Mark	Stevens	director	staff	Counseling Services	2008–2016
William C.	Watkins	vice president	staff	Student Affairs	2008–2010
Faculty					
Linda S.	Bowen	associate professor	faculty	Journalism	2010–2016
Sakile K.	Camara	professor	faculty	Communication Studies	2008–2012
Irene	Clark	associate professor/director of composition	faculty	English	2008–2016
Shoeleh	DiJulio	professor	faculty	Engineering and Computer Science	2010–2011
Kiren	Dosanjh-Zucker	faculty development	faculty	Business Law	2008–2011
Abel	Franco	associate professor	faculty	Philosophy	2008–2011
Monica	Garcia	assistant professor	fellow	Secondary Education	2015–2016
Steven M.	Graves	associate professor	faculty	Geography	2008–2016
Patricia	Juarez-Dappe	assistant professor	faculty	History	2008–2014
Sharon	Klein	WRAD coordinator/professor	faculty	English	2008–2016

First Name	Last Name	Title	Role	Department	Years
Daisy	Lemus	codirector, faculty development	faculty	Communication Studies	2011–2016
Brennis	Lucero-Wagoner	emeritus professor	faculty	Psychology	2010–2013
Lauren	McDonald	associate professor	fellow	Sociology	2015–2016
Ani	Nahapetian	associate professor	fellow	Computer Science	2015–2016
Donal	O'Sullivan	assistant professor	faculty	History	2010–2016
Bonnie	Paller	director of assessment and prog. review (professor)	faculty	Undergraduate Studies (and Philosophy)	2008–2014
Vicki	Pedone	professor and chair	faculty	Geological Sciences	2008–2015
Adrian	Perez-Boluda	assistant professor	faculty	Modern and Classical Languages	2008–2015
Jennifer L.	Romack	professor	faculty	Kinesiology	2008–2014
Carrie S.	Rothstein-Fisch	associate professor	faculty	Educational Psychology and Counseling	2008–2016
Abe	Rutchik	associate professor	fellow	Psychology	2015–2016
Siva	Sankaran	professor	fellow	Systems and Operations Management	2015–2016
Diane	Schwartz	professor	faculty	Computer Science	2011–2015
Whitney	Scott	faculty development	faculty	Child and Adolescent Development	2015–2016
Katherine F.	Stevenson	assistant professor	faculty	Mathematics	2008–2013
Christina	Von Mayrhauser	associate professor and GE coordinator	faculty	Anthropology	2008–2014
Theresa	White	associate professor	fellow	Africana Studies	2015–2016

Support Staff

First Name	Last Name	Role	Department	Years
Ana	Quiran	support staff:	Institutional Research	2008–2016
Sabrina	Rife	support staff:	Institutional Research	2010–2016
Amy	Matsubara	support staff:	Institutional Research	2008–2010
Ryan	Feyk-Miney	support staff:	Institutional Research	2010–2015
Vana	Khachatourian	grad asst.	Institutional Research	2015–2016
Andrew	Takimoto	grad asst.	Institutional Research	2015–2016
Patricia	Lara	grad asst.	Institutional Research	2015–2016
Jose	Perez	grad asst.	Institutional Research	2011–2012

Appendix 2

Master List of Questions Posed during Face-to-Face Learning Habits Interviews

Freshman Interview

Introduction to project and interview procedures (confidentiality, etc.)

Now, let's begin with the questions proper by talking a bit about how you approach your studies these days.

A. Please tell me a little something about your study habits in high school. For example, how and where did you do your homework?

B. How have your study habits changed since you became a student here at CSUN?

Things to look for in responses to questions A & B
(ask for elaboration if mentioned in passing):

- Academic difficulties in high school and how handled (e.g., trouble with math)
- Academic difficulties/challenges at CSUN and how being handled (i.e., amount of reading required)
- Reliance on group work in high school or college, regardless of how groups are constituted
- Use of CSUN services and resources (including faculty office hours)
- Influence of family context and/or living conditions
- Motivation underlying desire to learn

C. Instructional Techniques

Let's change focus a bit and talk about your classes rather than about how you study.

C.1.a. In the classes you have taken at CSUN thus far, can you think of approaches or techniques used by some of your instructors that were particularly helpful in enhancing your learning?

C.1.b. Are there things some of your instructors do that establish a classroom climate particularly conducive to learning?

C.2. Now for the other side of the coin: have there been practices employed by some of your instructors that tended to hinder your learning?

D. Are there things that you routinely do in your classes that help you learn (e.g., sitting at the front of the class, getting to know your instructors or other students)?

Junior Interview

Introduction to project and interview procedures (confidentiality, etc.)

Now, let's begin with the questions proper.

Question #1: I'd like to begin by asking you to tell me a little something about how you approach your studies these days. In other words, what strategies are you using inside and outside the classroom to do your assignments and prepare for tests?

Follow-Up:

1.a. How do these strategies differ from those you used when you first entered CSUN?

1.b. Has your academic experience at CSUN been different from what you expected it to be when you first started college?

If yes, how has it differed?

*If experience has **not** differed,* what do you think accounts for the fact that you knew what to expect from college?

1.c. If you ran into your freshman self at the Freudian Sip here on campus, what advice would you give that younger self about improving your academic performance?

Possible Prompts: What about
> the primary purpose of college?
> where to turn for help if you run into academic difficulty?
> writing papers?
> managing your class schedule?
> preparing for class?

1.d. Has your motivation to learn changed since you entered CSUN?

> 1.e.1. If yes, how?
> 1.e.2. Has this changed perspective affected how you study?
> 1.e.3. If no, would you say that your motivation to learn influences how you study? If yes, in what ways?
> 1.e.4. Are there other aspects of your experiences during the last two years that have affected your learning or how you approach your studies?

Possible Prompts: What about
> interactions with faculty members?
> cocurricular activities?
> paid employment on or off campus?
> changes in your life circumstances?

Now let's change the topic a bit.

Question #2: How do you balance the academic demands here at CSUN with your other responsibilities?

Follow-Up:

> 2.a. Have these nonacademic responsibilities changed during the last two years?
> 2.b. If so, has this affected how you deal with academic demands?
> 2.c. If no, do you think the stability of these responsibilities has made it easier for you to focus on your college work?

Question 3a: Looking back over the last two years, can you identify any turning points or "aha" moments that have changed how you approach college or your studies? If yes, could you tell me a little about this experience?

Question 3b: Are there skills or knowledge that you have acquired or strengthened during the last two years that you will rely on when you leave CSUN?

Follow-Up:

> 3.b.1. If yes, what are these skills or knowledge?
> 3.b.2. Why do you consider these things important?

3.b.3. If no, why do you think your coursework has provided so little that will be useful to you after graduation?

Question 3c: Are there skills or knowledge that you still hope to acquire or strengthen before graduating from college?

Follow-Up:

3.c.1. If yes, what are these skills or knowledge?
3.c.2. Why do you consider these things important?

Is there anything else that has affected your experience here at CSUN that we have not discussed yet? Anything that my questions have overlooked?

Interviews with Graduating Seniors

Introduction to project and interview procedures (confidentiality, etc.)

Now, let's begin with the questions proper.

Question #1: As you think back over your time at CSUN, what learning strategies have served you best during your college years?

Question #2: Changes in how students approach their studies.

#2.A. Are there events and/or issues that emerged in class sessions during your years at CSUN that have affected your learning or how you approach your studies?

Possible Prompts: What about
the structure of the syllabus?
the evolving face of classroom technology?
the increasing emphasis on SLOs?
the contributions made by other students?

#2.B. What about experiences and events outside the classroom? Have they affected your learning or how you approach your studies?

Possible Prompts: What about
interactions with faculty members?
cocurricular activities?
paid employment on or off campus?
changes in your life circumstances?

#3. How has the diversity of the university's student body contributed to your learning experiences during your years at CSUN?

Follow-Up:

#3.A. When you talk about diversity, what do you mean?

#3.B. Is CSUN more or less diverse than your high school was?

#4. If you were starting college over, what, if anything, would you do differently?

#5. If CSUN's president hired you as a consultant, what would you advise her to change about current procedures and practices at CSUN?

What Lies Ahead

Question #6: What skills or knowledge have you acquired or strengthened during your time at CSUN that you expect to rely on after you graduate?

Follow-Up: Why do you think that these skills/knowledge will prove useful?

Question #7: Tell me about your plans for your first year as a CSUN graduate?

Follow-Up:

7.a. Are you planning to seek further education?

7.b. Are you planning to seek paid employment?

Question #8: As you begin to look ahead beyond college, what are you particularly looking forward to or worried about? Are there any things you hope for or fear?

Closing Questions:

#9a. Has your participation in the Learning Habits Project made any difference in your experience here at CSUN? For example, has it affected the time it has taken you to obtain your degree?

#9b. Which, if any, aspects of your periodic face-to-face interviews have been helpful to you?

Appendix 3

Questions Posed at Project Registration and in All End-of-Term Assignments

1. Full name

2. Current home address
Street (2 lines)
City, State Zip

3. Telephone
Cell:
Home (if different):

4. Personal e-mail address:

Question about Student's Major:
   5. Have you decided upon a major?
   6. What do you currently consider your major? (If you are uncertain, just say "Undecided.")

Questions Posed in Every Fall Term

1. Thinking back on the courses you took in fall [year], was there one in which you learned a great deal more than in the other courses you took?

2. If yes, please list the department abbreviation and course number of that course in the space below (e.g., EDUC 100).

Course Abbreviation and Number: _____

3. What was it about this course that made it such a good learning experience for you? Please be as specific as possible in responding, and mention all relevant aspects of the course in question (e.g., its structure and organization, your interest in its content, your fellow students, the instructor's style, the exercises required in class or as homework, etc.). [open-ended]

4. In the courses you attempted this past term (other than the one mentioned above), were there techniques, exercises, or approaches that your instructors used in one or more that made a significant contribution to your learning?

5. If yes, please describe the techniques or exercises that were so helpful. (If you covered one or more of these in your response to question #1 above, confine your response here to helpful techniques in the other courses you took this past term.) [open-ended]

6. Were there other aspects of your CSUN experience this term (e.g., cocurricular activities, paid employment) that made a significant contribution to your learning?

7. If yes, please describe the most important such experience. [open-ended]

Questions Posed in Every Spring Term

All of the above, plus the question below.

8. Is there anything else that was particularly important to your learning during the last year that we have not asked you about in either this or last fall's end-of-term survey? If yes, could you please briefly describe it? [open-ended]

Unique End-of-Term Questions

Assignment #1 (First Fall Term)

8. Did you read *Title of Freshman Common Reading* this past summer or fall?

9. Did you attend the freshman convocation at the beginning of the fall term?

10. If yes, did the speech by [name of convocation speaker] enhance your understanding of the book? [responses: not really; yes, a bit; yes, a good deal; yes, a great deal]

11. Was *Title of Freshman Common Reading* discussed in one of the classes you took in fall [year]?

12. If yes, did the discussion increase your understanding of the issues raised in the book? [responses: not really; yes, a bit; yes, a good deal; yes, a great deal]

13. If yes, what aspects of the class discussion did you find most useful? [open-ended]

Assignment #2 (First Spring Term)

9. Are you currently planning to return to CSUN next fall?

10. What aspects of your CSUN experience over the past year contributed to your decision about returning in the fall? [open-ended]

11. Were there classes in which you performed less well than you would have liked during your first term at CSUN? [For no, append the following: (skip to question #13)]

12. If yes, what changes did you make in your study habits or course-taking patterns to strengthen your academic performance during this past spring term? [open-ended]

Assignment #3 (Second Fall Term)

7. Has the way you approach your writing assignments changed since you came to CSUN?

8. Why or why not? [open-ended]

9. If you have taken courses here at CSUN that were particularly helpful in strengthening your writing skills, what was it about them that proved so helpful? (Please be as specific as possible in responding.) [open-ended]

10. Has the way you approach your reading assignments changed since you came to CSUN?

11. Why or why not? [open-ended]

12. If you have taken courses here at CSUN that were particularly helpful in strengthening your reading skills, what was it about them that proved so helpful? (Please be as specific as possible in responding.) [open-ended]

Assignment #4 (Second Spring Term)

7. Do you think your ability to think critically and analyze intellectual problems has improved since you came to CSUN? Why or why not? [open-ended]

8. Since coming to CSUN, have you changed the way you approach assignments involving mathematics or quantitative reasoning?

9. Why or why not? [open-ended]

10. If you have taken courses here at CSUN that were particularly helpful in strengthening your quantitative reasoning skills, what was it about them that proved so helpful? (Please be as specific as possible in responding.) [open-ended]

Assignment #5 (Third Fall Term)

7. Now that you have begun to take courses in your major, would you say that you study differently for them than you did for the lower-division GE courses you took in previous terms?

8. If yes, how do your study habits differ in the two types of courses? [open-ended]

9. What does succeeding in college mean to you? [open-ended]

10. How have your notions of college success changed since you first entered CSUN? [open-ended]

11. Has the way you think about civic responsibility and/or political involvement changed since you came to CSUN?

12. If yes, how? [open-ended]

13. If you have taken courses here at CSUN that had an impact on how you think about civic responsibility and/or political involvement, what was it about them that proved important? (Please be as specific as possible in responding.) [open-ended]

Assignment #6 (Third Spring Term)

7. Do you think your ability to find and use information has improved since you first enrolled at CSUN?

8. In which areas do you think you have improved the most (e.g., finding background material for papers, using electronic search media devoted to specialized areas, using the Web to locate relevant information, evaluating the reliability of sources, etc.)? [open-ended]

9. If you have taken courses here at CSUN that were particularly helpful in strengthening your ability to find and use information, what was it about them that proved so helpful? (Please be as specific as possible in responding.) [open-ended]

10. Were there aspects of your CSUN experience during the last year that you consistently found scary or stressful? For example, being called on in certain classes, talking to some instructors, finding the funds to pay your fees, or doing poorly on a test.

11. If yes, please briefly describe why these fearful situations were difficult for you.

Assignment #7 (Fourth Fall Term)

7. Looking back over your last three and a half years at CSUN, what do you know now that you wish you had known when you first entered the university in fall [year]? Put somewhat differently, what advice would you give to a new freshmen about the best means of succeeding at this university? [open-ended]

8. CSUN, like many other CSU campuses, has a student body that is quite diverse in several respects. Would you say that your high school was:
    a. More diverse than CSUN
    b. Less diverse than CSUN
    c. Much like CSUN in terms of diversity

9. Has the diversity of students you encountered at CSUN during the last three years:
    a. Enhanced your learning? Y/N
    b. Hindered your learning? Y/N
    c. Made no difference to your learning? Y/N

10.Why do you think the diversity of the student body at CSUN has affected your learning in the way that it has? If it has helped in some cases, but hindered in others, please try to explain the circumstances that gave rise to the different effects. [open-ended]

Assignment #8 (Fourth Spring Term)

7. During your years at CSUN, have you taken a class that you started out having no interest in—that is, you just took it to fulfill a requirement or because it fit into your schedule—but that you ended up learning a great deal in? (Y/N)

8. If yes, what was it about the class that awakened your interest in the subject matter and/or allowed you to learn so much? [open-ended]

9. Conversely, have you enrolled in a class at CSUN that you were really looking forward to taking but in which you ended up learning very little? (Y/N)

10. If yes, what was it about the class that undercut your interest and/or prevented you from learning? [open-ended]

Assignment #9 (Fifth Fall Term)

7. When you first enrolled at CSUN, were you expecting to graduate within four years?

a. If yes, what academic or personal circumstances have prevented you from doing so? [open-ended]

b. If no, what academic or personal circumstances led you to plan on taking more than four years to complete your baccalaureate degree? [open-ended]

Assignment #10 (Fifth Spring Term)

7. As you begin to think about graduating from CSUN and are exploring your immediate job prospects, are there topics or areas of study that you wish you had learned more about? (If no, skip to question #9.)

8. If yes, please name one neglected topic or area of study, and describe why or how it represents a gap in your education. [open-ended]

9. Conversely, are there topics or areas of study that you explored in greater depth than you now think was necessary?

10. If yes, please name one overexplored topic or area of study, and describe why you think the preparation you acquired in it will not be as useful as you initially expected. [open-ended]

Index

About the Editors

Elizabeth Berry is professor emerita, California State University, Northridge (CSUN). A professor of communication studies and faculty member in gender and women's studies for 34 years, Berry served as a chair of the Communication Studies Department, associate dean of her college, and associate vice president for undergraduate studies. She initiated and was director of the Center for Teaching and Learning, the faculty pedagogy support center at CSUN.

Berry's research focuses on pedagogy, feminism, and rhetoric. She has published in national and international journals and facilitated workshops on effective communication, sexual harassment, and communication and the sexes. She has served as codirector of the Learning Habits Project since 2007.

Bettina J. Huber served as CSUN's director of Institutional Research (IR) until her retirement in 2017. While managing IR's multifaceted responsibilities for providing the analytic, research, and descriptive data needed by university departments and offices, Huber prepared periodic in-depth reports that drew on an array of longitudinal data to provide insight into CSUN's success in enabling its increasingly diverse students to complete their studies and earn their degrees.

Prior to coming to CSUN in the fall of 2005, Huber directed the Office of Analytic Studies at Cal State San Marcos, a unit she established when she arrived in fall 1998. She also served as director of research at the Modern Language Association in New York City and deputy executive officer at the American Sociological Association in Washington, D.C. After completing a PhD in sociology at Yale, Huber spent the better part of a decade as a faculty member in the Sociology Department at the University of California, Santa Barbara. She has served as codirector of the Learning Habits Project since 2007.

Cynthia Z. Rawitch is professor and administrator emerita at CSUN. At the university for 44 years until her retirement in 2017, Rawitch taught journalism and chaired the department before moving into administration, where she served as associate dean and interim dean of the Mike Curb College of Arts, Media, and Communication and associate vice president for undergraduate studies. At the time of her retirement, Rawitch was the university's vice provost. In addition to her PhD in higher education administration from UCLA, Rawitch earned a master of science in journalism at Northwestern University.

Prior to coming to CSUN as a part-time instructor in 1972, she was a reporter and editor at the Associated Press in Los Angeles. She served as "professor in residence" for the *Los Angeles Times'* Minority Editorial Training Program (METPRO) for eight years. Her areas of interest include journalism ethics, diversity in the media, and student success.

About the Contributors

Linda S. Bowen is a professor of journalism at CSUN and has been on the faculty for more than 17 years, including five years as department chair. Bowen was a newspaper reporter and editor in California before joining academia. Her research interests include integrating media literacy concepts into teaching journalism skills and fostering civic engagement through community and K–12 projects, such as the nationally recognized Media Mentors.

Irene L. Clark is a professor of English at CSUN, has been on the faculty since 2000, and serves as director of the Composition Program for the Department of English. Her research interests include composition theory and pedagogy, genre theory, rhetoric, and brain research.

Steven Graves is a professor of geography at CSUN and has been on the faculty since 2003. His areas of research interest include economic geography, pedagogy, social justice, and hip-hop music. One of his recent scholarly initiatives focused on documenting the social ecology of payday lending.

Harold Hellenbrand teachers in the Department of English since retiring in 2017 after nearly a decade as provost and vice president for academic affairs at CSUN. Amid a wide variety of interests, his current focus is on the state of higher education in the United States.

Sharon M. Klein is a semiretired professor of English at CSUN and has held teaching assignments in English, linguistics, and liberal studies since 1986. Her research interests center on linguistic theory, language development, and the role of linguistics in K–12 classrooms.

Daisy Lemus is a professor of communication studies at CSUN and has served on the faculty since 2005. She is also associate vice president for faculty affairs after several years as a codirector of the faculty development office. Her research interests center on organizational change and learning and personal and professional development.

Peter Mora is a part-time faculty member in the Department of Educational Psychology and Counseling and earned his master's degree in counseling, with an emphasis on marriage and family therapy, at CSUN. He works with the Experience Confidence and Enjoyment in Learning (ExCEL) interventions program. His research interests are in depression, anxiety, academic motivation, academic success, self-efficacy, first-generation students, and student success in higher education.

Donal O'Sullivan has been a member of the history faculty at CSUN since 2007, and his research interests include Russian/Soviet history, modern European history, and pedagogy. In spring 2010, he received CSUN's Distinguished Teaching Award.

Carrie Rothstein-Fisch is a professor in the Department of Educational Psychology and Counseling, co-coordinates the Master of Arts in Early Childhood Education program, and is celebrating her 31st year at CSUN. Her research interests include culture and learning (bridging cultures), science and math in early childhood, and advocacy and leadership in early childhood education.

Mary-Pat Stein is an associate professor of biology and has been teaching at CSUN for 11 years. Research interests include intracellular trafficking of *Legionella pneumophila* and pedagogical approaches to using technology for learning.

Mark Stevens is a faculty member in the Department of Educational Psychology and Counseling, Marriage and Family Therapy program, at CSUN, and has returned to teaching after 10 years as director of university counseling services. He serves as coordinator of Experience Confidence and Enjoyment in Learning (ExCEL) interventions programming. His research interests include psychotherapy with men and culturally responsive pedagogy.